Designing Software Synthesizer Plugins in C++

Designing Software Synthesizer Plugins in C++ provides everything you need to know to start designing and writing your own synthesizer plugins, including theory and practical examples for all of the major synthesizer building blocks, from LFOs and EGs to PCM samples and morphing wavetables, along with complete synthesizer example projects.

The book and accompanying SynthLab projects include scores of C++ objects and functions that implement the synthesizer building blocks as well as six synthesizer projects, ranging from virtual analog and physical modelling to wavetable morphing and wave-sequencing that demonstrate their use. You can start using the book immediately with the SynthLab-DM product, which allows you to compile and load mini-modules that resemble modular synth components without needing to maintain the complete synth project code. The C++ objects all run in a stand-alone mode, so you can incorporate them into your current projects or whip up a quick experiment. All six synth projects are fully documented, from the tiny *SynthClock* to the *SynthEngine* objects, allowing you to get the most from the book while working at a level that you feel comfortable with.

This book is intended for music technology and engineering students, along with DIY audio programmers and anyone wanting to understand how synthesizers may be implemented in C++.

Will C. Pirkle is a Staff Scientist at Audio Media Research, Inc. and Music Engineering Technology program director at the University of Miami Frost School of Music. He teaches a range of classes, from audio electronics to digital signal processing and audio programming. In addition to 16 years of teaching, Will has 20+ years of experience in the audio industry, working and consulting for such names as Korg Research and Development, XM Radio, and National Semiconductor Corporation. An avid guitarist and studio owner, Will enjoys projects that combine his skills.

T0386620

Designing Software Synthesizer Plugins in C++

With Audio DSP

2nd Edition

Will C. Pirkle

Routledge
Taylor & Francis Group

NEW YORK AND LONDON

First published 2021
by Routledge
605 Third Avenue, New York, NY 10158

and by Routledge
2 Park Square, Milton Park, Abingdon, Oxon, OX14 4RN

Routledge is an imprint of the Taylor & Francis Group, an informa business

Library of Congress Cataloging-in-Publication Data
A catalog record for this title has been requested

ISBN: 978-0-367-51048-0 (hbk)
ISBN: 978-0-367-51046-6 (pbk)
ISBN: 978-1-003-05220-3 (ebk)

Typeset in Times New Roman
by codeMantra

James Robert Pirkle

Contents

Figures

Tables

Preface

This book is the complete opposite of the first edition. A main influence for this change is a documentary I watched a few years ago that involved a Canadian rock power trio and the soul searching they did regarding their fourth album and its content. I followed their design pattern for my fourth offering, in more ways than one.

In early May 2020, I sat on my couch, enjoying my Saturday morning ritual of Bugs Bunny, coffee, and guitar practice (it was Bach's cello suites), glad that the COVID-semester was finally over and thinking about how I was going to change the way the synth projects would be presented for the new book, including distribution from my website. The first edition was overblown, and both my writing and coding styles had changed dramatically, so I wanted a different approach. I had already assembled the bulk of the code during that spring semester. It had been through layers of kaizen-ing over the last few years, but I had also added some newer components, like morphing wavetables, and I had moved part of my synth class at the University of Miami into note-sequencing rather than just the synth signal processing. A short consulting gig the previous winter had provided me with some advance notice on a killer new synth that would make its debut at the 2020 National Association of Music Merchants (NAMM) show shortly thereafter, and I had since combed through the well-written manual repeatedly, deciding to redo my LFOs to mimic some of that synth's features. And I simply had to create my own version of its brilliantly imagined, independent loop, multi-lane sequencer for the book. But, as I listened to Stalling's "Powerhouse Theme" – of which I will never tire – and watched Bugs torment a construction worker who was trying to exterminate him, I kept thinking that I was only making things more complicated and difficult with my new trick LFOs and wacky looping sequencer that would also work with morphing wavetables and fixed tables or samples. This new book needed simplicity, not more overblown complexities; it needed to be the opposite of the first edition.

I had received an advance copy of Gabrielli's *Developing Virtual Synthesizers with VCV Rack* from my editor to use as a reference and to ensure that my book would not overlap with much of its content (it doesn't), and it was sitting on my coffee table. I had read the text and found myself very jealous. Designing a synth module – a tiny part of a much larger synth structure – was much different than designing a semi-modular software synth. I sat in my Saturday morning daydream bliss, thinking about how cool it would be to just write modules rather than dealing with voice-stealing, MIDI decoding, synth engines, modulation matrixes, and voice architectures. And, having watched students struggling with large synth projects with complicated compiler setups, I thought of how refreshingly nice it would be to work on a tiny plugin component requiring only a handful of files that would compile almost instantly and could be immediately tested within the context of a full synth product on Windows and MacOS alike. But I also knew from experience that a book formatted with projects like that would be met with ire from the many engineers; potential readers; and, of course, the numerous forum post authors who would disagree vehemently, wanting to see the design of completed synths, polyphony, voice-stealing, and all the gory details.

As Bugs wrapped up his final gag, involving dynamite, blasting caps, and concrete, I had one of those Saturday morning ideas that makes you cock your head and smile. I imagined a synth plugin that allowed users to compile and load their own relatively tiny synth modules into it at runtime, but not in the modular fashion, with patch cables and flashing lights. Modules for LFOs, EGs, oscillators, and filters, or other kinds of components and processors, could be loaded and attached to the existing GUI controls – after all, every LFO has a frequency knob, every EG has an attack control, and oscillators are just begging to be detuned. What if there were four assignable controls that could map to anything the programmer desired, whose labels could be changed during the module loading operation? And how about incorporating a dynamically filled string control that would allow the programmer to display a set of waveform names, filter types, or other parameters for the user? That modular option would provide readers of all levels a path to understanding each module's functionality, which roughly corresponds to each book chapter. You could start out testing, modifying, and designing these small modules with only a few source files, and if you were interested in building modules for VCV Rack® or Cherry Audio's Voltage Modular®, you could lift most of that code directly.

For readers who want to incorporate the synth objects into their own plugins external to any other product, the objects need to have a stand-alone mode of operation and should not need the rest of the synth components, or the container synth plugin that manages the small modules, to function. And, for readers that want the whole shebang, each entire synth needs to be packaged in a single C++ object for easy integration with the user's chosen plugin framework. Finally, the C++ objects and synth modules need to be framework and plugin-API agnostic, not requiring any third-party code. Thus, I would need to write a tiny API to use for the synth modules, which would need to be as lean and thin as possible, and, likewise, could not be platform dependent. This would become a kind of open-architecture synth platform, and groups of programmers could convert the skeleton synth into any kind of synth they wanted while allowing the underlying engine and voice objects to handle the MIDI and other chores.

SynthLab™ was born that morning, and the module core API was completed by lunchtime. It was so lean and light, the test modules compiled in a matter of seconds. And having written numerous custom plugin APIs, I already knew the pitfalls to avoid, involving crossing the thunk barrier – an imaginary line that separates a process and the DLL it loads, and over which function calls pass their arguments. The test AU and VST plugins worked flawlessly; I now had a simple platform to use for teaching, and users would have an open-architecture platform for experimenting with new ideas. The book could certainly detail and expose all of the operations of the lower-level engine and voice objects, and users could implement them in their own products. But the individual chapters could focus just on these "cores" – the mini-plugins you load into SynthLab that are the modular building blocks of all synths. There are six complete synth projects in the book and available for download. All of them have precompiled AU and VST plugins for Windows and MacOS that you can demo and, of course, modify with your own individual module cores of all flavors.

Thanks to Hannah Rowe, my Focal Press editor, who encouraged me and helped in the premise for the 2nd edition. In addition, I need to say thanks to all those at the University of Miami's Frost School of Music, who've both supported and entrusted me with the Music Engineering Technology program. They include Dean Shelly Berg, Rey Sanchez, and Serona Elton, along with my faculty colleagues Joe Abbati; Chris Bennett; Dana Salminen; and, of course, my old boss, Ken Pohlmann. I must include gracious thanks to my colleagues at Audio Media Research, Scott Mire, Michael Ljunggren, and José Paiz, for their encouragement and patience during the writing process, and their thoughts on the SynthLab paradigm and what it may bring to the future of music technology education.

As with all my books, I look forward to hearing what you've cooked up in SynthLab. You can always find me at www.willpirkle.com!

Will Pirkle
October 15, 2020

1 SynthLab Introduction

SynthLab™ is the name of a set of C++ objects, structures, and functions designed to encapsulate and implement each of the functional blocks in a software synth, or soft-synth. There are scores of objects and structures, including abstract base classes, abstract interfaces, and all of the derived classes that implement the SynthLab synth projects. There are multiple projects for different types of synths, and you have access to all of the code for all of the objects and synth projects. But I've gone a step further to get you playing with the code and learning SynthLab without needing to integrate the objects into your plugin framework and then compile, debug, and test the complete synth projects, which are more complex than the audio effect plugins in my *Designing Audio Effect Plugins in C++*, 2nd ed. (I refer to this as "my FX plugin book" in this text).

In addition to the C++ code and objects that you may compile and integrate into your own projects, you may also download the pre-compiled versions of each of the six different synths for VST3 (Windows® and MacOS®) and AU (MacOS). These are called the SynthLab Dynamic Module (SynthLab-DM) projects. I designed SynthLab in a highly modular format to include the use of "module cores" that are small, complete synth objects which implement the soft synth building blocks. You may design, compile, and then *dynamically load your own modules into the host DM synths*. This will allow you to study and learn each synth component, modify the code, or invent your own designs, then load those modules into the synth at runtime to debug, test, and voice. If you are interested in designing modular components for systems like VCVRack, then these tiny synth modules represent each of those modular building blocks – oscillators, filters, envelope generators, and the like.

In addition, all of the underlying building block objects feature a "stand-alone mode" of operation, so you can integrate them into existing projects right away without needing to manage entire synth projects.

The base classes and interfaces, like all of the smaller helper objects and functions, may be accessed with just two includes: *synthbase.h* and *synthfunctions.h*, and their *.cpp* implementation files. You can find the C++ code and projects at www.willpirkle.com or https://github.com/willpirkleaudio/synthlab.

1.1 What You Need to Know to Use SynthLab Objects and Projects

You will notice that there is no mention of plugin APIs in this book – AAX, AU and VST are absent as they are covered in detail in my FX book. There is no discussion about specific plugin frameworks – ASPiK, JUCE, IPlug2, etc. Likewise, there are no analog or DSP theory chapters, so you will need to bring your own knowledge to the table or be willing to study it alongside this book. There is also no "intro to MIDI" chapter. You need to know how MIDI messages work, what a MIDI "CC" means, and the like. There are numerous books and sources available on all of these topics. These are prerequisites for getting the most out of this text.

   This book is not designed to feature any particular framework or API but rather shows how I create software synthesizers in C++ using DSP theory and coding implementations. Most chapters begin with theory of operation, then show the C++ objects I use to implement that theory. You will need to download the code and study it side-by-side with the text as the book only includes very specific C++ code: stuff that is non-intuitive or very specific to audio or synthesis. Since all of the synth components use the same module-core paradigm and ten-control GUI implementations, the book figures and specifications are cleaner and easier to understand. This is in stark contrast to the book's first edition, in which each project was vastly different in architecture and components.

   If you intend to build the complete synth projects in this book, you need to have a solid grasp on your chosen plugin framework, and you especially need to understand how to generate your own GUIs within that framework; you will also need to understand some advanced GUI design topics, such as dynamic loading of string lists (remember that you are free to pick and use individual C++ objects and code as you like for your own synth projects). You will find that adding the synth objects to your framework's processing object is very straightforward, but the GUI details may be challenging. Chapter 5 covers the details on using the module cores, designing with objects in stand-alone-mode, and connecting the synth engines to your framework, and you can always get more help and information from www.willpirkle.com/forum.

1.2 SynthLab Synth Projects

To demonstrate how to use and combine these objects, and how they work together, I have created a set of synth projects based on the same fundamental architecture which only differ in their oscillators and waveform rendering. All synths feature monophonic, unison, and polyphonic operational modes. These projects include:

SynthLab-WT: four-oscillator wavetable synth that includes ordinary wavetable, morphing wavetable, and one-shot drum and sound effect (SFX) wavetable implementations; the various oscillators may be used in any combination

SynthLab-PCM: PCM sample playback synth with four separate PCM oscillators; this synth uses. wav files for its PCM sample storage and retrieval

SynthLab-VA: four-oscillator virtual analog synth using virtual analog oscillators and filters

SynthLab-KS: physical modeling synth that uses the Karplus-Strong plucked string algorithm to generate realistic acoustic and electric guitar and bass sounds

SynthLab-DX: four-operator FM synth that produces the classic Yamaha DX synth sounds

SynthLab-WS: wave sequencing synth based on the Korg Wavestate's ® multi-lane, independent looping wave sequencer that allows use of both normal and morphing wavetable oscillators during the sequencing operation; the wave sequencing oscillator demonstrates how to create an amalgam of modules encapsulated in a single object

In addition, each of these has a precompiled dynamic module (*DM*) version which you can download from www.willpirkle.com/synthlab using the DM subscript/prefix: for example, SynthLab-WS$_{DM}$ is the dynamic module version of the wave sequencing synth, and the dynamic module synths are collectively referred as SynthLab-DM.

1.2.1 SynthLab Documentation

SynthLab is fully documented with the Doxygen® tool and is available to download at www.will-pirkle.com/synthlab-docs/. This includes every C++ object, interface, structure, and function, with every member variable and member function. You should bookmark this page and refer to it often. Synth projects are considerably complex, and there is not enough room in the book to document every object.

> The C++ listings in this book represent the interesting, difficult, or highly synth-oriented code that connects to the theory portions of each chapter. You will need to use the documentation and review the sample project code to get the most out of this book and understand how to select and use whichever C++ objects you like in your own plugin projects.

1.3 Synth Components

Most hardware and software synthesizers are designed from the same set of basic building blocks that will be used throughout this book. Table 1.1 lists these components, their abbreviations, and their descriptions, as applied to the SynthLab projects.

Table 1.1 Synthesizer components, my abbreviations, and descriptions, as used in *SynthLab*

Component	Abbreviation	Description
Synth engine	Engine	The entire synth, in one object that manages a set of voices
Synth voice	Voice	This term is not always used the same way, but for SynthLab, it is the object that renders each note-event; a voice contains a collection of one or more of the components below (LFO, EG, etc.)
Low frequency oscillator	LFO	An oscillator with frequency f_o on the range of about 0.02 to 20.0 Hz, though numerous variations on these limits are allowable
Envelope generator	EG	Produces a unipolar control signal used to modulate other components; it is most closely associated with the output amplifier, where it sets the time-domain contour of the rendered signal
Digitally controlled amp	DCA	A variable gain and panning amplifier used on the output of each voice
Virtual analog filter	VAFilter	A synth filter designed using digital integrator replacement in analog block diagrams
Biquad filter	BQFilter	A synth filter designed using the bilinear z-transform (see my FX plugin book)
Wavetable oscillator	WTOsc	A pitched oscillator that reads data from a table or array

(Continued)

Component	Abbreviation	Description
FM operator	FMOp	A combination of a sinusoidal wavetable oscillator and an EG that controls its output amplitude; FM operators are combined to modulate each other
PCM oscillator	PCMOsc	A pitched oscillator that reads pre-recorded PCM data from a table, array, or audio file
Virtual analog oscillator	VAOsc	An algorithmic oscillator that simulates the output of analog oscillators
Karplus strong oscillator	KSOsc	Contains an exciter and one or more resonators to simulate the behavior of plucked strings; may be modified to produce bowed string sounds – technically not an oscillator but behaves like one in the synth implementation
Wave sequence oscillator	WSOsc	An amalgam of four inner oscillators that generates the wave sequences from the Korg Wavestation® and Wavestate® synths; works in conjunction with the *WaveSequencer* object
Modulation matrix	ModMatrix	A component that connects modulation sources (LFOs and EGs) to modulation destinations, such as filter cutoff frequency or oscillator amplitude
Wave sequencer	WS	A modulation source that generates a sequence of modulation values used to create both melodic and evolutionary sounds; may be extended to use as a traditional step sequencer – this is based heavily on the Korg Wavestate's wave sequencer

1.4 Basic Software Synth Architecture

In the early 1990s, the MIDI Manufacturers Association (MMA) produced a specification for a software synth called the Down Loadable Sound (DLS) synth. You can get a copy of the Level I (L1) specification from www.midi.org/specifications-old/item/dls-level-1-specification. This file and the DLS Level II version are excellent sources as they define the synth architectures, GUI controls and their limits, and the transform functions that are used to manipulate GUI and MIDI control signals. I use some of these transforms and functions in SynthLab, so this is an excellent and perhaps mandatory resource for you to acquire. Figure 1.1 shows how the MMA diagrams a software synth. The LFOs and EGs are articulators that control parameters of the audio engine, and the control logic ties everything together.

The block diagram in Figure 1.1 will render a single note, so a polyphonic synth would include multiple sets of these blocks, one for each note that is rendered. In SynthLab, Figure 1.1 is called a "synth voice" block diagram, and the "synth engine" is a set of these voice blocks. This is detailed in Chapters 2 and 3, but you need to know the lingo now.

1.5 SynthLab Voice Architecture

All SynthLab projects use the same basic voice architecture, shown in Figure 1.2. Each synth has a different quad oscillator bank, and SynthLab-WS includes the additional wave sequencer object, but the projects are otherwise the same. Take note of the names of the components – *ampEG*, *filter1*, *wtOsc3*, etc. – as these are used throughout the text; being C++ member variable names, they will be italicized. All SynthLab synth projects include the following in their voice architectures:

- Four pitched oscillators – these are named according to the oscillator type, e.g. *wtOsc1* (wavetable oscillator 1) or *fmOp1* (FM operator 1)

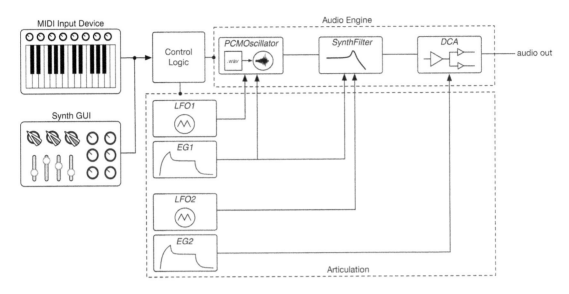

Figure 1.1 The MMA representation of a software synth includes control logic, articulation, and an audio engine that renders the synthesized signal

- Two LFOs (*lfo1* and *lfo2*)
- Three EGs (*ampEG*, *filterEG*, and *auxEG*)
- Two virtual analog filters that may be placed in series or parallel (*filter1* and *filter2*)
- One modulation matrix with multiple sources and destinations (*modMatrix*)
- One output DCA with EG control and panning function (*dca*)
- One ping-pong delay FX on the output
- One wave sequencer object (SynthLab-WS only)

Note that SynthLab's audio path is fully stereo – all oscillators feature stereo outputs and the filters, DCA and delay FX process stereo signals. Each note-event is rendered through its own voice object, so for a polyphony of 16 notes, we need 16 voices.

1.6 SynthLab C++ Implementation

Every SynthLab component is a C++ object or structure, from the top-level *SynthEngine* object down to the *SynthClock* – a tiny modulo counter that is the time-base for most oscillators. Figure 1.3(a) shows the C++ object hierarchy – take some time to study this diagram since I use the same paradigms throughout the text.

- Rounded corner blocks are C++ objects or structures
- Many objects contain an interface pointer to another object, shown with the familiar interface circle-bar on the left
- Square boxes contain string lists, or non-C++ objects
- C++ objects, structures, and their member variables and methods are always *italicized*

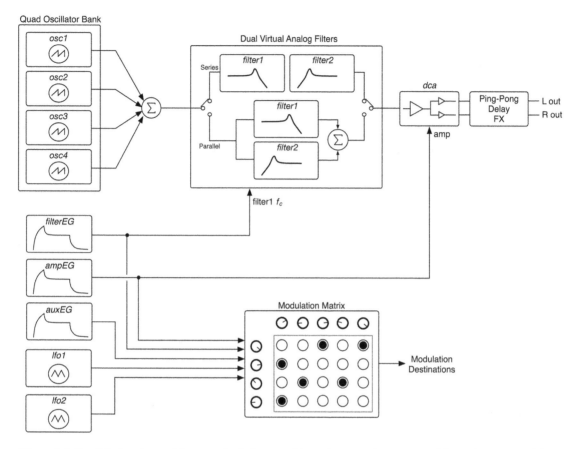

Figure 1.2 SynthLab voice architecture includes two filters that may be processed in series or parallel, or individually bypassed; the SynthLab-WS project also includes a wave sequencer object

Figure 1.3(a) shows how each sub-component is made of smaller components, and some of them reveal string lists that wind up on the GUI.

- The *SynthEngine* contains a set of 16 *SynthVoices*, one for each note of polyphony
- Each *SynthVoice* (voice 0 is shown here) contains a set of *SynthModules* that encapsulate the functionality of each row in Table 1.1
- All *SynthModules* <u>except</u> the wave sequencer, mod matrix, and DCA include four *ModuleCore* objects – I will always provide at least one core per module, and some include bonus cores to boot
- Each *SynthModule* exposes the names of its module cores
- Each *ModuleCore* object implements a variation on the module's theme and exposes a list of up to 16 strings for selecting core-specific parameters; for oscillators, these are waveform string names, and for filters, they are filter types, etc.

The module-plus-core paradigm is not only central to the way in which SynthLab is able to generate professional results, exposing banks of waveforms or sets of filters, but also part of the way in which it helps teach how each of the modules – which correspond to chapters in the book – operate within the synth structure. It also allows you to focus on only one part of the project at a time, and you are free to add your own modules so you can really personalize the synth projects without having to build new synths from scratch. In addition, the cores demonstrate variations on the module functionality. Examine the module cores in Figure 1.3:

- *ClassicWTCore*: wavetables of classic sounds, like analog and FM waveforms, as well as some tables taken from slicing instrument samples
- *MorphWTCore*: wave morphing oscillator that uses banks of wavetables to crossfade-morph
- *DrumWTCore*: one-shot wavetables of classic electronic drums, one drum sound per voice
- *FourierWTCore*: demonstrates dynamic wavetable creation using Fourier synthesis

There is a bonus *SFXWTCore* that implements one-shot sound effects that are useful in the wave sequencing synth.

1.6.1 Core, Module, and Mod Knob Strings

To maximize flexibility, SynthLab uses a dynamic GUI interface that allows loading string lists and GUI labels on-the-fly. The sizes of the lists are fixed to allow proper handling of automation and DAW state save and restore operations. You may also decide to implement a static GUI and not use the dynamic core paradigm – that is up to you and is covered as an option in Chapter 5. Figure 1.3(b) shows a typical GUI implementation for *wtOsc1*, the first of four wavetable oscillators (C++ object named *WTOscillator*) in the *SynthVoice* object. On the right side, there are four "mod knob" controls named A, B, C, and D which are specific to each module core. Most cores have at least one unassigned mod knob for you to experiment with. Examine Figure 1.3(a) and (b), and notice how the GUI controls connect to the module and its cores:

1   The GUI exposes the module core names that the *WTOscillator* provides in a list for the user – Classic WT, etc.
2   When the user selects a core, the module strings are dynamically loaded into the next control, named "Waveform" here (or "Filter Type" for the filters, "EG Contour" for the EGs, etc.)
3   In addition, the mod knob labels (A, B, C, and D) are re-named for that particular core to show the functionality; un-assigned knobs show only the alphabetical letter
4   Each object includes four hard-wired controls that are specific to that module: for example, in the oscillator object, these are tuning, output, and pan controls, while for the EG object, these are attack, decay, sustain, and release

You will see that almost all of the synth modules follow this paradigm and include exactly ten GUI controls per module; the exceptions are the sequencer, mod matrix, and DCA, which are either too complex to shoehorn into this format or too simple to require multiple cores and GUI controls.

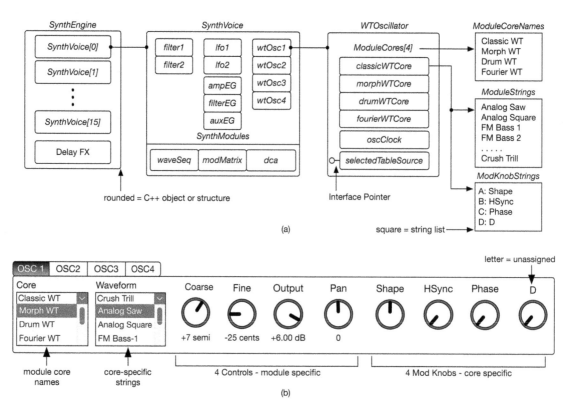

Figure 1.3 (a) SynthLab C++ objects include the engine, voice, modules, cores, and their associated string lists; (b) typical GUI layout for the wavetable oscillator

1.7 Why SynthLab Uses This Architecture

You may be wondering why SynthLab has this module-core paradigm with the dynamic strings and mod knobs. The short answer is that it is a result of both reader comments on the first edition of this book and, more importantly, years of teaching at the university level, where the class must be brought up to speed in only one semester. It is not uncommon for grad students from other universities to contact me for advice about very specific synth components – such as the virtual analog filters or FM operators they are researching for their thesis work. SynthLab's modules and cores make it easy to focus on just one concept and study that in depth. In addition, you can personalize your own components. For example, suppose you want to create your own morphing oscillator and make your own wavetable banks. If you only want to change the waveform banks, you can simply modify my object to supply the bank names. If you want to do the chapter home-work problems or invent your own variation on my objects to add some interesting functionality that you want to investigate, you can subclass the *ModuleCore* base class; implement the object, name the core, and choose the names of the morphing banks that the user sees; and implement the functionality of the free-agent mod knobs and your own added ideas.

In addition, I usually break my classes into groups and have them each work on their own variation on a specific module. I use a three-step approach to facilitate their understanding. The first two steps are usually done as homework or a "pre-lab," while the third is for a larger project. The goal of the project is to implement something new and interesting, so the students must brainstorm and research to think of new ideas.

1   First, I assign homework and projects that only involve altering my code that extends the object in a simple but interesting manner.
2   Next, I assign a variation-object (which changes some specific behavior or functionality) or a combination-object (which amalgamates two or more modules in an interesting or intelligent manner) so they must subclass the base class object and work on implementing either their own variations or completely new functionality. This is when the students really begin to understand how the theory connects to the code as they are forced to go in and dissect and debug the existing code.
3   Finally, I assign an open-ended project that involves adding new objects or orchestrating big-picture parts of the synth that require brand new types of components (note sequencers, weird oscillators, and bizarre filters are some student favorites).

With SynthLab, you can start with the first wavetable synth project and design its GUI, which takes time because there are many components and controls, then debug and implement the synth. To move to the next project, you only need to change the oscillator-rendering core as everything else is the same. This means you can re-use the same project and GUI over and over, and if you implement the dynamic string loading and core selection, you only need to change a few lines of code to generate what appears to be a completely different synth. The only project that would require more GUI work is the wave-sequencing synth, which exposes the sequencer controls but also hides the underlying oscillator controls, so you can make it fit into the same GUI real-estate area as the rest.

1.8 SynthLab Object Operational Phases

In Chapter 3, you will see that all synth modules implement the same set of five functions plus the constructor; these perform the majority of the synth operations. When these objects appear in future chapters, I use the same paradigm for describing the C++ coding details based on the functions that correspond to the six operational phases of the modules and are named in the same way.

1.8.1 Construction Phase

Each object's constructor performs specific construction related to that module. The *SynthEngine* is instantiated first and creates its set of *SynthVoice* members, along with the delay FX object. The *SynthVoice* object creates its set of *SynthModules* and wires the modulation matrix. At the *SynthModule* level, the constructor creates the audio buffers used to shuttle data between objects and creates and initializes any other member objects. It also sets up the processing structure used to communicate with its set of cores. At the *ModuleCore* level, the constructor is mainly involved in exposing the set of 16 core strings and text labels for the mod knobs.

1.8.2 Reset Phase

The reset phase usually only happens once after the DAW loads the plugin, but it will also happen if the user changes the DAW sample rate. For synth plugins, the sample rate is usually established only once and not changed again; however some DAWs, such as Reaper®, may implement the reset operation many times prior to streaming audio. Therefore, each module implements a function named *reset* whose only argument is the current sample rate. The details of the reset phase and function are dependent on the object: for example, the wavetable oscillators use the reset phase to query the wavetable database to make sure the necessary tables are available.

1.8.3 Note-On Phase

Each module and core implements a *doNoteOn* function that accepts the MIDI data for the particular note-event. Most modules perform some meaningful operations during note-on: for example, the oscillators reset their internal clock objects and store the MIDI pitch of the incoming note. The note-on phase must fully prepare the object for its operation of rendering or processing audio data.

1.8.4 Update Phase

The update phase is one of the most important and can be the source of CPU bottlenecks. Each module will be updated once per audio block processing cycle, as detailed in Section 2.4, and implements the *update* function to perform these operations. The update phase consists of two parts: updating the component state due to changes made on the GUI and updating the rendering variables based on modulation from other components. Usually, the equations are combined for both of these parts. For example, an oscillator's state may change because the user adjusted the coarse tuning control, which affects the pitch. At the same time, an LFO connected to the oscillator's modulation input may also alter the oscillator pitch. The values of both of these are combined to generate a single pitch shift for that audio block processing cycle. The details of pitch modulation, which is key to almost every synth module in some fashion, are discussed in Section 6.8.1.

1.8.5 Render Phase

There are two fundamental types of synth components: those that render information (audio or control signals) and those that process information (usually audio but may also apply to control signals in some cases). All synth modules implement a *render* function that performs each module's functionality; clearly, there will be numerous differences based on the kind of module. Modulation objects render their output into special arrays called modulation inputs and outputs. Pitched oscillators render audio into audio-only buffers. Filters and DCAs process audio input buffers and write to audio output buffers; all of these are detailed in their corresponding chapters.

1.8.6 Note-Off Phase

Interestingly, most modules do nothing during the note-off operation, with the exception of the envelope generators, which play a critical role in the note-event lifecycle, as described in Section 4.1. If nothing occurs during the note-off phase, then it is not documented in the chapter.

1.8.7 Why No Destructor Phase?

Almost all SynthLab objects and their members are instantiated dynamically and use the *std::unique_ptr* or *std::shared_ptr* for maintenance, freeing us from worrying about calling the *delete* operator and keeping track of reference counts and lifecycles. Use of these auto-deleting pointers goes all the way down to some of the lowest-level objects. But still, there are a handful of exceptions, such as dynamic wavetable creation that is sample-rate dependent, wherein the destructor has meaningful code. In many of these cases, you will likely implement your own object to handle these operations in a way that makes sense to you, such as creating tables or reading files, so in general, that will be your issue to deal with.

Bibliography

MIDI Manufacturer's Association. 1999. *Downloadable Sounds Level 1*. https://www.midi.org/specifications-old/item/dls-level-1-specification, Accessed October 14, 2020

MIDI Manufacturer's Association. 1999. *Downloadable Sounds Level 2*. https://www.midi.org/specifications-old/item/dls-level-2-specification, Accessed October 14, 2020

Roads, Curtis. 1996. *The Computer Music Tutorial*, Chap. 2. Cambridge: The MIT Press.

2   The Synth Engine

The synth engine implements the entire synth architecture, and *SynthEngine* is the single C++ object you need to add to your plugin framework's processing object. In the example plugins designed with ASPiK, this is the *PluginCore* C++ object; for JUCE, it is the *AudioProcessor* object. Each of the synth projects is packaged in a single *SynthEngine* object, which is implemented in *synthengine.h* and *sythengine.cpp*, and located in a directory with the other supporting object files. These objects are framework agnostic, meaning they are pure C++, have no bindings to any plugin framework, and do not require additional libraries beyond the built-in standard template libraries included in your compiler. In Chapter 5, you will learn how to wire up the engine to render audio and how to send GUI parameter information to it. This chapter focuses on the synth engine's duties and overall architecture.

2.1 Engine Behavior

The engine performs three tasks during the synth's operation: (1) initialization, (2) applying GUI control changes, and (3) rendering the synthesized audio. I designed the *SynthEngine* object to expose simple functions that service these operational functions, with an interface that is not dependent on any plugin framework. Your plugin framework's processing object will create and use the engine object – it is the sole C++ object and interface that you need to wire into your plugin. After instantiation, the plugin will call five methods on the engine for the three engine functions, as seen from the plugin/DAW side:

1   **Initialization**: the plugin calls the engine's *reset* and *initialize* functions
2   **Set GUI parameters**: the plugin calls *getParameters* for a shared pointer to the engine's GUI connected parameters and *setParameters* to instruct the engine to update its states, causing a trickle-down transfer of parameters using shared pointers and without data copying
3   **Rendering audio**: the plugin calls the engine's *render* function, passing it audio buffers to fill one a block-by-block basis

2.2 Engine Architecture

The *SynthEngine* objects are identical for all of the SynthLab. Each *SynthEngine* owns a set of *SynthVoice* objects, each of which renders a single note-event for that particular synth flavor, so there is a different *SynthVoice* for the FM synth, the virtual analog synth, etc. For a synth with a polyphony of eight notes, you will need eight *SynthVoice* objects. You can create a multi-timbral synth by mixing *SynthVoice* objects of different types. The engine mixes the audio outputs of the active voice objects as it renders the final synth output for your framework's processor object to handle. The *SynthEngine* objects use a statically declared array of *std::unique_ptrs*, one for each voice. The unique pointer object deletes the underlying resource automatically when no other object references it and doesn't require memory maintenance or the *delete* operation.

```
std::unique _ ptr<SynthVoice> synthVoices[MAX _ VOICES];
```

If you are an experienced programmer, you will want to modify the object in your own way: for example, you could put each voice on its own thread and include another mixer-thread to mix the outputs. Or you could dynamically control the number of voice instances based on CPU power. For this chapter, you don't need to think about the internal voice operation, only that you will be creating, initializing, and calling the voice rendering function from the *SynthEngine* instance.

Figure 2.1 shows the *SynthEngine* architecture in block diagram form. The GUI, MIDI input, and audio output connections are inside of dotted boxes – this is where your plugin framework processor object makes its interface connections. You can see that there are three connection points:

1   GUI information, sent to a shared voice parameter and the sole engine parameter data structures
2   Incoming MIDI information for CCs and other common messages, collectively called "global MIDI data"
3   Audio output rendering, delivering data from the engine to the processor object

Figure 2.2 shows the big-picture block diagram of objects and function calls. The circle-bar on the left edge of each object represents an external function call or interface. Most objects also include a few functions that are only used within that object. In this chapter, we focus on the *SynthEngine*, its exposed functions, and their operations, shown in the bold box in Figure 2.2. In Chapter 5, you will see details of the framework side. In the next chapter, we look at the voice, module, and core objects.

2.3 Shared Data

Sharing data across C++ objects is a necessity for a software synth. Even a complex FX plugin still only has one main target for the GUI controls, but in a polyphonic synth, each note-rendering object (*SynthVoice*) shares the same voice GUI controls with all the others – the filter f_c, oscillator detuning, and EG settings are applied identically to each voice object. In addition, SynthLab modules are designed so that each component has full access to all incoming MIDI data, allowing you to tailor your objects specifically for custom MIDI message processing – for example, MIDI Polyphonic Expression (MPE). The wavetable and PCM sample data is generally large and likewise must be shared across the voices to prevent redundancy and memory consumption.

2.3.1 *The Singleton*

If you don't know what a singleton is, some programmers will tell you that you are better off not knowing. The singleton is a source of heated debate among programmers. You were probably

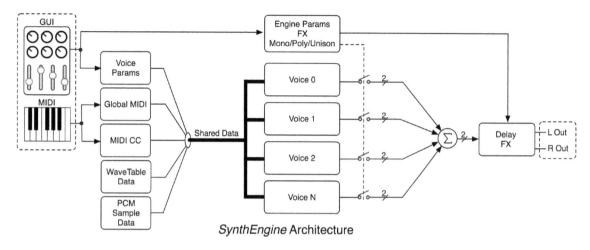

Figure 2.1 The *SynthEngine* object architecture; the dotted boxes show the interface points to your plugin framework's processor object

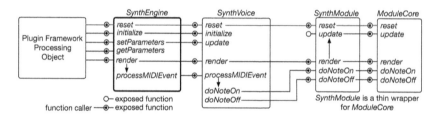

Figure 2.2 Hierarchy of SynthLab objects responding to function calls from the host plugin framework processor object

taught that declaring global variables is a bad design choice; these exist through the lifetime of the process in which they are created, even if they are created in a DLL, loaded into that process address space, and later deleted. Essentially, a singleton is a global variable that points to a data structure or C++ object which often acts as a database, using get/set functions to store data that persists for the lifetime of the process. Singletons are delightfully simple to implement and use. They are also disastrous in some cases, especially where class factories are involved. Having been burned with singletons in the past, I avoid them unless there is no other option. This book will not use singletons in any manner. That said, if you poke around the AAX, AU, and VST API base classes and lower-level code, you might be interested in what you find – while eschewed in the academic world, global variables and singletons are known for appearing in real-world applications.

2.3.2 *The Shared Pointer*

The standard library's *std::shared_ptr* object is designed to allow the safe sharing of resources with lifecycle control, which deletes the underlying resource automatically when no other object references it. Objects that use the shared pointer cannot harm the underlying data. For the SynthLab projects, I am using *std::shared_ptrs* to share engine and voice data structures across objects as well as to share MIDI, wavetable, and PCM sample data. As thin wrappers, the shared pointers require a function call to use the underlying "naked" pointer, but that bit of overhead is outweighed by the benefits of safe data sharing and automatic lifecycle control. Within the SynthLab objects, there are a handful of instances in which old-fashioned (naked) pointers are used; generally, this involves access to floating point arrays that are audio input and output buffers, dynamically created wavetables, and ultimately connected to the plugin framework.

2.3.2.1 Shared GUI Parameters

The SynthLab architecture consists of one engine that owns a set of *SynthVoice* objects. Each voice owns a set of *SynthModule* objects that encapsulate the synth building blocks. Each module includes a custom data structure that is used to pass GUI control data into the object. Consider the array of four synth voice objects stacked together in Figure 2.3(a), in which each voice consists of the following *SynthModules*: LFO, EG, filter, wavetable oscillator, and DCA. Figure 2.3(c) shows that the voice's custom parameter structure, *SynthVoiceParameters*, contains a set of module parameter structures that are maintained with *std::shared_ptrs*, one for each module, and shown in dotted boxes.

This means that the *LFOParameter* structure and its contents for the voice's *lfo1* member object are shared across all *lfo1* members and, thus, the stack of objects connected to the parameter structure box. Each of the module's custom structures are shared across the same objects and across all voices. In Figure 2.3(c), the engine object owns a single instance of a *SynthVoiceParameter* structure, also implemented with a shared pointer that is likewise shared across all voices. In order to force programmers to maintain this important architecture, all voice and module constructors require shared pointers to their specific data structures. Note that this is not required when using the objects in stand-alone mode as they will synthesize their own parameter structures.

The *SynthEngine* contains a shared parameter member, created during instantiation, that is used for updating from the GUI. It is a shared pointer because the plugin framework's processor object will need to obtain it to update the GUI control information.

```
std::shared _ ptr<SynthEngineParameters> parameters =
                    std::make _ shared<SynthEngineParameters>();
```

Within the *SynthEngineParameters* definition, you will find the shared pointer of voice parameters:

```
std::shared _ ptr<SynthVoiceParameters> voiceParameters =
                    std::make _ shared<SynthVoiceParameters>();
```

When the synth engine creates the voice objects, it passes the identical shared pointer to each one during construction.

2.3.2.2 Engine-Specific GUI Parameters

In addition to the shared voice parameters, the engine parameters also include some top-level controls, which apply at the engine level only. The most important parameter is a strongly typed *enum* that sets the synths mode: monophonic (one note at a time), unison (one note at a time, but the note is made of layered voices) and polyphonic (multiple notes can be played simultaneously). Operational modes are covered in Chapter 4.

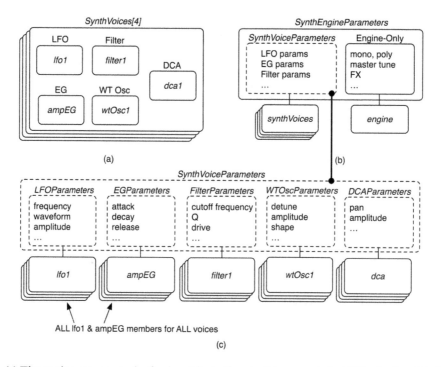

Figure 2.3 (a) The engine owns a stack of voice objects (four in this example but 16 in the SynthLab projects), each of which includes an identical set of LFO, filter, EG, oscillator, and DCA objects; (b) the engine owns a voice parameter structure that is shared across these voices; and (c) the shared voice parameters structure consists of a set of shared module parameter structures

```
enum class synthMode { kMono, kLegato, kUnison, kUnisonLegato, kPoly};
```

The other members include global controls for volume, pitch bend sensitivity, and overall instrument tuning. These are mapped to their corresponding MIDI data values, and use names that define their functionality.

2.3.2.3 Shared MIDI Input Data

The engine receives and decodes MIDI messages from your plugin framework's processor object, as described in Section 5.4.3. All decoded messages are then stored in two arrays of *uint32_t* data types, one for the MIDI continuous controller (CC) data and the other for a selected set of messages relevant to the SynthLab projects. The two sets of messages are called MIDI CC and Global MIDI data, respectively. A third array of DAW data, comprising BPM and time signature information, is included, though it is not specifically MIDI and is called "aux DAW data." This is likewise shared with the modules. A simple C++ class named *MIDIInputData* manages the three arrays and allows for read-only access to incoming data for all synth modules, simplifying MIDI modulation calculations and allowing for MPE.

This class is derived from *IMIDIInputData* that allows module core objects to access the data. The *SynthEngine* contains a single member, created during instantiation, that is used for sharing the MIDI input data:

```
std::shared_ptr<MidiInputData> midiInputData =
                                std::make_shared<MidiInputData>();
```

When the synth engine creates the voice objects, it passes each one the identical shared pointer during construction.

The engine is set up to allow for the generation of MIDI output data for MIDI effects, but this is not implemented for the SynthLab projects as it is unnecessary for their operation. On occasion, you will see *midiOutputData* variables in the code, but they are only there if you want to get into MIDI effect programming, which is outside the scope of the synth signal processing presented here.

2.3.2.4 Shared Wavetable and PCM Sample Data

The wavetable and PCM sample data is shared across the voices, as are their modules using shared pointers. The *WavetableDatabase* and *PCMSampleDatabase* objects maintain the data for the wavetable and PCM sample oscillators. You will notice that the engine, voice, and MIDI input data shared pointers are all created with *std::make_shared* right in the *synthengine.h* file and are generated during instantiation but before the constructor function is executed. The engine is the original creator and owner of this data. To provide maximum flexibility in the modules and their cores, the wavetable and PCM sample databases are created empty, lacking content of any kind. The wavetable and PCM sample oscillators bring their own data, either creating it at construction time or reading from compiled data arrays or *.wav* files included with the plugin. The module chapters contain details about the databases and their interfaces.

As the wavetable and PCM sample oscillators are instantiated, each will query the corresponding database to see if the required tables or sample arrays exist. If not, the oscillator object will create them and add them to the database. This means that the very first wavetable oscillator of a given core type will create and register its tables with the database. All subsequent wavetable oscillator cores will find the data and will not need to create it. The same paradigm holds true for PCM sample oscillators that use *.wav* files to package their multi-sample sets such that the files are only accessed once. The engine's members are therefore declared with *nullptr*:

```
// --- shared tables
std::shared_ptr<WavetableDatabase> wavetableDatabase = nullptr;

// --- shared samples
std::shared_ptr<PCMSampleDatabase> sampleDatabase = nullptr;
```

Then, in the engine's constructor, the empty databases are generated and passed to the voice objects during construction, which, in turn, construct their modules passing in the shared database pointers. You can see how the shared pointers trickle down from engine to voices, and then from voices to modules, each during construction.

2.4 *SynthEngine* Constructor

We can put all of this information together by examining the *SynthEngine's* constructor which does the following set of tasks:

1   Initialize some of the MIDI global and CC data to values that will prevent the synth from starting up without audio: for example, MIDI CC7 (volume) is set to the maximum value 127, while MIDI CC10 (pan) is set to the center value 64; the code below is a partial listing as there are numerous other defaults to make

```
// --- volume/pan prevent accidental silence, pan
midiInputData->setCCMIDIData(VOLUME _ CC07, 127); // --- MIDI VOLUME max
midiInputData->setCCMIDIData(PAN _ CC10, 64); // --- MIDI PAN center
```

2   Create the wavetable and PCM sample database shared pointers

```
// --- these databases are empty at this point
if (!wavetableDatabase)
    wavetableDatabase = std::make _ shared<WavetableDatabase>();

if (!sampleDatabase)
    sampleDatabase = std::make _ shared<PCMSampleDatabase>();
```

3   Create the set of voice objects that will render audio, passing MIDI; notice the unused *midiOutputData* (also a shared pointer) and the *blockSize* parameter which we will investigate next

```
// --- create the voices
for (unsigned int i = 0; i < MAX _ VOICES; i++)
{
    // --- reset is the constructor for this kind of smartpointer
    //
    synthVoices[i].reset(new SynthVoice(midiInputData,
                                 midiOutputData, /* unused */
                                 parameters->voiceParameters,
                                 wavetableDatabase,
                                 sampleDatabase,
                                 blockSize));
}
```

The last line of code sets up a special structure for rendering from the voice and is discussed in Section 2.4.4.

```
// --- voice render
voiceProcessInfo.init(NUM _ INPUT _ CHANNELS,
                 NUM _ OUTPUT _ CHANNELS,
                 blockSize);
```

2.5 Audio and MIDI Block Rendering

The engine is also responsible for accepting incoming MIDI data and rendering the final output signal. All plugin frameworks, like ASPiK, JUCE, and iPlug2, ultimately process and render audio in blocks named "audio I/O buffers" here. This is covered in detail in the second edition FX book. In addition, the frameworks gather incoming MIDI messages that are queued and time-stamped to align in a sample-accurate manner with the audio data. This package of information in applied to the processor object's audio processing or rendering function. For some synth APIs, like VCV Rack, the processing must be done on a sample-by-sample basis in which processing occurs on each sample interval. If you are rendering stereo audio, there are two samples to render on each sample interval.

In SynthLab, audio is rendered in blocks with a preferred size of 64 stereo samples at a time; this is the designated default *blockSize* variable you see in the *SynthVoice* construction in Section 2.2.2.4. A stereo sample means one sample each for the left and right channels, and the *blockSize* value indicates the number of stereo samples. When you instantiate the engine in your framework, you send it the default block size; you thus have the ability to change this value, but there is a reason for the preferred size of 64 samples/channel. All plugin frameworks deliver audio samples in independent left and right data buffers, and SynthLab expects you to render into individual buffers as well. The SynthLab projects are set up with the ability to accept incoming audio data that you may process through filters or use as a side-chain, vocoder, or other control generator. The stock SynthLab projects only render audio, so we will only be discussing the audio output buffers.

Incoming MIDI data is also applied in the same block fashion, with all MIDI messages sent to the engine via a *std::vector* of *midiEvent* objects. However, as with many commercially available synth products, the MIDI messages are serviced all at once, before the audio block is rendered. This means that they are not sample-accurate and are part of a SynthLab scheme to granulize MIDI data and internal modulator signals over blocks of data that generate a massive increase in efficiency and a lowered CPU usage. The tradeoff in efficiency is well worth the loss of perfect sample accuracy between MIDI and audio, and follows a law of diminishing returns – as the block size becomes larger, the savings flatten out.

The amount of MIDI "slop" in the system is a function of the block size since all messages will be processed first, placing a maximum error in MIDI event timing that is equal to the block size multiplied by the sample interval. At 44.1 kHz, 64 samples of MIDI slop will equate to a worst-case time offset error of 1.4 mSec, and the performer will not notice this slight latency in playing keys or using MIDI controllers. You may also up the block size to 128 samples and experiment with your own tactile limits. However, if you demand perfect sample accuracy, set the *blockSize* variable to one (1) during engine construction; just be prepared to pay the price in CPU usage.

2.5.1 *The* AudioBuffer *Object*

The *AudioBuffer* object plays several roles in SynthLab and is used not only for moving audio data between your processor object and the engine but also within the synth modules themselves as the voice renders them, in turn. The *AudioBuffer* object is designed with plugin frameworks and native APIs in mind; the input and output buffers are independent per channel and passed *float*** parameters that are compatible with all plugin APIs and frameworks that process channel buffers (i.e. everything but VCV Rack). In addition, it includes members that store channel counts, maximum block size, and current block size if a partial block needs rendering, which may happen. Details for preparing the buffers can be found in Chapter 5.

2.5.2 *The* midiEvent *Structure*

The *midiEvent* structure contains the raw MIDI data that has been converted from BYTE to *uint32_t* in your framework. The sample-offset value is transmitted, but it is ignored during block processing.

```
uint32 _ t midiMessage = 0;          //< BYTE message as uint32 _ t
uint32 _ t midiChannel = 0;          //< BYTE channel as uint32 _ t
uint32 _ t midiData1 = 0;            //< BYTE data 1 as uint32 _ t
uint32 _ t midiData2 = 0;            //< BYTE data 2 as uint32 _ t
uint32 _ t midiSampleOffset = 0;     //< sample offset
```

2.5.3 *The* SynthProcessInfo *Object*

Your plugin framework's processor object prepares a *SynthProcessInfo* object that is passed to the engine on each block processing cycle. The object inherits from *AudioBuffer* and therefore includes the protected members and methods mentioned in Section 2.3.1. The object includes a member vector of *midiEvents* to be decoded for the render operation. The engine's render function uses this information for MIDI and for rendering audio. The framework duties are discussed in Chapter 5.

2.6 *SynthEngine* Operational Phases

We discussed the engine constructor in Section 2.2.2.4. The *SynthEngine* does not have a base class but is set up with virtual functions and a virtual destructor so that you may use it as a base class, overriding its behavior with your own functions and allowing you maximum freedom in implementing your own ideas. Aside from a few functions dedicated to voice-stealing and polyphony, discussed in Chapter 4, there are only five functions to deal with, and two of them are trivial. Let's examine the guts of each method and discuss its role in engine functionality.

2.6.1 SynthEngine *Reset and Initialization*

The engine initialization phase is shown in Figure 2.4(a), and your plugin framework only needs to make five function calls to the engine for operation. The first two are *initialize* and *reset*. Your framework will call the engine's *reset* function whenever the sample rate is established or changed for the plugin. In many DAWs, this will be called only once. The *reset* function for the *SynthEngine* is trivial in that it simply forwards the reset call to its array of *SynthVoice* objects and FX module.

```
bool SynthEngine::reset(double _ sampleRate)
{
    // --- reset array of voices
    for (unsigned int i = 0; i < MAX _ VOICES; i++)
    {
        // --- reset them
        synthVoices[i]->reset( _ sampleRate);
    }
    // --- FX
    pingPongDelay->reset( _ sampleRate);
    return true;
}
```

The SynthLab-PCM project uses *.wav* files to load PCM sample data. For the precompiled and ASPiK versions, these files are located in a folder in the same directory as the plugin component or DLL. You have the freedom to move this location as you see fit. The *initialize* function is used to forward the path to your DLL's container directory to the voice objects for use in parsing the PCM samples. The PCM database objects assume that the PCM sample folder is in a subfolder of this directory. Your plugin framework or your personal plugin project needs to know the folder name at instantiation time, so if you want to change this path, just make sure it is in a directory with an established location. The *initialize* function simply forwards this path to the member voices. A *const char** is used for maximum flexibility across frameworks and APIs, and to allow dynamic core loading across a thunk barrier. See the documentation for more information on the DLL path.

```
bool SynthEngine::initialize(const char* dllPath)
{
    // --- loop and init
    for (unsigned int i = 0; i < MAX _ VOICES; i++)
    {
        // --- init
        synthVoices[i]->initialize(dllPath);
    }
    return true;
}
```

2.6.2 *Setting* SynthEngine *Parameters*

Your plugin framework will take GUI control information and send it to the *SynthEngine* via the *getParameters* and *setParameters* method that uses a shared pointer to shuttle parameters to the voice objects and engine-specific components. This is shown in Figure 6.4(b) and occurs at the top of the buffer processing cycle.

```
void setParameters(std::shared _ ptr<SynthEngineParameters>& _ parameters)
```

The framework side of the code is discussed in Chapter 5. The engine parameters allow the *SynthEngine* GUI to expose the following controls (this is your decision, and they may be omitted):

- Global volume control
- Global pitch bend sensitivity, coarse and fine adjustments
- Global tuning, coarse and fine adjustments (as with analog synths)

These parameters may be sent directly to the engine, voice, and oscillator objects, but I have set them up to be converted into the appropriate MIDI data values. The MIDI specification includes data variables for all of these items and is detailed at www.somascape.org/midi/tech/spec.html#usx7F0401 (note that the MIDI spec uses the term "master" where I use the term "global"). The MIDI data values are written to the *globalMIDIData* array and require massaging to be converted from 7-bit MSB/LSB into uint32_t values.

The *setParameters* function performs three operations for the engine:

1   Set up the global MIDI data with information from the global parameters for volume, pitch bend, and tuning; some code is straightforward, such as the pitch bend range (sensitivity), while others require work; remember that this is optional, and you may remove it if you like.

```
// --- pitch bend range in midi data table; for a released synth, you
// want to decode this as SYSEX as well
// --- sensitivity is in semitones (0 -> 127) and cents (0 -> 127)
uint32 _ t pbCoarse = parameters->globalPitchBendSensCoarse;
boundMIDIValueByte(pbCoarse);

unsigned int pbFine = parameters->globalPitchBendSensFine;
boundMIDIValueByte(pbFine);

midiInputData->setGlobalMIDIData(kMIDIMasterPBSensCoarse, pbCoarse);
midiInputData->setGlobalMIDIData(kMIDIMasterPBSensFine, pbFine);
```

2   Call the *update* function on the voices one at a time; this is only required for changing module cores, as described in Chapter 5, and requires little overhead; no calculations are performed.

3   If unison mode is chosen, this function also sets the unison voices' detuning and panning parameters; this is also discussed in Chapter 5.

2.6.3 SynthEngine *Render Operation*

The plugin framework's processor object will call the *render* function once per data block during its own audio processing function. The render operation consists of three phases:

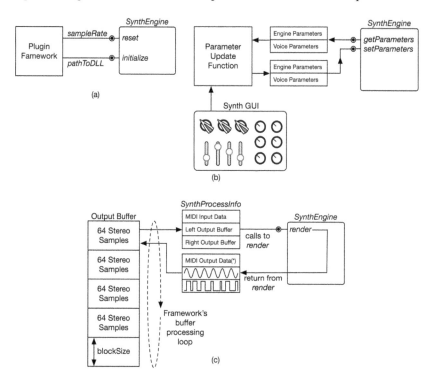

Figure 2.4 SynthEngine operation consists of three phases: (a) initialization, (b) GUI updates, and (c) audio rendering

1   Update the engine's GUI parameters with calls to *getParameters* and *setParameters* that use shared pointers for setting parameters, as shown in Figure 2.4(b)

2   Prepare a *SynthProcessInfo* structure with the incoming MIDI data and pointers to audio buffers for rendering

3   Enter a block processing loop that sends the *SynthProcessInfo* structure into the engine repeatedly, using MIDI data and audio buffer pointers for each *blockSize*; if the last buffer is smaller than *blockSize*, just call the render function, and set the current *blockSize* value, as shown in Figure 2.4(c)

This function processes the incoming MIDI using the *processMIDIEvent* function and then calls the voice render methods.

2.6.4 SynthEngine *MIDI Processing*

All MIDI messages are decoded at the top of the block processing cycle in the function *processMIDIEvent* that is called once for each incoming MIDI event. This function is split into three parts, as shown in Figure 2.5: one part decodes and stores all MIDI CC messages in the CC database, another stores global non-note messages, while the third handles MIDI note-on and note-off messages only. The engine is set up to respond to all MIDI channels, which you can change easily since this function is the primary MIDI receiver.

The top portion of the *processMIDIEvent* function that decodes note-on and -off events is key to the mono/unison/polyphonic operation and is covered in Chapter 4.

```
bool SynthEngine::processMIDIEvent(midiEvent& event)
{
    if (event.midiMessage == NOTE _ ON)
    //
    // --- ALL NOTE ON/NOTE OFF MESSAGES
    //
    // --- Covered in Chapter 4
```

The second part deals with the MIDI CC messages. You can easily modify this function to add more data to the global MIDI data array. For the pitch bend message, the LSB and MSB are placed

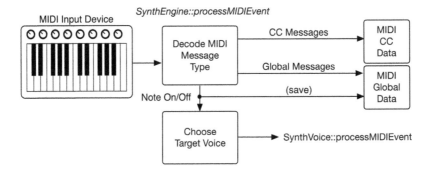

Figure 2.5 SynthEngine MIDI processing

into the *globalMIDIData* array using the *set* function call; for the CC messages, the data is simply stored as-is in *uint32_t* format.

```
// --- store the data in our arrays
if (event.midiMessage == PITCH_BEND)
{
    midiInputData->setGlobalMIDIData(kMIDIPitchBendDataLSB,
                                              event.midiData1);
    midiInputData->setGlobalMIDIData(kMIDIPitchBendDataMSB,
                                              event.midiData2);
}

if (event.midiMessage == CONTROL_CHANGE)
{
    // --- store CC event in globally shared array
    midiInputData->setCCMIDIData(event.midiData1, event.midiData2);
}
```

After that, you may add code to store any other MIDI input data you wish to include, such as tuning, pitch bend, and global volume/pan messages. These are implemented on the SynthLab GUI and stored as their MIDI counterpart data.

2.6.5 SynthEngine *Audio Synthesis*

The engine calls the voice's render function repeatedly, as shown in Figure 2.3(c). The *SynthVoice::render* function takes the same kind of argument as the engine – a *SynthProcessInfo* structure – but it is an engine member object and has been prepared in advance. The last line of code in the engine's constructor from Section 2.2.2.4 is:

```
// --- for voice objects
voiceProcessInfo.init(NUM_INPUT_CHANNELS,
                NUM_OUTPUT_CHANNELS,
                blockSize);
```

This function sets up the *AudioBuffer's* input and output arrays using the arguments as channel counts. The parameters NUM_INPUT_CHANNELS = 0 NUM_OUTPUT_CHANNELS = 1 set up no audio input buffer and two output buffers, one for each stereo channel. The *blockSize* parameter sets the maximum size of these buffers. Let's step through the render function:

```
bool SynthEngine::render(SynthProcessInfo& synthProcessInfo)
```

First, a call is made to flush the output buffers in the incoming *synthProcessInfo* object as they may contain old data; it is not uncommon for plugin frameworks and APIs to leave old data in these arrays.

```
// --- clear out
synthProcessInfo.flushBuffers();
```

Next, all of the MIDI events in the vector are serviced using the member function:

```
// --- issue MIDI events for this block
uint32_t midiEvents = synthProcessInfo.getMidiEventCount();
for (uint32_t i = 0; i < midiEvents; i++)
{
    // --- get the event
    midiEvent event = *synthProcessInfo.getMidiEvent(i);
    // --- process it
    processMIDIEvent(event);
}
```

Next, we set up for the render operation. When summing many voices (notes) together, the synth may overload the output, so this chunk of code sets a scaling factor for each voice depending on the mode; this is further discussed in Chapter 4.

```
double gainFactor = 1.0;
if (parameters->mode != synthMode::kUnison)
    gainFactor = 0.5;
```

Next, the *midiInputData* and *voiceProcessInfo* objects are refined with data for the current block; note the use of *getSamplesInBlock* to determine how many of the maximum *blockSize* samples need to be rendered. Also, notice how the DAW information is transferred into the MIDI *aux-DAWData* array; this makes it instantly available to every component.

```
// --- important
voiceProcessInfo.setSamplesInBlock(
                             synthProcessInfo.getSamplesInBlock());


midiInputData->setAuxDAWData(kBPM, synthProcessInfo.BPM);
midiInputData->setAuxDAWData(kTSNumerator, etc…
midiInputData->setAuxDAWData(kTSDenominator, etc…
midiInputData->setAuxDAWData(kAbsBufferTime, etc…
```

Lastly, the engine loops over the voices calling the *render* function on each of the active voices. A voice state is set to *active* only if the voice is currently processing a note-event. A helper function is used to accumulate the voice output buffers together (the audio mixer operation). The final application of global volume and delay FX is covered in Section 16.4.

```
// --- loop through voices and render/accumulate them
for (unsigned int i = 0; i < MAX_VOICES; i++)
{
    // --- blend active voices
    if (synthVoices[i]->isVoiceActive())
    {
        // --- render and accumulate
        synthVoices[i]->render(voiceProcessInfo);
        accumulateVoice(synthProcessInfo, gainFactor);
    }
}
```

Bibliography

MIDI Manufacturer's Association. 1999. *Downloadable Sounds Level 1*. https://www.midi.org/specifications-old/item/dls-level-1-specification, Accessed October 14, 2020

MIDI Manufacturer's Association. 1999. *Downloadable Sounds Level 2*. https://www.midi.org/specifications-old/item/dls-level-2-specification, Accessed October 14, 2020

somascape.org. 2019. *Guide to the MIDISoftware Specification*. http://www.somascape.org/midi/tech/spec.html#usx7F0401, Accessed October 14, 2020

SynthLab Documentation. 2020. www.willpirkle.com/synthlab-docs, Accessed on October 14, 2020

3 Synth Voices, Synth Modules, and Module Cores

The SynthLab *SynthVoice* object is responsible for rendering note-events, and there is one voice object per note of polyphony in the synths. As with the engine, the *SynthVoice* object has no base class but is set up to be a base class with the virtual functions and destructor, so feel free to subclass your own when you are ready. The term "voice" has several meanings in synth lingo, but here, it also includes the synth type. The voice architecture is covered in Section 1.5.

3.1 Voice Behavior

The voice performs three tasks during the synth's operation: (1) initialization, (2) responding to MIDI note-on and note-off messages, and (3) controlling the audio signal flow through a set of member objects called modules. The voice object's central responsibility is maintaining the set of *SynthModule* objects that make up the synthesizer components, such as oscillators and filters. I designed the *SynthVoice* object to expose simple functions that service these three areas of operation. The voice object also processes incoming MIDI data for note-on and note-off events, which it uses to control its set of modules.

1. **Initialization**: the voice calls the module's *reset* function
2. **Note-on and note-off**: the voice calls the *doNoteOn* and *doNoteOff* methods on its set of modules
3. **Controlling audio signal flow**: the voice calls the module's *update* and *render* functions during each block processing cycle and delivers the rendered audio back to the engine

Figure 3.1 shows the big-picture block diagram and connection from the engine to the voice to an individual module. This chapter focuses on the blocks in bold: voice, module, and core.

3.2 *SynthVoice* Modules

The SynthLab-DX and SynthLab-PCM synths only differ in their *SynthVoice* objects – everything else is identical. Furthermore, the only thing that differentiates the FM voice from the PCM voice is the set of oscillators used to render the signal. This means that the code for the voice objects is about 95% similar. Each *SynthVoice* object owns a set of objects subclassed from *SynthModule*. Each module is a synth building block and can be grouped into modulators, oscillators, processors, and controllers, as shown in Figure 3.2. The voice object also needs to update these modules with new GUI control information once per buffer process cycle. A voice is a collection of these objects, plus all the code needed to manage them.

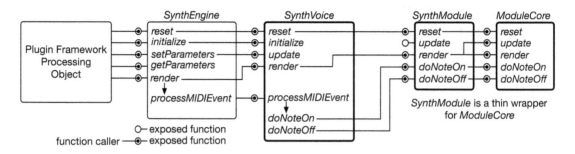

Figure 3.1 Flow of function calls from host plugin framework processing object to the *SynthEngine*, then to the voices, modules, and their cores

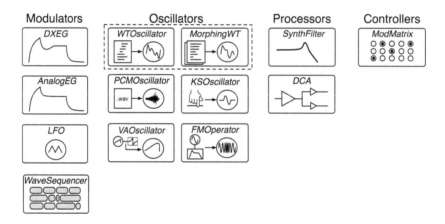

Figure 3.2 SynthLab modules each implement one synth building block; all are subclassed from *SynthModule*; note that the normal and morphing wavetable oscillators are combined (dotted box) and may be mixed freely

3.3 *SynthVoice* Parameters

The *SynthVoiceParameters* structure contains all of the GUI information for programming the voice object and all of the controls for all of the modules in Figure 3.1, plus the additional parameters for the chosen oscillators. All of these are implemented with shared pointers within the *SynthVoiceParameters* structure.

The engine object creates the global *SynthVoiceParameters* during its construction, and all of the shared pointers and parameter structures for each of the voice's modules are also created since they are members of the voice parameter structure. The top part of the declaration is for voice parameters whose names indicate their target functionality.

Next, each parameter structure is declared with *make_shared,* thereby constructing each underlying structure and generating the safe pointer, in a series of declarations. This is the underlying mechanism that allows both the voice object and its modules to share common parameters exclusive to each of them. These structures are where you will place the GUI control information, as described in Chapter 5.

```
// --- LFOs
std::shared _ ptr<LFOParameters> lfo1Parameters =
                               std::make _ shared<LFOParameters>();
std::shared _ ptr<LFOParameters> lfo2Parameters =
                               std::make _ shared<LFOParameters>();


// --- EGs
std::shared _ ptr<EGParameters> ampEGParameters =
                               std::make _ shared<EGParameters>();
std::shared _ ptr<EGParameters> filterEGParameters =
                               std::make _ shared<EGParameters>();
// --- etc . . .
```

3.4 *SynthModule* Members

Each voice's member modules are exclusive to that voice and are not shared with other objects. The modules are all maintained with an *std::unique_ptr* and are declared in the class definition, then constructed in the *SynthVoice* constructor. Table 3.1 lists the modules that are identical across all voices – of course, you may add, remove, or change the modules for your own designs.

The declarations are simple:

```
// --- modules common to all voices:
std::unique _ ptr<DCA> dca;
std::unique _ ptr<AnalogEG> ampEG;
std::unique _ ptr<SynthLFO> lfo1;
std::unique _ ptr<SynthFilter> filter1;
etc . . .
```

The *SynthVoice* members include shared pointers to the MIDI input, wavetable, and PCM sample databases in Section 2.3. These are declared along with the modules, then populated during the voice constructor.

```
std::shared _ ptr<MidiInputData> midiInputData = nullptr;
std::shared _ ptr<WavetableDatabase> wavetableDatabase = nullptr;
std::shared _ ptr<PCMSampleDatabase> sampleDatabase = nullptr;
```

Table 3.1 SynthVoice modules that are identical across all synth projects

Module Object Name	SynthVoice std::unique_ptr< >	Notes
DCA	*dca*	Output only DCA
AnalogEG	*ampEG;*	Hardwired to DCA
AnalogEG	*filterEG;*	Hardwired to filter 1
AnalogEG	*auxEG*	Assignable EG modulator
SynthLFO	*lfo1*	LFO1 may modulate LFO2
SynthLFO	*lfo2*	General purpose LFO
SynthFilter	*filter1*	18 different filters, plus bypass
SynthFilter	*filter2*	18 different filters, plus bypass
ModMatrix	*modMatrix*	Modulation matrix object
WaveSequencere	*waveSequencer*	Generates modulation values only; specific to SynthLab-WS

3.5 *SynthVoice* Construction

The voice object must create all of its modules and pass them the MIDI input, wavetable, and PCM sample database pointers at construction time. The *SynthVoice* constructor prototype is shown here; the *midiOutputData* is not used but is available for your own experimentation. Notice the maximum block-size parameter – this is needed for the modules to create their audio output buffers at that maximum size.

```
SynthVoice(std::shared _ ptr<MidiInputData> _ midiInputData,
           const std::shared _ ptr<MidiOutputData> _ midiOutputData,
           std::shared _ ptr<SynthVoiceParameters> _ parameters,
           std::shared _ ptr<WavetableDatabase> _ wavetableDatabase,
           std::shared _ ptr<PCMSampleDatabase> _ sampleDatabase,
           uint32 _ t _ blockSize = 64);
```

During construction, the voice object needs to do the following:

1 Create all sub-modules using *std::unique_ptr* and its *reset* function, passing in the shared module parameter structures from its voice parameters structure
2 Add sources and destinations to the modulation matrix (covered in detail in Chapter 14)

The module creation follows the same paradigm – each module receives a shared pointer to a structure within the voice's shared parameters for GUI updates. The wavetable and PCM sample oscillators are also given database pointers; the database details and usage are explained in each oscillator chapter, as are the constructor prototypes, but they are all fundamentally similar. Here is the construction of a few of the modules: it is easy to see where the shared parameters and databases are part of each constructor; the modulation matrix object only requires the shared parameters. Stand-alone mode construction is generally simpler and is covered in Section 5.3.1.
LFO:

```
lfo1.reset(new SynthLFO(midiInputData,      /* shared midi data */
           parameters->lfo1Parameters,      /* shared parameters */
           blockSize));                      /* max blocksize */
```

Filter:

```
filter1.reset(new SynthFilter(midiInputData,    /* shared midi data */
              parameters->filter1Parameters,    /* shared parameters */
              blockSize));
```

Wavetable Oscillator:

```
wtOsc.reset(new WTOscillator(midiInputData,     /* shared midi data */
            parameters->wtOscParameters,        /* shared parameters */
            wavetableDatabase,                  /* shared wavetables */
            blockSize));
```

PCM Sample Oscillator:

```
pcmOsc.reset(new PCMOscillator(midiInputData,   /* shared midi data */
             parameters->pcmOscParameters,      /* shared parameters */
```

```
                  sampleDatabase,       /* shared PCM data */
                  blockSize));
```

Modulation Matrix:

```
modMatrix.reset(new ModMatrix(parameters->modMatrixParameters));
```

3.6 *SynthVoice* **Operational Phases**

You can see from Figure 3.1 that the voice and module object share nearly identical member functions, and many of the voice functions simply call the same named functions on the modules.

3.6.1 SynthVoice *Reset*

This function calls the *reset* functions on all of its modules. It also sets the *currentMIDINote* flag to −1, indicating that no notes are playing. This will be used for polyphony and voice-stealing in the next chapter. We will look into each *reset* function in the corresponding module chapters.

```
pcmOsc->reset( _ sampleRate);
dca->reset( _ sampleRate);

lfo1->reset( _ sampleRate);
lfo2->reset( _ sampleRate);

ampEG->reset( _ sampleRate);
filterEG->reset( _ sampleRate);
auxEG->reset( _ sampleRate);

filter1->reset( _ sampleRate);
filter2->reset( _ sampleRate);

etc...
```

3.6.2 SynthVoice *Update*

The *update* function is called after the GUI parameters have been set on the engine. For the *SynthVoice*, this only consists of swapping module cores in or out, as described in Section 3.7, when the user selects them from the GUI. The modules are identified with index values that you use in your GUI's control so they are not related to any framework.

3.6.3 SynthVoice *doNoteOn and doNoteOff*

The voice's *processMIDIEvent* function is called repeatedly at the top of each processing block to service all MIDI messages for that audio block. This function only looks for note-on and note-off messages, then calls the voice's corresponding functions that accept *midiEvents* as arguments (see Section 2.3.2). These methods perform two main functions: calling the note-on or note-off message on all of the sub modules, and setting a state variable so the voice knows its state, which is used for voice-stealing.

```
enum class voiceState { kNoteOnState, kNoteOffState };
```

SynthVoice::doNoteOn(midiEvent& event)

The note-on function is a bit more complex as it involves portamento, which uses the *GlideModulator* object described in Section 6.7.1. Each SynthModule has its own pre-defined glide modulator member object. The MIDI note number is converted to a pitch and stored as the current note, and the previous note is recalled. If portamento is enabled in the voice parameters (which would have come from a GUI control), the note information and glide time are used to start the glide modulator.

```
// --- calculate MIDI -> pitch value
double midiPitch = midiNoteNumberToOscFrequency(event.midiData1);
int32_t lastMIDINote = currentMIDINote;
currentMIDINote = (int32_t)event.midiData1;

GlideInfo glideInfo(lastMIDINote, currentMIDINote,
                    parameters->glideTime_mSec, sampleRate);

if (parameters->enablePortamento && lastMIDINote >= 0)
{
        xxxOsc1->startGlideModulation(glideInfo);
        xxxOsc2->startGlideModulation(glideInfo);
        xxxOsc3->startGlideModulation(glideInfo);
        xxxOsc4->startGlideModulation(glideInfo);
}
```

Next, the series of note-on message handlers is called, and the state variable and *voiceIsRunning* members are set.

```
MIDINoteEvent noteEvent(midiPitch, event.midiData1, event.midiData2);


// --- start oscillators
vaOsc1->doNoteOn(noteEvent);
vaOsc1->doNoteOn(noteEvent);
vaOsc3->doNoteOn(noteEvent);
vaOsc4->doNoteOn(noteEvent);

// --- modulators/processors
dca->doNoteOn(noteEvent);
ampEG->doNoteOn(noteEvent);
filterEG->doNoteOn(noteEvent);
etc...

// --- set the flag
voiceIsRunning = true; // --- we are alive!
voiceNoteState = voiceState::kNoteOnState;
```

The note-off handler is simpler, merely calling the module functions and saving the state variable.

```
SynthVoice::doNoteOff(midiEvent& event)
```

```
// --- lookup MIDI -> pitch value
double midiPitch = midiFreqTable[event.midiData1];
```

```
MIDINoteEvent noteEvent(midiPitch, event.midiData1, event.midiData2);
```

ampEG->doNoteOff(noteEvent);
filterEG->doNoteOff(noteEvent);

etc…

```
// --- set our current state
```
voiceNoteState = voiceState::kNoteOffState;

3.6.4 SynthVoice *Render*

The rendering function in the *SynthVoice* is quite simple as the modules do the hard work. The function accepts the *SynthProcessInfo* structure that the engine sends in and uses the *samplesTo-Process* during the calls to the sub-modules.

SynthVoice::render(SynthProcessInfo& synthProcessInfo)

The function follows this pattern:

1   Call a *render* on all modulator member modules
2   Run the modulation matrix to transfer modulator sources to destinations (see Chapter 14)
3   Process the audio from the oscillators through the filters and DCA, managing the flow of audio buffers; this is somewhat dependent on the voice type

Each module's *render* function makes a call to the core's *update* method first. The *update* functions will set the modulator's parameters for the current block, then each modulator will generate one output value for the block during the *render* operation. The modulation matrix applies the modulator values to the destinations. This chain of update/render is identical across all SynthLab voice objects.

```
// --- render modulators
```
lfo1->render(samplesToProcess);
lfo2->render(samplesToProcess);

ampEG->render(samplesToProcess);
filterEG->render(samplesToProcess);
auxEG->render(samplesToProcess);

```
// --- do all mods
```
modMatrix->runModMatrix();

Next, the oscillators are rendered; this will depend on the voice type. We will look at this process for each synth project in Chapter 16. It is more important to understand how the audio is transferred from the oscillators to the filters to the output DCA. All processes are done with helper functions that perform fast *memcpy* operations on the audio buffers, transferring blocks of audio data down the signal path. These are named *copyOutputToInput* and *copyOutputToOutput*, and take buffer pointers, samples to copy, and a channel indicator (mono to mono, stereo to stereo, etc.).

Here are some examples:

1   Render and transfer audio from the virtual analog oscillator (*vaOsc*) output into the *filter1* input:

```
vaOsc->render(samplesToProcess);


copyOutputToInput(vaOsc->getAudioBuffers(),     /* source */
                  filter1->getAudioBuffers(),   /* destination */
                  STEREO _ TO _ STEREO,         /* channel info */
                  samplesToProcess);            /* samples to copy */
```

2   Run *filter1*, and copy its output to the input of *dca*:

```
filter1->render(samplesToProcess);


copyOutputToInput(filter1->getAudioBuffers(),   /* source */
                  dca->getAudioBuffers(),        /* destination */
                  STEREO _ TO _ STEREO,
                  samplesToProcess);
```

3   Run the *dca*, and copy its output to the output buffers, which the engine passed to the voice when the render was called – note that the *copyOutputToInput* function includes multiple versions that accept different types of input pointers so they are simple to use

```
// --- update and render
dca->render(samplesToProcess);


// --- copy to mains out
copyOutputToOutput(dca->getAudioBuffers(),      /* source */
                   synthProcessInfo,            /* NOTE: destination! */
                   STEREO _ TO _ STEREO,
                   samplesToProcess);
```

The MIDI note-on message places the voice into its active state, notifying the engine to call its render operation. The MIDI note-off message places the voice into the note-off state, but the voice does not fully finish operations until the output EG that is connected to the output amplifier has finished its release state and expired into the off state. At this point, the voice may be shut down.

The very last part of the *render* function is also one of the most important – checking for the note-off state and an expired *ampEG* object. This will be covered in detail in Chapter 4.

3.7 SynthModules and ModuleCores

The module-core paradigm is fundamental to SynthLab. Each module is subclassed from the *SynthModule* base class, and each implements the same set of overridden base class functions which correspond nearly identically with the voice object functions. Figure 3.2 shows how I diagram the modules, using the *PCMOscillator* as an example. The figure shows everything you need to know without needing large data tables.

At the top of the diagram, you can see the GUI control knobs. There are always four assigned knobs at the top and four assignable controls called "mod knobs" shown below, labeled A, B, C, and D. In some modules, all are assigned; others have "free" controls with which you can easily perform experiments without needing to modify a bunch of code. These controls funnel into the *parameters* block, which represents the shared parameter structure for this module. The parameters are applied to the active *ModuleCore* object, which is an internally owned member that has access to the *SynthModule's* input and output ports, labeled with icons and text. Different modules require access to different ports, which are shown as enabled when connected to the core with a bar, also shown in Figure 3.3(a). You will sometimes see a dotted box around a module core's sting list – this indicates a separate downloadable project that can be used for building only the module core in the SynthLab-DM projects.

3.7.1 SynthModule *I/O Ports*

The I/O ports connect a module to its input and output sources. Figure 3.3(b) shows a block diagram of the *SynthModule* with inputs and outputs. Modulation inputs and outputs are arrays of *double* values, one modulation value per audio block, but with numerous slots in the arrays for various modulator types. Audio data is transferred via the *AudioBuffer* described in Section 2.5.1.

3.7.1.1 Input Ports

- MIDI input is provided via the engine's shared structure
- Modulation input values arrive in a pre-defined modulation array with one active modulation value processed per block; there may be many inputs, each with its own slot in the array (e.g. bipolar input (from LFO)), unipolar input (from EG), etc.
- FM inputs are from outputs of other oscillator modules and include one block's worth of audio data
- Audio inputs allow you to send external audio data to the module (e.g. from a side chain or vocoder microphone input); these are declared for you but not used in the book projects

3.7.1.2 Output Ports

- Modulation output values are written into an array that has pre-defined slots for the various modulators; e.g. the LFO writes to the bipolar array slot, while the EG writes to the unipolar slot
- FM outputs are identical to the audio output for a given module; all oscillator module output buffers may be used as FM input buffers for other modules

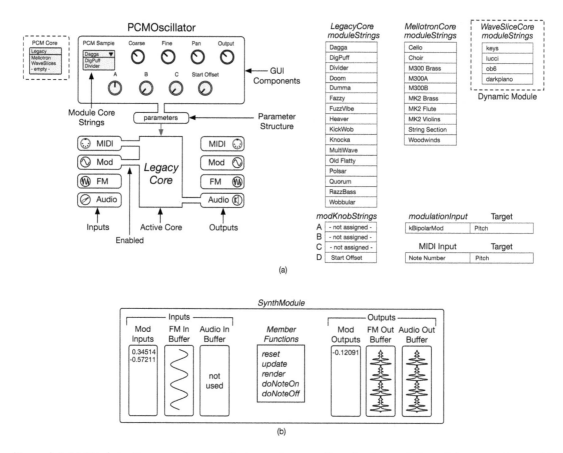

Figure 3.3 (a) Module diagrams show attributes and connections in the module and its core, along with module and mod knob strings for each core; notice that the *moduleStrings* show up in the GUI as a selection list and (b) the *SynthModule* block diagram

- Audio output is written into a pre-prepared *AudioBuffer* object that always has two channels (for dual-mono or stereo operation) and is only valid for oscillators as the modulators write to the modulation arrays
- A MIDI output structure is provided but not used in the projects

3.7.2 SynthModule *Virtual Functions*

All modules must override the five *SynthModule* virtual functions: *reset, update, render, doNoteOn*, and *doNoteOff*. These correspond to the five *SynthVoice* virtual functions with identical names. The engine calls the voice object functions, which, in turn, call the individual module functions. Table 3.2 lists these virtual functions, along with a brief description; they are also shown in Figure 3.2. We will look deeper into these functions as they apply to the different modules inside

Table 3.2 SynthModule virtual functions that all modules must override and descriptions

Function Name	Description
reset	Sets the sample rate and resets member objects
update	Using GUI and modulation input, calculate the object variables for the current block of data (e.g. filter f_c, EG release time,…)
render	Render output; modulators write to modulation outputs, oscillators write to audio buffers, processors read from and write to audio buffers
doNoteOn	Perform note-on activities
doNoteOff	Perform note-off activities (used on EG only)

of their respective chapters. The main point here is that the synth voice will call these functions directly from its own functions of the same name.

3.8 Module Cores

Each *SynthModule* owns an array of up to four *ModuleCore* objects. The module cores are specialized components that operate within the overall behavior of the module but with individualized functionality. For example, the *SynthFilter* is a *SynthModule* that has two module cores: *VAFilterCore* and *BQFilterCore*. Both of these implement audio filters, but one is used specifically for the virtual analog filters described in Chapter 12, while the other provides alternate but useful filters based on the biquad algorithms in the first edition FX book. When the user selects a core, two things happen: first, the new core object becomes the "active core," and second, its specialized string list of up to 16 items is loaded into a GUI control for the user. In Figure 3.2, you can see the module core names in a list in the dotted box; this GUI control is available for all modules and is not shown in the individual module chapter diagrams.

3.8.1 ModuleCore *Strings*

The *VAFilterCore* and *BQFilterCore* will likely expose different strings for their different filters, and if some stings have the same name, that is fine. In Figure 3.2, you can see the core module strings for the PCM oscillator's *LegacyCore* object as it appears in the module chapter. This array of strings is a *ModuleCore* member, and you supply the string names in the core's constructor. Figure 3.4(a) shows how the module strings are related to their cores and how these will appear to the user on a typical GUI using the *PCMOscillator* and its cores that expose the bank waveforms. For this object, each core is slightly different: the legacy core uses transient + loop PCM samples, while the Mellotron uses single long recordings of notes, and the wave slice core uses the Aubio audio tool to slice up the *.wav* files that are its data arrays.

3.9 SynthModule/ModuleCore Relationship

The *SynthModule* is an ultra-light wrapper around the active core; examine the class definition in *synthbase.h*, and you will see that the *ModuleCore* base class virtual functions have the same names as the *SynthModule* functions in Table 3.2. The difference is in the argument that is passed

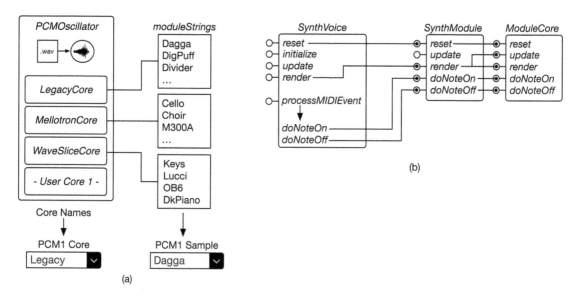

Figure 3.4 (a) The PCM oscillator includes three pre-written cores and one empty (user) core that allow the PCM oscillator to implement banks of waveforms; (b) the relationship between voice, module, and core is tight

to the core virtual functions. Figure 3.2(b) shows a module with its module I/O and parameters. The core sits inside and does the real work for each of the module's functions. In order to give the core access to the I/O buffers, modulation arrays, and parameters, the module passes it a data *CoreProcData* structure that contains mainly interface pointers and references to these resources, and the core uses them during its function calls. There are some advantages to using this paradigm for SynthLab:

1   Cores are simple and compact; if you want to focus your work on just one type of module and not the entire synth, then you only have a few files to edit – usually just two
2   Cores follow the idea of C++ encapsulation; each one hides the details of functionality of a concept that is encapsulated; the filter cores generate filters in drastically different ways (virtual analog versus biquad), but the user only sees another bank of filters
3   Cores allow for the concept of program and data "banks" in which each core implements 16 different variations on its basic theme, each being presented to the user in a list every time the core changes; each wavetable oscillator core generates a bank of waveforms, each PCM sample oscillator generates a bank of samples, each filter core creates a set of filters, etc.

Cores allow me to make a version of SynthLab that can dynamically load the cores you write and compile as a plugin-within-a-plugin; my version of the SynthLab-DM projects is able to load core DLLs into itself at startup time (you can add this functionality yourself if you know how to user your plugin framework).

If you are using my SynthLab pre-compiled plugins, you can build a "core plugin" – a plugin that is loaded <u>into</u> the SynthLab plugin at startup time – allowing you to customize each module for yourself. This allows you to go through the book, learning about each module and its parameters, and understanding its inner code and theory of operation. The cores are pure C++ and are not tied to any plugin framework, requiring a minimal compiler setup that is so simple, you won't need *CMake*. You can also build your own modules in any component flavor and add them to the existing plugin. This means that my SynthLab plugins are dynamic, and you may modify and change their core operations – all of the modules in Figure 3.1, if you like – to suit your own research or interest areas.

3.9.1 CoreProcData *Structure*

The cores require access to the module's I/O ports and parameters, accomplished with the *Core-ProcData* structure that is setup with only basic C++ data types and agnostic C++ interfaces, whose functions likewise only contain the basic data types. Unlike most of SynthLab, this structure does not use the *std::* library and has no shared pointers and no *std::strings*. This allows for the dynamic loading of core modules (mini-plugins); any function calls from the host (the plugin DLL) to the server (the core DLL) must cross the "thunk" barrier, meaning that arguments passed back and forth must have C++ memory footprints that are exactly described and known a-priori. The *CoreProcData* consists of input and output audio buffer pointers, along with several safe interfaces for accessing the outer module's resources, including *IModulator*, *IWavetableDatabase*, *IPCMSampleDatabase*, and *IMIDIInput*, all of which are documented online. Since each module has a separate custom parameter structure, a *void** is used to pass this structure in and out of the core using *void** cloaking and un-cloaking.

3.9.2 SynthModule *Constructor*

The *SynthModule* constructors follow a three-step pattern:

1   Setup the audio input and output buffers; oscillators only have outputs, while processors (filters and amplifiers) have both inputs and outputs
2   Set up a *CoreProcData* member structure that will be used for communication with the core
3   Instantiate the cores, store them, and select the default core

This code is fundamentally identical in every module-core relationship and only varies with the kind of core and audio capabilities; there is no need to repeat it in every chapter. Here is the constructor for the *PCMOscillator* that creates three member cores.

Create audio buffers for inter-module signal flow; note use of constants with 0 inputs and 2 outputs:

```
// --- create our audio buffers
audioBuffers.reset(new SynthProcessInfo(SMPL _ OSC _ INPUTS, /* 0 */
                                        SMPL _ OSC _ OUTPUTS, /* 2 */
                                        blockSize)); // prefer 32 or 64
```

The *coreProcessData* structure gets its interface pointers from the module's resources: audio I/O buffers, modulation I/O arrays, MIDI data, and databases. Examine each core's constructor for the details:

```
// --- setup the core processing structure for dynamic cores
coreProcessData.inputBuffers = getAudioBuffers()->getInputBuffers();
coreProcessData.outputBuffers = getAudioBuffers()->getOutputBuffers();
coreProcessData.modulationInputs =
                                modulationInput->getModulatorPtr();
coreProcessData.modulationOutputs =
                                modulationOutput->getModulatorPtr();
etc. . .
```

Finally, create the cores, and store them on the module's array, then select the first core as the default.

```
// --- setup the cores
for (uint32_t i = 0; i < NUM_MODULE_CORES; i++)
    moduleCores[i] = nullptr;


std::shared_ptr<PCMLegacyCore>
                defaultCore = std::make_shared<PCMLegacyCore>();
addModuleCore(std::static_pointer_cast<ModuleCore>(defaultCore));

etc…


// --- core[0]
selectDefaultModuleCore();
```

3.9.3 SynthModule *Wrapper Functions*

Most of the module-to-core functions are trivial as they simply call the selected module's functions of the same name with the *coreProcData* argument. The *reset* function must reset all of the cores, while the rest of the functions operate on the selected core. Here is the *reset* function for the *PCMOscillator*:

```
bool PCMOscillator::reset(double _sampleRate)
{
    // --- PCM cores need path to DLL for adding to database
    coreProcessData.dllPath = dllDirectory.c_str();
    coreProcessData.sampleRate = _sampleRate;

    for (uint32_t i = 0; i < NUM_MODULE_CORES; i++)
    {
        if(moduleCores[i])
            moduleCores[i]->reset(coreProcessData);
    }
```

```
        return true;
}
```

The update function merely calls the core version:

```
bool PCMOscillator::update(){
        return selectedCore->update(coreProcessData);
}
```

The render function parses the *samplesToProcess* variable and updates the *coreProcData* structure:

```
bool PCMOscillator::render(uint32_t samplesToProcess){
        // --- update
        coreProcessData.samplesToProcess = samplesToProcess;

        return selectedCore->render(coreProcessData);
}
```

The note-on and note-off functions apply the current *MIDINoteEvent*:

```
bool PCMOscillator::doNoteOn(MIDINoteEvent& noteEvent)
{
        coreProcessData.noteEvent = noteEvent;

        return selectedCore->doNoteOn(coreProcessData);
}
```

3.10 Review

Chapters 2 and 3 contain the fundamentals of how the synth engine, voices, modules, and their module cores are related and used to create the synth projects, and show the main coding details of each object connection. The idea is to give you an understanding of how Figure 3.1 works on the different levels – from engine to voice to modules to cores. Go back and review Figure 3.1, and follow the function calls from the framework to the engine's *render* operation. The engine calls the voice *render*, which calls *render* on all modules, which, in turn, call *update* and *render* on the active core.

Chapters 7–13 and 14–15 contain *SynthModule* and *ModuleCores* for each of the building blocks used for the SynthLab projects. Each of these "module chapters" has the theory of operation, followed by the module and core descriptions and implementation strategies. There are a considerable number of interfaces, synth objects, helper objects, and functions included, and these are documented online at www.willpirkle.com/SynthLab-docs. You will need to download the code for the projects and spend time comparing the code with what you read in the text as you go through the book, which will also take considerable patience. After the module chapters, we will put the pieces together in the complete SynthLab projects. You have several options for their implementation, which are discussed in Chapter 5.

Bibliography

Gabrielli, Leonard. 2020. *Developing Virtual Synthesizers with VCV Rack*, Chaps. 1, 3. New York: Routledge.
SynthLab Documentation. 2020. www.willpirkle.com/synthlab-docs, Accessed on October 14, 2020

4 Synth Operational Modes

Polyphony and Voice-Stealing

Synthesizers have three basic operational modes: monophonic (mono), monophonic-unison (unison), and polyphonic (poly). The two monophonic modes include an option for legato operation in which the amp EG does not re-trigger for new note-events; this is covered in Section 7.1.3. Note that legato mode only applies if the user holds a key down, then presses another key without releasing the first key, generating two note-on events in succession. It does not apply when playing mono but releasing each key before triggering a new note. On some synths, the legato mode has its own dedicated switch; for SynthLab, I combined legato mode with the two mono modes to produce a total of five synth modes of operation:

1 **Mono**: basic monophonic operation that uses the same voice object for every note-event; new note-events re-start the amp EG and produce transient edges (clicks)
2 **Legato**: monophonic mode with legato slurring
3 **Unison**: monophonic mode with multiple voice objects mixed together and each detuned slightly, producing a thick sound
4 **Unison legato**: unison mode with legato slurring
5 **Polyphonic**: polyphonic mode; when all voices are exhausted, and a new note-event arrives, an existing voice is sacrificed to play the new note, aka voice-stealing

When dealing with mono and unison modes (non-legato), we must make an important decision on handling the re-triggering of the amp EG when the new note-event arrives. One of our options is to trigger the new note immediately, placing the EG back into the attack state from wherever the EG was in its cycle. The second is to shut down the EG through an ultra-fast release time of about a millisecond, thereby bringing the output down to zero, then moving to the attack state and re-starting the EG. The second mode is called *return-to-zero* (RTZ). Both modes are covered in Sections 7.1.2 and 7.1.3, and shown in Figure 7.3. The EG objects expose an additional virtual function named *shutdown* that places the EG into this fast-release state, allowing the voice to quickly shutdown the EG. The *shutdown* function is also used in polyphony during voice-stealing so that one voice may be quickly silenced to make way for a new note-event.

> The SynthLab projects all implement RTZ mode for the monophonic non-legato modes such that the monophonic voice steals from itself if a new note is triggered while the single monophonic voice is playing. The legato modes ignore the *shutdown* operation and are therefore simpler to implement and understand.

4.1 The Note-Event Lifecycle

It is important to clarify the difference between the note-off event and the end-of-note signal. As it turns out, the amp EG plays a major role in the grand scheme of things. The amp EG is the envelope generator attached to the output DCA; it produces the synthesized signal's time domain envelope. Figure 4.1 shows a synth voice consisting of an oscillator and a DCA that is connected to the amp EG and shows the four parts of the note-event lifecycle:

1   **Note-on message**: resets objects and starts amp EG in attack state
2   **Note-off message**: places amp EG into the release state; all other modules continue operation as normal
3   **Waiting for release**: the voice monitors the state of the amp EG, waiting until its release state has finished
4   **Release complete**: when the amp EG finishes its release phase, it goes into the off state; only at this point is the note-event finished and the voice off

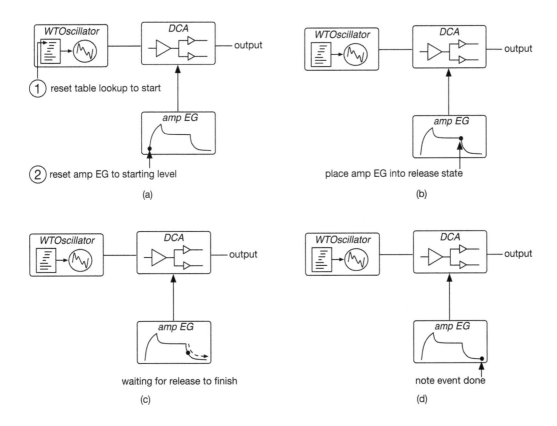

Figure 4.1 The four states of the note-event lifecycle: (a) the note-on message resets objects and places the amp EG into the attack state; (b) the note-off message places the amp EG into the release state; (c) the voice waits for the amp EG to finish, rendering output the entire time; and (d) the note-event is finished when the amp EG reaches the off state

4.2 *SynthEngine* MIDI Processing

The engine and voice object both handle the note-on and note-off messaging. The engine's *process-MIDIEvent* method splits the incoming MIDI messages into note-events and CC events, then calls the voice's *processMIDIEvent*, which handles the more complicated details; it is shown in Figure 4.2. The block marked "Choose Target Voice" represents the logic for the five modes of operation. For mono and unison modes, the choice is hardwired but more complex for the poly mode that involves voice-stealing. This chapter is all about making that choice.

4.2.1 SynthEngine *Mono Modes*

The engine parameters include a variable for the operational mode coded as an index-based parameter from the GUI control that displays the modes for the user. The index is compared to a strongly typed *enum* for easier code readability:

```
enum class synthMode { kMono, kLegato, kUnison, kUnisonLegato, kPoly };
```

The *SynthEngine* performs the initial MIDI message processing, as covered in Section 2.3.2.3, and implements the engine-side of the synth operational modes. For mono and legato modes, the *SynthEngine* uses the first *SynthVoice* object in its array for all note-events and simply forwards the MIDI event to the voice object for processing. The engine's *processMIDIEvent* function is blissfully simple for mono and legato. The note-on and note-off code is shown here, using the GUI index parameter for decoding the mode:

```
bool SynthEngine::processMIDIEvent(midiEvent& event)
```

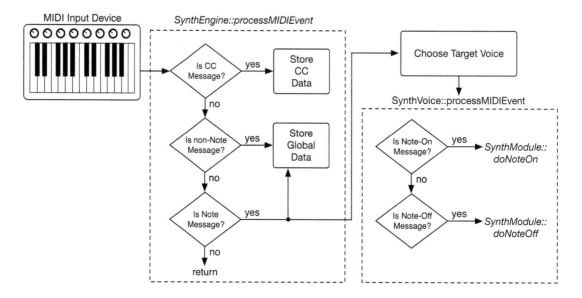

Figure 4.2 The engine decodes the incoming MIDI messages; for note-on and note-off, the engine first finds a target voice, then forwards the MIDI processing function call

For note-on operation the engine saves the current note number and velocity in the global MIDI data for the objects to share – for example, filter key-tracking and oscillator portamento both require knowing the MIDI note number.

```
if (event.midiMessage == NOTE _ ON)
{
    // --- set current MIDI data
    midiInputData->setGlobalMIDIData(kCurrentMIDINoteNumber,
                                     event.midiData1);
    midiInputData->setGlobalMIDIData(kCurrentMIDINoteVelocity,
                                     event.midiData2);


    // --- mono mode
    if (parameters->synthModeIndex == enumToInt(synthMode::kMono) ||
       parameters->synthModeIndex == enumToInt(synthMode::kLegato))
    {
        // --- just use voice 0
        synthVoices[0]->processMIDIEvent(event);
    }
```

For note-off operation, the engine first queries the voice with *isVoiceActive*, then sends the MIDI message to the voice and returns immediately.

```
else if (event.midiMessage == NOTE _ OFF)
{
    // --- for mono, we only use one voice, number [0]
    if (parameters->synthModeIndex == enumToInt(synthMode::kMono) ||
        parameters->synthModeIndex == enumToInt(synthMode::kLegato))
    {
        if (synthVoices[0]->isVoiceActive())
        {
            synthVoices[0]->processMIDIEvent(event);
            return true;
        }
    }
}
```

4.2.2 SynthEngine *Unison Modes*

Unison and unison legato are handled just like the mono modes except that multiple voices are all called at once with the same MIDI messages, placing multiple voices into the running state. Both unison modes involve detuning the voices slightly and setting the oscillators to start at slightly different phases so they do not sum together in a way that produces a click or pop due to the in-phase components. For SynthLab, unison mode uses four voices: *synthVoice[0] – synthVoice[3]*. The engine's MIDI processing is identical to the mono modes, except for the fact that it uses multiple voices.

For both note-on and note-off operation, the engine calls the four voice functions in succession, and the code is identical for both messages:

```
if (parameters->synthModeIndex == enumToInt(synthMode::kUnison) ||
    parameters->synthModeIndex == enumToInt(synthMode::kUnisonLegato))
{

            // --- SynthLab: 4 voices
            synthVoices[0]->processMIDIEvent(event);
            synthVoices[1]->processMIDIEvent(event);
            synthVoices[2]->processMIDIEvent(event);
            synthVoices[3]->processMIDIEvent(event);

}
```

4.3 *SynthEngine* Unison Detuning

The engine is also responsible for setting the detuning, panning, and phase offsets of some of the unison voice objects. This happens in the engine's *setParameters* method so that the detuning is updated if the user changes the control while notes are playing. The engine parameters include the global detuning that the user controls. The voice parameters include their own unison detuning value, which is set differently for each voice to thicken up the sound, as well as a phase offset variable. The code in the engine's *setParameters* method sets these variables, and you have the ability to customize this code as you like. Note that for many synths, unison mode also involves panning the voices differently, but all SynthLab oscillators are stereo in nature, and individual oscillators may be panned. If you want to override this, feel free to do so; a *unisonPan* variable is already declared for you in the voice parameters, but you will need to modify the rendering function accordingly. The engine's *setParameters* function has all the action; notice how the global unison detuning is applied differently to each of the four voices. The phase offsets were set with experimentation and prevent clicks and pops. The engine cycles though the voice objects in order to call their corresponding *update* methods:

```
for (unsigned int i = 0; i < MAX _ VOICES; i++)
{
    // --- update voices
    synthVoices[i]->update();
```

Inside this for-loop, we check the mode parameter and issue the detuning and phase offsets – note that the phase offsets only apply during note-on operation.

```
if (parameters->synthModeIndex == enumToInt(synthMode::kUnison) ||
    parameters->synthModeIndex == enumToInt(synthMode::kUnisonLegato))
{
// --- voice 0
    if (i == 0)
    {
            parameters->voiceParameters->unisonDetuneCents = 0.0;
            parameters->voiceParameters->unisonStartPhase = 0.0;
            parameters->voiceParameters->dcaParameters->panValue = 0.5;
    }
```

```
// --- voice 1
else if (i == 1)
{
    parameters->voiceParameters->unisonDetuneCents =
                parameters->globalUnisonDetune _ Cents;
    parameters->voiceParameters->unisonStartPhase = 13.0;
    parameters->voiceParameters->dcaParameters->panValue = -1.0;
}
etc . . .
```

Table 4.1 lists the voice detuning and phase offsets for unison mode – feel free to change these or add more voices for a thicker unison sound.

4.4 Voice State and MIDI Event Storage

The voice object maintains a few Boolean flags, which it uses to help implement the synth modes. The voice keeps track of a simple state variable named *voiceIsActive* that is true as long as the voice is rendering output in the first three phases of Figure 2.1 and is accessed via the *isVoiceActive* method. When a new MIDI note-on event is received, the data is stored in the member structure *voiceMIDIEvent*, which persists until the note is either turned off or stolen. During steal operations, the voice keeps track of a Boolean flag *stealPending* during the steal operation and another MIDI structure *voiceStealMIDIEvent* that stores information about the new note. The voice state variable and steal flag are used along with the MIDI event structures to implement the steal operation.

4.5 Voice-Stealing

Voice-stealing is usually associated with polyphonic operation. The *SynthEngine* declares some number of voice objects based on the synth type, target device, CPU power, and other information. For simplicity, the SynthLab projects have a fixed number of voices, but you can override that behavior in the constructor for your own experiments. If the user presses enough keys or generates enough note-on messages, the engine will run out of voices at some point. If this happens and a new note-on message arrives, the engine will need to implement a plan for stealing an existing voice to use for the new note-event. This involves code on both the engine's and the voice object's sides. The engine will need to use a heuristic technique to choose the voice to steal, but after that, it simply issues a note-on message to that voice, as with other voices. On receiving the note-on message, the voice determines that it is being stolen and sets up logic on its side to handle that part.

Table 4.1 Voice detuning, panning, and starting phase offsets for unison mode

Voice Index	Detuning Coefficients Multiplied with globalUnisonDetune_Cents	Pan Value	Oscillator Start Phase Offset
0	0	0.5 (center)	0
1	(+1.0)	−1.0 (left)	13 degrees
2	(−1.0)	+1.0 (right)	−13 degrees
3	(0.707)	−0.5 (halfway left)	37 degrees

4.5.1 Voice-Stealing for RTZ Operation

SynthLab uses the RTZ EG operation in the non-legato mono and unison modes to avoid inconsistent clicks and pops. However, this requires quickly shutting down the current voice, then stealing it once it completes its shutdown. In this mode, voice actually steals itself. The voice implements the *processMIDIEvent* function, which usually calls either its *doNoteOn* or its *doNoteOff* sub-functions during normal operations.

4.5.2 Note-On Steal Operation

The steal operation starts with logic in the voice's note-on message handler, which determines whether the voice is being stolen. Once that determination is made, the following events occur:

1 Voice stores the current note-on MIDI message in a member structure *voiceStealMIDIEvent* – this contains the note number and velocity information for the stolen event
2 Voice calls the *shutdown* function on the amp EG to quickly shut itself down
3 Voice sets *stealPending* so it will know how to handle the end-of-note event when the amp EG expires

4.5.3 Post-Shutdown Steal Operation

During the one-millisecond shutdown time, the voice's oscillators and other modules will continue normal operation for the length of the render process. The voice will need to monitor the amp EG and wait for it to complete its shutdown cycle at the end of the *render* function, as described in Section 4.5.5. Once detected, the voice performs the following:

1 Check the *stealPending* flag to see if the voice is being stolen, and if so:
2 Call the voice's note-off handler – this was never called because the event was stolen
3 Copy the *voiceStealMIDIEvent* structure into the *voiceMIDIEvent* structure
4 Call the note-on handler with the new MIDI event information, switching the pitch and velocity to the stolen note – the steal operation is complete

The RTZ voice self-steal operation is simpler than poly mode stealing because there is no selection of a target voice, so the engine-side code does nothing more than call the voice's *processMIDIEvent* method. Studying RTZ operation first allows you to see the voice-side code in isolation, and it is identical to the poly mode operation.

4.5.4 SynthVoice *Stealing Code Part 1*

The code that implements the steps in Section 4.5.2 is located in the *SynthVoice:: processMIDIevent* function and is triggered when the voice gets a note-on message while it is still active. Once the EG is shut down, and flags are set, the function returns. If it is not stealing, it simply calls its *doNoteOn* handler.

```
if (event.midiMessage == NOTE _ ON)
{
        // --- steal detection
        if (isVoiceActive())
```

```
        {
                // --- save information
                voiceStealMIDIEvent = event;

                // --- set amp EG into shutdown mode
                ampEG->shutdown();

                // --- set the steal flag
                stealPending = true;
                return true;
        }

// --- call the subfunction if NOT stealing
        doNoteOn(event);
}
```

Notice that the note-off message is always handled the same way, with a simple call to the note-off handler.

```
else if (event.midiMessage == NOTE _ OFF)
        doNoteOff(event);
```

4.5.5 SynthVoice *Stealing Code Part 2*

At the end of each *render* function call, the voice checks to see if the amp EG has expired into the off state; if not, it simply returns as usual.

```
if (voiceIsActive)
{
        if (ampEG->getState() == enumToInt(EGState::kOff))
        etc . . .
```

At this point, the voice knows that the note-event is finished and will either shut off or perform the steal operation, depending on the state variable we set. For the steal operation, we implement the steps in Section 4.5.3. If no steal is pending, then the voice goes into the inactive state, setting its state variable to *false*.

```
// --- check for steal pending
if (stealPending)
{
        // --- turn off old note event
        doNoteOff(voiceMIDIEvent);

        // --- copy new note MIDI info
        voiceMIDIEvent = voiceStealMIDIEvent;

        // --- turn on the new note
        doNoteOn(voiceMIDIEvent);
```

```
    // --- stealing accomplished!
    stealPending = false;
}
else
    voiceIsActive = false;
```

The two functions here comprise the two-part steal operation that the voice implements for RTZ and poly modes. To complete the chapter's discussion, we just need to examine the engine-side code for polyphonic operation.

4.6 Polyphony and Voice Timestamps

For polyphony, the engine services the note-on message in two stages. First, it tries to find a free, unused voice in its array. If all voices are active, then it finds a suitable voice to steal. This code is implemented in the engine's *processMIDIEvent* function and uses *getFreeVoiceIndex* and *getVoiceIndexToSteal* – note that these return the index in the engine's array of the suitable voice object.

```
else if (parameters->synthModeIndex == enumToInt(synthMode::kPoly))
{
    // --- get index of the next available voice (for note on events)
    int voiceIndex = getFreeVoiceIndex();

    // --- find a voice to steal
    if (voiceIndex < 0)
        voiceIndex = getVoiceIndexToSteal();

    // --- start/steal the voice
    if (voiceIndex >= 0)
        synthVoices[voiceIndex]->processMIDIEvent(event);
```

Once that index is found, the engine simply calls the corresponding voice's *processMIDIEvent* as usual – there are no extra functions or Boolean variables to set since the voice operates in a very strict manner, as described in Sections 4.5.4 and 4.5.5, and knows when it is being stolen. This means that the engine-side code involves selecting the voice to steal and nothing else. Selection of the voice involves a heuristic technique, which is a decision-making operation that has no optimal solution (other than making a new voice object). For voice-stealing, several common heuristics apply, including:

1   Stealing the "oldest" voice's note – the voice that has been playing longer than all the others
2   Stealing the voice with the oldest note that is also *not* the lowest MIDI pitch since drone notes are common across many musical styles
3   Stealing a voice based on the chord being played; choosing inner or outer voices, or other advanced selection criteria
4   Stealing notes based on MIDI channels (e.g. MIDI channel 10 has priority as the general MIDI drum channel)

We are going to use the first heuristic: steal the oldest voice. This requires us to know something about the ordering of the voice note-on events. For this heuristic, we only care about the absolute age of the voice's active state and can use a simple time-stamping method. We don't care about the *actual* DAW system time that the note-events occur at, just the ordering. This is accomplished with a simple counter named *timestamp*, which is a *SynthVoice* member variable and includes three functions for manipulating it:

```
uint32_t timestamp = 0;
```

```
uint32_t getTimestamp() { return timestamp; }
void incrementTimestamp() { timestamp++; }
void clearTimestamp() { timestamp = 0; }
```

During the voice's note-on handler, the timestamp is cleared just before we detect the voice steal.

```
if (event.midiMessage == NOTE_ON)
{
    // --- clear timestamp
    clearTimestamp();

    // --- detect if we are being stolen:
```

This means that after the *processMIDIEvent* function call returns to the engine, the newly active voice will have a *timestamp* value of 0. Immediately after issuing a note-on call to a voice, the engine loops over its array, incrementing the timestamps of all active voices.

```
// --- increment all timestamps for note-on voices
for (int i = 0; i < MAX_VOICES; i++)
{
    if (synthVoices[i]->isVoiceActive())
        synthVoices[i]->incrementTimestamp();
}
```

This means that the newly triggered voice will have *timestamp* = 1, while the previous voice will have *timestamp* = 2, and so on. The voice with the highest timestamp value is the oldest one that's active – the voice to steal has been identified. Figure 4.3 shows a sequence of voice activations and time stamping for an engine with four total voice objects. In Figure 4.3(a), all voices are free, while Figure 4.3(b)–(e) show how the voice timestamps are incremented for one, two, three, and four note-on events. When a new note-on event arrives, the engine finds voice 0 with the largest timestamp and selects it. During the voice note-on handler, the timestamp is reset to 0; it is then immediately incremented with the preceding code and becomes the youngest voice.

The function *getFreeVoiceIndex* is trivial and simply loops over the voices, testing the *voiceIsActive* flag on each one, returning the free index or −1 if not found. The function *getVoiceIndexToSteal* is where you implement your heuristic. To find the oldest voice, you simply examine the timestamps of the active voices:

```
int SynthEngine::getVoiceIndexToSteal()
{
    int index = -1;
    int timestamp = -1;
    int currentTimestamp = -1;
```

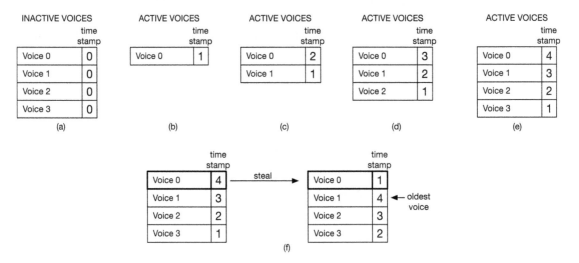

Figure 4.3 An engine with four voices: (a) prior to any notes triggered (b) when the first note is triggered, voice 0 is selected then (c) second note and (d) third note and (e) fourth notes are triggered with timestamps incremented each time and (f) after the oldest voice is stolen, it becomes the youngest and so on

```
for (int i = 0; i < MAX_VOICES; i++)
{
        currentTimestamp = (int)(synthVoices[i]->getTimestamp());

        // --- find index of oldest voice
        if (currentTimestamp > timestamp)
        {
                timestamp = currentTimestamp;
                index = i;
        }
}
return index;
}
```

In addition, the voice has query functions for its MIDI note number, so you may use heuristics that involve a note's pitch in relation to the other voices. For example, to find the oldest voice that is not playing the lowest note, you would modify the function above to find the two oldest voices, then query each one for the MIDI note number and return the index of the voice with the higher of the two values.

```
uint32_t getMIDINoteNumber() { return voiceMIDIEvent.midiData1; }
```

4.7 Review

The MIDI note lifecycle depends on the amp EG's state to determine when the note-event has finished so that plays a role in the synth modes. The legato modes do not reset the amp EG, so there is no click to suppress, and their operation only involves informing the EG that it is in legato mode. For mono and unison non-legato modes, RTZ is implemented so that depressing a note while another is held will shut down the existing note before starting the next, an operation that is a voice self-steal operation. This operation only involves voice-side code. In polyphonic operation, the engine gets involved as it uses a heuristic function to select a suitable voice to steal.

Bibliography

Braut, Christian. 1994. *The Musician's Guide to MIDI*, Appendix A. Alameda: SYBEX.
Sound on Sound Magazine. 1999. "Synth Secrets." http://www.soundonsound.com/sos/allsynthsecrets.htm, Accessed October 14, 2020
SynthLab Documentation. 2020. www.willpirkle.com/synthlab-docs, Accessed on October 14, 2020

5 Learning and Using the SynthLab Objects & Projects

Now that we've covered the SynthLab architecture, synth modules, cores, and their operational phases, we can learn how to use SynthLab. You have numerous options here, and you can move around easily, from testing modules in the precompiled SynthLab-DM versions to integrating small bits and pieces into your existing projects to cloning the entire engine and voice architecture and building the GUIs to go with them. Remember that SynthLab is not tied to any third-party plugin framework and does not use any third-party libraries or code as a result.

5.1 Designing Modules with the SynthLab-DM Projects

The easiest way to start using SynthLab is with the *DM* projects. In this case, you will compile a tiny *.dll* file (Windows) or *.dylib* file (MacOS), which encapsulates a single synth module – a specific type of EG, filter, LFO, or pitched oscillator. The only difference between the various *DM* synths is the quad oscillator bank, described in Section 1.5. This means that any LFO, EG, or filter module you design will instantly work as a dynamic module in any of the other synths. In the ensuing chapters, each time you are introduced to a module core, you have the ability to copy, modify, or redesign that core as you like and then test it within the SynthLab-DM project.

There are example dynamic modules with code for every type of component. Suppose you created your own wavetable oscillator module that generates drum sounds, and you named it "Drum WT DLL." You set up your tables and assign a list of your waveform strings: "Kick 1, Kick2," etc. You also have a cool idea for filtering and reversing the audio, so you implement four of your own mod knob functions, and you assign the labels. You then compile your module mini-plugin and place the result in the proper location (detailed in Section 5.2.2). When you open your DAW and instantiate the wavetable synth, your new module will appear in the list of cores along with the others, and the mod knob labels will change to reflect your ideas, as shown in Figure 5.1. This allows you to design as many modules as you like and truly customize the synth in your own unique way.

5.2 SynthLab-DM Modules Are Dynamic Linked Libraries

In order to make your own dynamic module, you will need to create a simple project in Visual Studio or Xcode that will generate a dynamic linked library (DLL) that is loaded at runtime. If you are unfamiliar with DLLs and how they relate to plugins, check out my FX plugin book for a

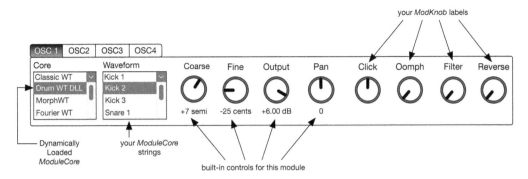

Figure 5.1 You can create internal modules for the SynthLab-DM synths without needing to recompile the entire project; this shows a module named Drum WT DLL that exposes a set of waveform and mod knob strings for the user to see

complete detailed description. The Visual Studio and Xcode DLL projects are so lean and simple, there is no need for a *CMake* script or other utility – there are less than five steps required for both OS platforms. You can find the exact step-by-step details in the SynthLab documentation at www. willpirkle.com/synthlab-docs; you will be delighted at how painless it is to set up these mini-plugin projects.

5.2.1 *SynthLab-DM Modules Generate a C++* **ModuleCore** *Object*

In Section 3.9, you learned about the overview of the *ModuleCore* and its relationship to the outer container *SynthModule*. You also saw how the *CoreProcData* structure is used as the function argument that connects and allows safe communication across the thunk barrier between the *DM* synth and your module. The *ModuleCore* object represents the SynthLab-DM API. Your derived class overrides five functions, plus a constructor, and the DLL project creates a new instance of this object that is delivered into the SynthLab-DM synth at startup time. It then shows up as a module core, along with the others that are built into each project. You have complete access to all of the module core code, so you can freely use any existing core as a basis for your own designs. And you can test and debug your module within the DAW of your choice – the debugger will show you how the core is being loaded and used. The *ModuleCore* virtual functions are shown below.

```
class ModuleCore


// --- ModuleCore pure virtual functions
virtual bool reset(CoreProcData& processInfo) = 0;
virtual bool update(CoreProcData& processInfo) = 0;
virtual bool render(CoreProcData& processInfo) = 0;
virtual bool doNoteOn(CoreProcData& processInfo) = 0;
virtual bool doNoteOff(CoreProcData& processInfo) = 0;
```

```
// --- for EG only
virtual int32_t getState() { return -1; }
virtual bool shutdown() { return false; }
```

Your module must override and implement the functions in bold (and the two extra functions *get-State* and *shutdown* for EG modules only); with that accomplishment, you have a proper module to dynamically load. To streamline the modules, I've already created your derived class named *SynthLabCore* and set up the virtual functions, which are mostly empty. You may freely cut and paste from the example core code, copy the core objects and use some text replacement, or start from scratch. The details of these functions as they apply to each synth component are given in the following chapters.

   The DLL instantiation mechanism is fundamentally the same for Windows and MacOS. Your DLL module project ultimately exposes an export function that you can find in *synthlabdll.h* and *synthlabdll*.cpp, which includes code for both MacOS and Windows.
MacOS:

extern "C" SynthLab::ModuleCore* createModuleCore()

Windows:

```
#define DllExport extern "C" __ declspec(dllexport)
DllExport SynthLab::ModuleCore* createModuleCore();
```

The function creates the object with the *new* operator and returns it.

```
SynthLab::ModuleCore* createModuleCore()
{
    SynthLab::ModuleCore* module = new SynthLab::SynthLabCore();
    return module;
}
```

5.2.2 *Loading the C++* ModuleCore *Object*

The code to load your modules into the SynthLab-DM projects is likewise textbook DLL code for both OS platforms. Windows projects use the *LoadLibrary* function from *windows.h*, while MacOS projects use *dlopen* from *dlfcn.h*; these are heavily documented functions and operations that have been in use for a long time, so there is no need to cover them here. However, the location of your module DLL is very important as the loading functions will fail if this is not correct. Both AU and VST3 plugins are packaged in a bundle rather than a single file. A bundle is a folder that appears to the user as a file. When you download the SynthLab-DM projects, you will receive either a *.vst3* or a *.component* bundle. On Windows, you simply double click on the bundle icon to enter it, while on MacOS, you right click and use "Show Package Contents." Both bundles feature a special folder named *Resources*, located within the outer *Contents* folder. If you open this folder, you will see the *coremodules* subfolder, which will already include at least one *.dll* or *.dylib* for each kind of module. When you build your own module, you will then need to place it inside of the *Contents/Resources/ coremodules* folder. When you instantiate the DM-synth in the DAW, it scans this folder and tries to load all of the libraries it finds.

5.2.3 *Differentiating Your* ModuleCore

You only need to write two lines of code to instruct the DM-synth on how to treat your module. At the top of each module core constructor are two statements – for example, in the *BQFilterCore* module, you will find the following:

```
SynthLabCore::SynthLabCore ()
{
    moduleType = FILTER _ MODULE;
    moduleName = "BQFilterDLL";
    etc…
```

The *moduleType* dictates the type of component, and you have eight choices that implement the eight different supported cores according to Table 5.1. The module name you expose will show up in the module core lists for that kind of component. For example, if you create a module with *moduleType* = WTO_MODULE and name it "GoldenTables," then each wavetable oscillator's GUI control will list "GoldenTables," along with the pre-compiled cores for the user to choose.

There are three SynthLab modules that do not include cores in their design patterns. The DCA object is so simple that there is no need for module cores as there isn't much variation you can add. The *ModMatrix* object is mainly a bunch of for-loops and multiplication of simple gain and intensity factors but it has a very specific way of initialization and programming. The *WaveSequencer* only generates modulation values, making it quite simple to replace with your own; however, the GUI design and programming are very different from any of the *SynthModules*, so creating cores would be cumbersome from the GUI aspect. If you want to modify these objects, you will need to integrate them directly rather than writing the simple module DLLs.

Table 5.1 SynthLab's module types, their container objects, and the downloadable examples

moduleType	*SynthModule Container*	*SynthLab Examples*
LFO_MODULE	*LFO*	*ClassicLFOCore*
		FMLFOCore
EG_MODULE	*EnvelopeGenerator*	*AnalogEG*
		DXEG
		LinearEG
FILTER_MODULE	*SynthFilter*	*VAFilterCore*
		BQFilterCore
WTO_MODULE	*WavetableOscillator*	*ClassicWTCore*
		MorphWTCore
		DrumWTCore
		SFXWTCore
		FourierWTCore
VAO_MODULE	*VAOscillator*	*VAOCore*
FMO_MODULE	*FMOscillator*	*FMOCore*
PCMO_MODULE	*PCMOscillator*	*LegacyPCMCore*
		MellotronCore
		WaveSliceCore
KSO_MODULE	*KSOscillator*	*KSOCore*

5.2.4 *Testing Your Module Core*

Once you have copied your core object into the bundle's resources according to the instructions in Section 5.2.2, you will want to test it; actively debugging the module will show you the sequence of operations that all cores and their respective module containers carry out and will prepare you for integrating the main C++ objects. In your compiler, set the debug executable to your favorite DAW, then attach to the running process. Place breakpoints in your constructor and in each of the five (or seven, if EG module) overridden functions it implements. Then instantiate the synth plugin, and catch the constructor in action. Once constructed, play a note, then watch the sequence of events that occurs cyclically for each note-event, covered as the operational phases in Sections 1.8.1 through 1.8.6. Make sure you can trace the behavior of the *update* and *render* functions specifically as these are the two most important for each module. For the wavetable and PCM cores, take special care to watch how the modules query the wavetable and sample databases, then install their data as required – this is likewise very important if you want to create your own oscillators, especially the morphing varieties.

5.3 Using *SynthModules* in Your Projects

The next step up from working with the *ModuleCores* is to use the *SynthModules* that aggregate these cores. All *SynthModules* feature a stand-alone mode of operation, making it simple for you to use them straightaway. There are three kinds of *SynthModules*: modulators, pitched oscillators, and processors (filters, DCA, and delay FX), and all are easy to use outside of SynthLab.

5.3.1 *Modulator Objects in Stand-Alone Operation*

The LFO and EG objects are modulators that write their outputs into an output modulation array and have simpler constructors than the pitched oscillators. For example, say you want to incorporate the *SynthLFO* object into your own project. You have learned that all of the synth module constructors include two similar arguments: a shared pointer to the special GUI parameter structure and another shared pointer to the MIDI input structure. All *SynthModules* will construct their own shared-pointer to their custom parameter structures if the constructor argument is a *nullptr*, then you may access the structure using a function for stand-alone mode that has the same name across all objects: *getParameters*. The *SynthModule* and *ModuleCore* base classes store a Boolean flag, *standAloneOperation*, that you may set or clear. You may find it helpful to know the stand-alone state when you aggregate objects – see the *FMOperator* and *FMOCore* for an example of using this variable.

   The MIDI input data offers two choices. If you do not want or need to send MIDI data to the object, then construction is simple – just pass a *nullptr* in for the MIDI data, along with the object parameters; here, I use a shared pointer, but you could also use old-fashioned naked pointers as well. If you want to process individual samples rather than blocks, just set the *blockSize* parameter equal to 1.

```
// --- blocksize
uint32_t blockSize = 64;

//--- unique_ptr
std::unique_ptr<SynthLFO> myLFO;
```

```
// --- pass nullptrs for the parameters
myLFO.reset(new SynthLFO(nullptr, nullptr, blockSize));
```

In this case, the LFO will synthesize its own MIDI input data structure that is initialized with zeros; this will have no effect on the update phase.

If you want to send MIDI into the object, just create your own shared pointer and use it during construction:

```
std::shared_ptr<MidiInputData> midiInput =
                                std::make_shared<MidiInputData>();


// --- create object
myLFO.reset(new SynthLFO(midiInput, nullptr, blockSize));
```

To send MIDI information, you transfer data into the proper slot in the array. To set a mod wheel CC value of 42 and set the MIDI note velocity to 79, you would write:

```
midiInputData->setCCMIDIData(MOD_WHEEL, 42);
midiInputData->setGlobalMIDIData(kCurrentMIDINoteVelocity, 79);
```

This MIDI data will be used on the next update phase of the LFO operation, and there is no set-function to call as it is automatic.

To connect the LFO to GUI controls, or to manipulate it programmatically, you get its parameter structure and set the values. As with the MIDI input data, these parameters will be applied on the next update phase, and likewise, there is no set-function to call.

```
std::shared_ptr<LFOParameters> params = myLFO->getParameters();
```

To manipulate the object directly, you set its values accordingly:

```
params->frequency_Hz = 333.333;
params->outputAmplitude= 0.707;
```

If you are interfacing to a GUI, you send in the values directly from your GUI controls using actual (not normalized) values, as shown above.

```
double lfoRate = myGUI->lfoFreq;      // in HZ!
double lfoAmplitude = myGUI->lfoAmp; // actual value!
params->frequency_Hz = lfoRate;
params->outputAmplitude= lfoAmplitude;
```

5.3.2 *Accessing Modulator Outputs*

The ensuing chapters will detail how the modulation values are rendered and where they are written into the module's MIDI output array. To render and then access the fresh modulation values, you write:

```
//--- render
myLFO->render(blockSize);
```

```
// --- access output
double lfoModOut = myLFO->getModulationOutput()->getModValue(kLFONor-
                        malOutput);
```

The modulation array constants (e.g. *kLFONormalOutput* here) for every SynthLab object are found in *synthlabparams.h* as well as in the future chapters.

5.3.3 Oscillator Objects in Stand-Alone Operation: VA and KS

The virtual analog (VA) and Karplus-Strong (KS) oscillators use the same construction as the EG and LFO, so these follow the same pattern as the modulators. In stand-alone mode, they will create their own MIDI input and parameter structures, and accessing them is identical to the EG and LFOs for connecting to GUI controls or direct manipulation. All pitched oscillators write their outputs to *AudioBuffer* objects.

To create a virtual analog oscillator in stand-alone mode with MIDI input, you write:

```
//--- unique _ ptr
std::unique _ ptr<VAOscillator> vaOsc;

std::shared _ ptr<MidiInputData> midiInput =
                            std::make _ shared<MidiInputData>();
```

```
// --- pass nullptrs for the parameters
vaOsc.reset(new VAOscillator (midiInput, nullptr, blockSize));
```

And to access and manipulate parameters:

```
std::shared _ ptr< VAOscParameters > params = vaOsc->getParameters();
```

```
params->outputAmplitude _ dB = -3.0;
```

or from a GUI of your own design:

```
params->fineDetune = myGUI->oscFineDetune;
```

5.3.4 Oscillator Objects in Stand-Alone Operation: WT and PCM

The WT and PCM oscillators have extra arguments that are likewise shared pointers to the wavetable and PCM databases; these are described in Sections 9.3 and 11.4, respectively. Each database subclasses a base class abstract interface (*IWavetableSource*, and *IPCMSampleSource*) so that you may design your own versions in the way that makes most sense to you; these are key to efficiently sharing the tables and sample arrays. Manipulating the object via its parameter structure is done the same way as the other SynthLab components.

For example, to use the wavetable oscillator with my database object, and your MIDI input structure (assuming you want to send MIDI CC or global data to the pitched oscillator), you write:

```
// --- create shared resources
std::shared _ ptr<WavetableDatabase> wavetableDatabase =
                            std::make _ shared<WavetableDatabase>();
```

```
std::shared _ ptr<MidiInputData> midiInput =
                            std::make _ shared<MidiInputData>();

// --- declare
std::unique _ ptr<WTOscillator> wtOsc;

// --- create
wtOsc.reset(new WTOscillator(midiInput, nullptr, wavetableDatabase,
                            blockSize));
```

For true stand-alone operation, in which each oscillator creates and owns the database, you pass a *nullptr* for the database argument:

```
// --- create
wtOsc.reset(new WTOscillator(midiInput, nullptr, nullptr, blockSize));
```

The PCM sample oscillator named *PCMOscillator* works the same way – either provide a shared *IPCMSampleSource* database or the oscillator will create and use its own.

5.3.5 *Accessing Pitched Oscillator Audio Outputs*

To render the pitched oscillator output and access the audio samples, you use the *getAudioBuffer* methods. Remember that all SynthLab oscillators output stereo. As with the LFO, you may choose to render individual samples or blocks of audio. To render a block of 64 samples and access the output samples in a loop, you would write:

```
// --- render 64 samples
blockSize = 64;
wtOsc->render(blockSize);

float* leftBuffer =
        wtOsc->getAudioBuffers()->getOutputBuffer(LEFT _ CHANNEL);

float* rightBuffer =
        wtOsc->getAudioBuffers()->getOutputBuffer(RIGHT _ CHANNEL);

for (uint32 _ t i = 0; i < blockSize; i++)
{
    float leftSample = leftBuffer[i];
    float rightSample = rightBuffer[i];

    // --- do something with the audio...
}
```

5.3.6 *Filter Object in Stand-Alone Operation*

The last category includes objects that process audio from input to output, such as the *SynthFilter*. The constructors of these objects are identical to the LFO, EG, VA oscillator, and KS oscillator, requiring the MIDI input data and custom parameter structure shared pointers, and you can instantiate them in stand-alone operation using the same paradigms of providing the resources or letting the object manufacture its own. To create the *SynthFilter* object without MIDI input so that it manufactures its own parameter structure, and then set its parameters, you write:

```
// --- create in pure standalone form
std::unique_ptr<SynthFilter> filter;


filter.reset(new SynthFilter(nullptr, nullptr, blockSize));

// --- set the filter cutoff and Q controls
std::shared_ptr<FilterParameters> filtParams = filter->getParameters();


filtParams->fc = 1000.0;
filtParams->Q = 0.707;
```

5.3.7 Accessing Filter Audio Inputs and Outputs

A single *AudioBuffer* object includes both input and output arrays. To send a block of audio (including a block of only one sample) into the filter, you first prepare the audio buffer object using either the specialized constructor or the *init* method, which have the same arguments:

```
AudioBuffer(uint32_t numInputChannels,
            uint32_t numOutputChannels,
            uint32_t blockSize);
```

For example:

```
std::unique_ptr<AudioBuffer> filterBuffers;


filterBuffers.reset(new AudioBuffer(STEREO_CHANNELS,
                                    STEREO_CHANNELS, blockSize));
```

Load up the input buffer using the same for-loop that you use to access the output buffer:

```
float* leftInBuffer = filterBuffer->getInputBuffer(LEFT_CHANNEL);
float* rightInBuffer = filterBuffer->getInputBuffer(RIGHT_CHANNEL);

for (uint32_t i = 0; i < blockSize; i++)
{
        leftInBuffer[i] = // set here...;
        rightInBuffer[i] = // set here...;
}
```

To simplify buffer copy operations, I've included several helper functions (*synthfunctions.h*) that will move buffers into and out of the objects. To write the buffer into the filter and render the output, you write:

```
// --- to Filter1
copyBufferToInput(filterBuffers,                /* pointer to source */
                  filter->getAudioBuffers(), /* pointer to dest */
```

```
                    STEREO _ TO _ STEREO, /* stereo in, stereo out */
                    blockSize);           /* sample count */
```

```
// --- render filter
filter.render(blockSize);
```

Then, to get the filter's processed data, you use another helper function and the same kind of loop to access the samples.

```
// --- copy filter output to buffer output
copyOutputToOutput(filter->getAudioBuffers(), /* pointer to source */
                   filterBuffers,             /* pointer to dest */
                   STEREO _ TO _ STEREO,
                   blockSize)
```

5.4 Using *SynthEngines* in Your Projects

Each synth has a single *SynthEngine* object that encapsulates the complete project, and you only need to instantiate that engine object, then send it blocks of buffers to render into, along with the MIDI messages that occurred during that block, and update its state with the current GUI parameters in order to create a working synth. You should not attempt this until you are comfortable working with the modules and their cores. Connecting the engine to your framework's processing object is actually quite simple and straightforward; the details lie more in the audio block processing and GUI updating than in the engine internals. These are described in detail in the SynthLab documentation (www.willpirkle.com/synthlab-docs), and therefore, this is just an overview of the operation.

For example, to implement the wavetable synthesizer, you download the folder that includes the engine, voice, and modules – this is a self-contained synth folder requiring no other libraries or files. You will usually add the engine object to your plugin framework's processor, then instantiate it, passing along the maximum block size that can occur, as detailed in Sections 2.3 and 2.4. Make sure you understand how the *SynthProcessInput* is used to provide the block processing. In your processor object, you set up the objects:

```
// --- structure for passing audio and MIDI into and out of the engine
SynthLab::SynthProcessInfo synthBlockProcInfo;
```

```
// --- the entire synth in one object
std::unique _ ptr<SynthLab::SynthEngine> synthEngine = nullptr;
```

Then, set up the two objects in your processor's initialize or constructor method. The arguments to the information structure include input audio channel count (zero here as there are no audio or side-chain inputs), output channel count (stereo synth), and maximum block size:

```
// --- setup audio buffers 0 channels in, 2 channels out
//   block size = 64 (64 stereo samples)
synthBlockProcInfo.init(0, 2, 64);
```

```
// --- reset engine with max block size
synthEngine.reset(new SynthLab::SynthEngine(64));
```

5.4.1 SynthEngine *Reset and Initialize Phases*

The engine is simple to reset when the sample rate changes – just call the reset method, and pass the sample rate:

```
synthEngine->reset(resetInfo.sampleRate);
```

The engine also includes an *initialize* method that is called only once and sends the path to the plugin DLL for several objects to use, including the PCM sample database, which needs to know the location of the audio sample files. Your framework will provide you with a method to get the path to your plugin, so you simply send that path to the engine. For maximum flexibility, a simple *const char** is used for the path.

```
// --- get the DLL path from your framework
const char* dllPath = myFramework->getComponentPath( );

// --- initialize
synthEngine->initialize(dllPath);
```

5.4.2 SynthEngine *Prepare for Render*

For each block of audio you render, you need to first set up the *SynthProcessInput* structure by clearing the MIDI events, then add the information you get from your plugin framework:

```
// --- clear MIDI events at top of buffer
synthBlockProcInfo.clearMidiEvents();

synthBlockProcInfo.absoluteBufferTime _ Sec = // get from your framework!
synthBlockProcInfo.BPM =  // get from your framework!
synthBlockProcInfo.timeSigNumerator = // get from your framework!
synthBlockProcInfo.timeSigDenomintor =      // get from your framework!
```

After this step, you fire off the MIDI events prior to rendering.

5.4.3 SynthEngine *Prepare MIDI Input*

As described in Section 2.5.3, you will need to prepare a *SynthProcessInfo* structure with the incoming MIDI data for rendering in blocks, as shown in Figure 2.4. This will be very framework-dependent, so you need to know how to modify your processor object's buffer processing function to operate on sub-blocks that are *blockSize* in length.

You also need to know how to get the MIDI messages that were input during that block of samples, which is likewise framework dependent. The *SynthProcessInfo* structure provides a few functions to make this operation simpler. To add MIDI messages to the *SynthProcessInfo* structure for processing, you need to fashion your framework's MIDI input data into a *midiEvent* structure, then add it to the queue with the helper function. Suppose you access a MIDI message that encodes the following:

- Message Type: Note On
- MIDI Channel 10

- MIDI Note number: 60 (middle C)
- MIDI Velocity: 127
- Sample offset: 12 (this is optional information and not required for normal operation)

In your framework's MIDI input queue or callback you create the event structure:

```
SynthLab::midiEvent synthEvent(0x90, /* note on */
                              10,    /* CH 10 */
                              60,    /* note #60 */
                              127,   /* velocity */
                              12);   /* offset (can be 0 for all) */
```

Then, use the helper function to queue the message:

```
synthBlockProcInfo.pushMidiEvent(synthEvent);
```

With the events queued, you then need to fire the events, which pushes them into a structure for the engine to use, in the same sequence that you acquired these events in your framework's MIDI callback function. You need to do this just prior to calling the engine's *render* function. Loop over the block, and fire the events:

```
// --- fire ALL MIDI events for this block
for (uint32_t sample = 0; sample < blockSize; sample++)
    processBlockInfo.midiEventQueue->fireMidiEvents(sample);
```

5.4.4 SynthEngine *Audio Rendering*

The *SynthProcessInfo* structure inherits from *AudioBuffer* and therefore carries the input and output audio sample buffers with it. *The SynthEngine does not require or accept input or output buffer pointers from your framework.* The engine will write its final synth output into the *SynthProcessInfo* structure's output buffers – you only need to copy them to your processor's output buffers. To render the audio, you first set the number of samples to process in the information structure. When you initialized the engine and the processing structure, you set the maximum samples per block. However, it is possible that your framework or DAW will deliver a buffer that does not divide into *blockSize* pieces, leaving a partial buffer to fill. Just pass the partial buffer, and set the block size, and the engine will process and fill it like the other blocks.

```
// --- in case of partial block
synthBlockProcInfo.setSamplesInBlock(64); //<- equal/less than max-size
```

```
// --- render it
synthEngine->render(synthBlockProcInfo);
```

The final step is to write the audio to your framework's output buffer; you may use a simple loop or a *memcpy* function. In the code below, *output_buffer* is your framework's audio output buffer pointer, and the *startSample* and *blockSize* variables are part of the sub-block processing loop that you maintain. Remember that we set up the input and output channel count (2) when we initialized the processing structure in Section 5.4.2.

```
// --- output
float** synthOutputs = synthBlockProcInfo.getOutputBuffers();

// --- block processing -- write to outputs
for (uint32_t sample = startSample, i = 0;
     sample < startSample + blockSize;
     sample++, i++)
{
    // --- copy to outputs
    for (uint32_t channel = 0; channel < 2; channel++)
    {
        output_buffer[channel][sample] = synthOutputs[channel][i];
    }
}
```

5.5 *SynthEngine* GUI Design and Parameter Update

To use the engine effectively, you will need to design the GUI and expose the parameters according to your plugin framework. All modern DAWs will provide a default GUI if you need it, but you will still need to set up the plugin parameters according to your framework. Each SynthLab project includes documentation on the GUI parameter setup, including recommended minimum, maximum, and default values, along with the type of GUI control – continuous, numerical controls or string-list-based controls. You may also examine the pre-compiled SynthLab-DM projects to see my various GUIs to use as a basis for your own and to better understand the core-module controls.

5.5.1 *SynthLab's Dynamic Strings*

Referring back to Chapter 3 and Figure 3.4, recall that each *SynthModule* exposes up to 4 *ModuleCores*, each of which exposes up to 16 core strings that the user sees as waveform names, filter types, and EG contours. Note that both the maximum core and module string counts are simple to change to increase or decrease the size; you may also set the maximum number of cores to one if you wish, greatly simplifying operation. When the user selects a new core from your GUI control, its module strings and mod knob labels are dynamically loaded into the appropriate locations on your GUI. This is an advanced GUI design technique that is going to be highly framework-specific, so you will need to have a strategy for setting up these GUI controls and populating them as required. There are several approaches here, and with the stock projects that you download, all of the module names, core strings, and mod knob labels are known a-priori. To populate these controls, you have two basic options: generate a master list from the documentation that you store and retrieve as the user selects different cores or query the engine for these strings as you need them during real-time operation.

5.5.1.1 *Getting Core Names at Runtime*

Each module features two dynamic GUI string list controls for the core and its associated strings, and four assignable mod knobs that are initially labeled A, B, C, and D. When the user loads a new module core, you need to update the module strings (16 of them) and the four labels that adorn the mod knobs. To query the engine at any time for a list of the four module core names that are exposed for a given type of module, use the *getModuleCoreNames* function that returns a vector of the four strings.

```
vector<string> getModuleCoreNames(uint32 _ t moduleType)
```

The *moduleType* argument is the module type code listed in Table 5.1. To get the four core names for the LFO module, you write:

```
vector<string> cores = synthEngine->getModuleCoreNames(LFO _ MODULE);
```

5.5.1.2 Getting Module Strings and Mod Knob Labels at Runtime

To use dynamic string loading for the 16 module strings and 4 mod knob labels, you call two similar functions that return vectors of the strings. A mask value indicates the exact target. To get modules strings for the LFO2 waveforms and the FILTER1 types at runtime, you write:

```
vector<string> lfowaves = synthEngine->getModuleStrings(LFO2 _ WAVEFORMS);
```

```
vector<string> fltypes = synthEngine->getModuleStrings(FILTER1 _ TYPES);
```

To get the mod knob string labels for oscillator #3 and the filter EG (which is EG #2 in all projects), you write:

```
vector<string> o3MK = synthEngine->getModKnobStrings(OSC3 _ MOD _ KNOBS);
```

```
vector<string> fegMK = synthEngine->getModKnobStrings(EG2 _ MOD _ KNOBS);
```

You can then populate your controls with these strings.

5.5.2 Setting Synth Parameters from GUI Controls

You will want to update the GUI parameters on the *SynthEngine* prior to each of your framework's buffer processing function calls. You may also place the update calls on block-boundaries; all of the synth modules and objects follow this pattern. The engine's parameter structure contains GUI control variables for the engine (global tuning, delay FX, etc.) along with a shared voice parameter pointer. These are detailed in Chapters 2 and 3, along with the shared data scheme in Section 2.3.

5.5.2.1 GUI Control Example: SynthLFO

Each SynthLab project includes documentation on the GUI parameter setup. The engine, voice, and modules all include custom parameter structures that are described in this book and detailed in the online documentation. These structures are used to pass GUI control information into the objects. Generally speaking, there is a one-to-one correspondence with the structure member variables and your GUI controls, though you do not need to expose every control. Each of these parameter structures includes a special array of four normalized values that correspond to the four mod knobs A – D. As an example, let's examine the custom parameter structure for the *SynthLFO*

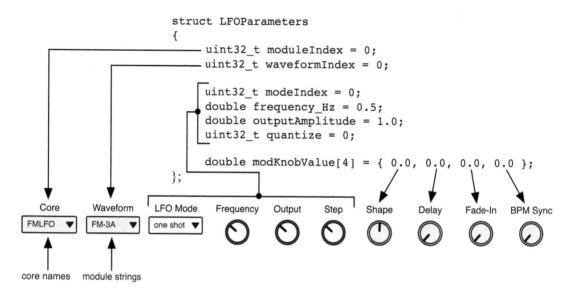

Figure 5.2 GUI controls and their relationship to the custom parameter structure; the controls in grey include the dynamic strings and are different for each kind of module and core

C++ object and compare it with a typical GUI implementation you might concoct, shown in Figure 5.2.

The *moduleIndex* and *waveFormIndex* variables are the selection values from your string list control (0 is the first item, 1 is the next, and so on). You send these integers into the module and core where they are decoded. The mod knob strings are normalized on the range [0, 1], and mod knob A always defaults to the center position. If Figure 5.2 represents connections to LFO2, you would update its variables using the engine and voice sub-parameters shown below, which are also discussed in Sections 2.6.2 and 3.3:

```
// --- declare and get shared pointer
shared _ ptr<SynthLab::SynthEngineParameters> engineParameters;
```

synthEngine->getParameters(engineParameters);

The engine's shared voice parameters are then used to update LFO2. In the code below, *myGUI* represents the GUI structure from which you parse your controls, which is also up to you and your framework.

shared _ ptr<SynthLab::SynthVoiceParameters>voiceParams = engineParameters->voiceParameters;

```
// --- LFO2 core and waveforms
voiceParams->lfo2Parameters->moduleIndex = myGUI->lfo2 _ coreindex;
```

```
voiceParams->lfo2Parameters->waveformIndex = myGUI->lfo2 _ waveform;

// --- normal parameters
voiceParams->lfo2Parameters->modeIndex = myGUI->lfo2 _ mode;
voiceParams->lfo2Parameters->frequency _ Hz = myGUI->lfo2 _ frequency _ Hz;
voiceParams->lfo2Parameters->outputAmplitude = myGUI->lfo2 _ outputAmp;
voiceParams->lfo2Parameters->quantize = myGUI->lfo2 _ quantize;

// --- mod knob parameters
voiceParams->lfo2Parameters->modKnobValue[0] = myGUI->lfo2 _ ModKnobA;
voiceParams->lfo2Parameters->modKnobValue[1] = myGUI->lfo2 _ ModKnobB;
voiceParams->lfo2Parameters->modKnobValue[2] = myGUI->lfo2 _ ModKnobC;
voiceParams->lfo2Parameters->modKnobValue[3] = myGUI->lfo2 _ ModKnobD;
```

Refer to the SynthLab documentation for complete examples that parse all GUI parameters with more detail on integrating the objects into your projects.

5.6 Programming the Modulation Matrix

The modulation matrix programming happens in the voice object's constructor. In addition, modulation routings may be added or removed at run-time; this is also needed when the user selects a new core to point the modulation matrix at the new object. These details are covered in Chapter 14 (modulation matrix), and you should examine the specific code in the voice object that loads new cores (e.g. *loadLFO1*, *loadFilter2*, etc.) to see how to remove and add new modulation routings. For this coding, the simplest option is to examine the sample code and notice how the routings are made, including the hardwired routings, such as *filterEG* to *filter1's* f_c value.

5.7 Getting *WaveSequencer* Status Meter Updates

The *WaveSequencer* object outputs status meter values to indicate which step is active for a given lane. Your processor may query the engine at any time to get an array of values that indicate an active (1) or inactive (0) status for any of the steps. The arrays return the status of the wave sequencer in the first voice that was triggered; you may modify this to return arrays for all voices, but this may be very confusing for the user. There are four sequencer lanes named *timing*, *wave*, *pitch*, and *step sequencer*, each of which has eight lane steps. The query functions are easily decoded using the lane name and step number:

```
// --- status for wave step 0
wave0 = engineParameters->wsStatusMeters.waveLaneMeter[0];

// --- status for step sequencer step 5
ssMod5 = engineParameters->wsStatusMeters.stepSeqLaneMeter[5];
```

Bibliography

SynthLab Documentation. 2020. www.willpirkle.com/synthlab-docs, Accessed on October 14, 2020

6 Modulation
Theory and Calculations

Modulation is fundamental to synthesis, and there are numerous sources and destinations for modulation values. The typical modulation sources include low frequency oscillators (LFOs), envelope generators (EGs), MIDI CCs, velocity, and note number. The output values are applied to modulate or change the destination's parameters. Typical destinations are pitched oscillator frequency, output amplitude, shape and filter f_c, Q, and drive. It is also possible for one modulator to modulate another: for example, one LFO may modulate the other LFO's oscillation frequency. Modulators have two general output types: unipolar on a range of [0, 1] and bipolar on a range of [−1, +1]. A modulation routing is a specific pair of modulation source and destination.

Some modulation calculations operate on the simple unipolar or bipolar values. Others require scaling or mapping the modulator to some new range: for example, a range of filter f_c values from 20 Hz to 18 kHz. Be sure to check out the online documentation, which lists numerous helper functions and simple C++ objects that will do much of the labor for our modulations.

6.1 SynthLab Mod Knob Mapping

All of the SynthLab core objects implement one to four functions that are controlled, with the four Mod Knobs included in every core. Some of these are already coded, and some are left as exercises for you. All cores expose the four mod knob controls, which are named A, B, C, and D. When you add strings to the *coreData.modKnobStrings*, they are exposed for the user in the GUI control. The four knobs are each unipolar in nature and transmit values on the range [0.0, 1.0]. The first mod knob (A) has its default in the center position (0.5), while the other three default to 0.0, so choose wisely when customizing these controls. For example, in the synth filter cores, the constructor sets up the four GUI strings; note that the "EG Int" and "BP Int" controls stand for "EG Intensity" and "Bipolar Intensity," respectively. Most modulation routings are controlled, with some kind of intensity value that may be unipolar or bipolar, and the filter has specialized intensity controls for each.

```
// --- modulation control knobs
coreData.modKnobStrings[MOD _ KNOB _ A] = "Key Track";
coreData.modKnobStrings[MOD _ KNOB _ B] = "Drive";
coreData.modKnobStrings[MOD _ KNOB _ C] = "EG Int";
coreData.modKnobStrings[MOD _ KNOB _ D] = "BP Int";
```

Since the mod knobs generate unipolar values, you will usually need to convert these to some other range of values. There are three helper functions to allow you to map these controls easily.

Each function accepts the normalized mod knob value, then maps it to a range that you set with the *min* and *max* parameters, and returns this value as a *double* data type.

```
getModKnobValueLinear(double normalizedValue, double min, double max)
```

```
getModKnobValueLog(double normalizedValue, double min, double max)
```

```
getModKnobValueAntiLog(double normalizedValue, double min, double max)
```

For example, the filter's "Drive" control needs to map to a linear range of 1.0 to 10.0, and this is easily accomplished as:

```
filterDrive = getModKnobValueLinear(
                parameters->modKnobValue[MOD _ KNOB _ B], 1.0, 10.0);
```

The three functions map linear, log, or anti-logarithmically, and allow you maximum ease in dealing with the incoming mod knob values.

6.2 MMA Transforms & Calculations

The MIDI Manufacturer's Association (MMA) published two documents called "DLS Level 1" and "DLS Level 2," which are specifications for two PCM sample-based software synths that used downloadable sounds (DLS) for samples. These documents are fantastic as they show two different software synth specifications, with Level 1 being the simpler of the two. The MMA documents several transforms that are used to convert lines into curves and are based on maintaining curvature between 7 and 14-bit control signals. These include *concave* and *convex* transforms that are complementary in nature. These are easily adapted to work with floating point values on both input and output ranges of [0.0, 1.0], as shown in Figure 6.1(a) and (b), and they are simple to make bipolar by mirroring each half across the *x*-axis. The simple equations for these adapted transforms are:

$$
\begin{array}{cc}
\text{Concave} & \text{Convex} \\
y = \begin{cases} 1.0 & x \geq 1.0 \\ -\left(\dfrac{5}{12}\right)\log(1-x) & 0.0 \geq x \geq 1.0 \\ 0.0 & x \leq 0.0 \end{cases}
&
y = \begin{cases} 1.0 & x \geq 1.0 \\ 1+\left(\dfrac{5}{12}\right)\log(x) & 0.0 \geq x \geq 1.0 \\ 0.0 & x \leq 0.0 \end{cases}
\end{array}
\tag{6.1}
$$

The 5/12 factor comes from the −96 dB lower limit for 16-bit digital audio and causes a tiny error near the 0.0 and 1.0 values. The functions in *synthfunctions.h* include a few more correction coefficients that I adapted from a similar transform which I use for logarithmic taper GUI controls and which performs a perfect mapping along the input/output ranges of [0, 1].

The MMA also defined an attenuation calculation for converting MIDI velocity on the range of [0, 127] into an attenuation value in dB, with −96 dB as the theoretical lower limit; this is shown in Figure 6.1(c). This transform is also used for converting linear MIDI CC 7 (volume) and CC 11 (expression) data into a curved form. This calculation is based off of a simple square law on the MIDI value, and we may convert the MIDI velocity into a direct scalar, bypassing the

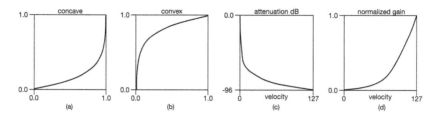

Figure 6.1 (a) MMA concave and (b) MMA convex transforms; (c) MMA velocity to attenuation in dB and (d) square law converted velocity to normalized gain graphs

log function altogether with the square law equation producing the familiar $y = x^2$ curve shown in Figure 6.1(d):

$$atten_{dB} = 20 \log \left(\frac{127^2}{vel^2} \right)$$
$$gain = \frac{vel^2}{127^2}$$

(6.2)

Since the convex and concave transforms involve a *log* operation, I've also created lookup table (LUT) versions for each, and the function will allow you to choose the method. The MMA velocity to normalized gain uses a simple square law, but you can experiment with this. Many synths offer multiple velocity curves for the users. The function prototypes of all these functions are below, and each has an LUT option that is disabled by default. Their implementations follow the equations and are simple and straightforward. There are also reverse (mirror image) versions that are used specifically in the DX EG object.

```
double concaveXForm(double xn, bool useLUT = false)
double bipolarConcaveXForm(double xn, bool useLUT = false)
double convexXForm(double xn, bool useLUT = false)
double bipolarConvexXForm(double xn, bool useLUT = false)
double mmaMIDItoAtten(uint32 _ t midiValue)
```

6.2.1 MIDI Velocity to Attack and Note Number to Decay Scaling

A MIDI modulation for the envelope generator that is useful when applied to the output DCA involves scaling the attack time with the velocity such that the attack time gets shorter as the velocity increases. Another common MIDI modulation involves scaling the note number to the decay time such that the decay gets shorter as the note number increases, similar to the way a piano note's envelope changes as you play in the higher register. These are both applied in the EG core object and may be enabled in the SynthLab synths. The calculation is simple and creates a scalar value that is multiplied against the attack or decay time during the note-on event, so this modulation only happens during note-on.

$$scalar_{VEL} = 1 - \frac{velocity}{127}$$
$$scalar_{NOTE} = 1 - \frac{note\ number}{127}$$

(6.3)

6.2.2 Constant Power Panning and Crossfading

Most SynthLab oscillators include a panning control to place the signal in the stereo field. The GUI control is set to move from −1 to +1 as the user pans from left to right, with zero as the center value. To get the imaging correct, you need to apply complementary constant power curves to generate the left and right channel. For crossfading between waveforms, as used in the morphing oscillators, the same principle applies to make the crossfading sound smooth, though, in some cases, linear crossfading may work better. For panning, the MMA DLS spec uses trigonometric curves with one quadrant each of a cosine and sine function; these are shown in the solid lines in Figure 6.2(a). In the center position, both functions evaluate to 0.707, which is exactly −3 dB. Alternatively, a square power law equation may be used, as shown in the dotted lines in Figure 6.2(a). At the center point, each function evaluates to 0.75. For panning, the x-axis moves from −1 to +1 as the user moves the panning knob clockwise from the hard-left position. For crossfading, the x-axis represents the crossfade time. Figure 6.2(b) shows the *XFader* C++ object that performs the crossfade operation on two input signals. This object allows you to choose between linear or either of the two constant power equations. It also allows you to set two crossfade times, one for each input; as shown, the crossfade times are identical. The constant power equations are given in Equation 6.4 for both panning (left/right) and crossfading (A/B).

Trigonometric   Square Law

$$A_{(LEFT)} = \cos\left(\frac{\pi}{4}(x+1)\right) \qquad A_{(LEFT)} = 1 - 0.25(x+1)^2$$

$$B_{(RIGHT)} = \sin\left(\frac{\pi}{4}(x+1)\right) \qquad B_{(RIGHT)} = 1 - (0.5x - 0.5)^2$$

(6.4)

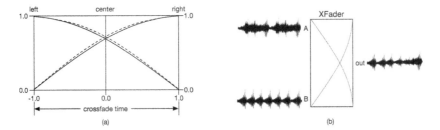

(a)   (b)

Figure 6.2 (a) Constant power curves for panning and crossfading with solid line for trigonometric and dotted line for square law transforms, and (b) the *XFader* C++ object crossfades between two signals, A and B, using linear, trig, or square law crossfading

6.3 Sequential Circuits Vector Joystick Envelope Modulation

The Sequential Circuits Prophet VS® introduced a new kind of envelope modulation for crossfading between either two or four different audio signals with a "vector joystick" known as vector synthesis. The Korg Wavestation® and Wavestate® synths include this modulation option as well. In essence, the user controls the relative mixes of the signals with an X-Y joystick, either manually, via MIDI CCs, or by programming a virtual path for the joystick to take during the note-event. Figure 6.3(a) shows the joystick as it appears on the synths, in a diamond shape. The four vertices marked A–D represent the four sources to be blended. The joystick's (x, y) coordinates are converted into four scalar values, which are used to attenuate each signal before mixing. The four values always add up to exactly 1.0, and when the joystick is in the center position, the values are all equal at 0.25.

Examining the Korg equations [Phillips], it is evident that the physical joystick unit was rotated 45 degrees clockwise prior to its mounting in the synth enclosure such that the true x and y-axes lie at 45-degree angles, shown with the dotted lines in Figure 6.3(a). For soft synth GUIs, it is simpler to get the true (x, y) coordinates by undoing the rotation, as shown in Figure 6.3(b), which places the x- and y-axes in the standard orientation. The vector mix equations use the square law functions, which are modified to produce the four envelope curves shown in Figure 6.3(c), in which the curves are linearized for easier viewing.

The equations are designed to accept MIDI CC values, and to keep the code identical to the original, you need to scale out the (x, y) coordinates to [0, 255] and rotate the incoming (x, y) point counterclockwise prior to computation to match the rotated original. Equation 6.5 combines the point rotation with the MIDI scaling of the (x, y) coordinates into (x_M, y_M) and then generates the vector multipliers as percentages that are easily converted into normalized values.

$$x_M = 127\left(\frac{x-y}{2}+1\right) \quad y_M = 127\left(\frac{x+y}{2}+1\right)$$

Coefficients as percentages [0, 100%]

$$B = \frac{x_M y_M}{645}$$
$$C = \frac{x_M(255-y_M)}{645}$$
$$D = \frac{(255-x_M)(255-y_M)}{645}$$
$$A = 100 - B - C - D$$

(6.5)

In addition to the four multipliers, two more potential modulation values are calculated: these are the x- and y-axis reflections of the current joystick location, called the AC and BD axis values. The function *calculateVectorMix* generates the A–D coefficients, along with the unipolar AC and BD reflection values. A structure is used to return the data. Notice that the joystick origin may also be adjusted.

```
struct VectorXFadeData
{
        double vectorA = 0.25;
        double vectorB = 0.25;
```

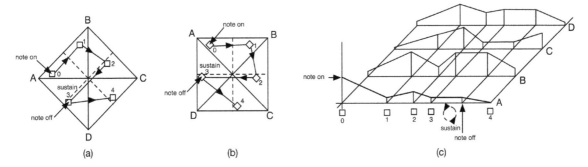

Figure 6.3 (a) The original Sequential/Korg vector joystick; (b) the rotated version is simpler for GUIs (the dotted lines show the actual *x*- and *y*-axes); and (c) visualization of the four envelopes that are generated as the stick moves from points 1 to 3, where it stays during the sustain period, and note-off moves the joystick to its final position 4

```
    double vectorC = 0.25;
    double vectorD = 0.25;

    // --- unipolar
    double vectorAC = 0.5;
    double vectorBD = 0.5;
};

VectorXFadeData calculateVectorMix(double joystick_X,
                                   double joystick_Y,
                                   double origin_X = 0.0,
                                   double origin_Y = 0.0)
```

6.4 Linear Frequency Modulation with LFO or EG

In the most basic version of FM, you simply add or subtract a value from the underlying frequency variable, then recalculate the new clock *phaseInc*. SynthLab uses bipolar modulation for linear FM, so first, you calculate the range and half-range of the modulation limits linearly. The reason for saving the full range is that you may wish to use a unipolar modulator such as the *AmpEG* in your variations. FCMOD_MIN is the minimum oscillator frequency, and FCMOD_MAX is the maximum value.

```
const double RANGE = ((FCMOD_MAX - FCMOD_MIN));
const double HALF_RANGE = RANGE / 2.0;
```

To implement bipolar modulation, you multiply a bipolar value by the half-range of the modulation limits. Linear frequency modulation means adding a frequency offset (positive or negative) to the underlying frequency value.

$$\text{mod} = biPolar Value * HALF\_RANGE$$
$$f_{OSC} = f_{OSC} + \text{mod}$$

(6.6)

The bipolar FM modulation value is always found in the module's *modulationInputs* array:

```
double mod = processInfo.modulationInputs[kFrequencyMod] * HALF_RANGE;
```

To apply the modulation, you simply add the half-range scaled value and then bound the value:

```
double newFrequency_Hz = parameters->frequency_Hz + mod;
boundValue(newFrequency_Hz, FCMOD_MIN, FCMOD_MAX);
```

At this point, you will use the *newFrequency_Hz* to alter the clock's *phaseInc*; then, the modulation is complete.

```
lfoClock.setFrequency(newFrequency_Hz, sampleRate);
```

6.5 BPM Sync

Synchronizing LFOs and delay FX to BPM is common today, and all DAWs and plugin frameworks have the ability to send the plugin BPM and time signature information. You can calculate timing values from the BPM and set the LFO frequency, or other time-based parameter, using a note duration, such as eighth note triplets. SynthLab features two different functions: one for the LFO and the other for the Wavestate wave-sequencer. The LFO function accepts a mod knob value from [0.0, 1.0] and quantizes it into eight integers that are used as index values in a lookup table. Moving the control from minimum to maximum steps through the sequence of note durations: whole note, half note, dotted quarter, quarter note, dotted 8th, 8th note, dotted 16th, and 16th note. The function returns the note duration in seconds:

```
double getTimeFromTempo(double BPM, double normalizedNoteMult)
```

```
// --- SynthLab code
double bpmSync = getTimeFromTempo(processInfo.midiData->auxData[kBPM],
                                  parameters->modKnobValue[MOD_KNOB_D]
```

```
if(bpmSync > 0.0)
   parameters->frequency_Hz = 1.0 / bpmSync;
```

The extended function that is used with the *WaveSequencer* object implements more note durations with a larger lookup table and returns the note duration in seconds or milliseconds. The function supports 16 different rhythmic values: 32nd note triplet, 32nd note, 16th note triplet, dotted 32nd note, 16th note, 8th triplet note, dotted 16th note, 8th note, quarter note triplet, dotted 8th note, quarter note, half note triplet, dotted quarter note, half note, whole note triplet, dotted half note, whole note, and dotted whole note. A strongly typed *enum* is used to send the note duration, and a static lookup table of multipliers is applied.

```
enum class NoteDuration { k32ndTriplet, k32nd, k16thTriplet, kDot32nd,
                     . . . kWhole, kDotWhole,
```

```
double getTimeFromTempo(double BPM, NoteDuration duration,
                        bool returnMilliseconds = false);
```

Both functions use the same core code, which simply converts the BPM into the corresponding duration for a quarter note in milliseconds or seconds, then uses a lookup table to scale the duration accordingly.

6.6 Quantizing

Several oscillators may implement step quantization on the output signal. Use the *quantizeBipolarValue* method, in which two mapping functions quantize the signal and remap it as a double value.

```
double quantizeBipolarValue(double d, uint32_t qLevels)
{
        uint32_t u = mapDoubleToUINT(d, -1.0 ,1.0 ,0 , qLevels, true);
        return mapUINTToDouble(u, 0, quantLevels, -1.0, 1.0);
}
```

To use the function, choose the quantization levels directly, or calculate to mimic bit-depth reduction:

```
// --- 12 steps
outputValue = quantizeBipolarValue(outputValue, 12);

// --- simulate 10-bit audio
outputValue = quantizeBipolarValue(outputValue, pow(2.0, 10));
```

6.7 Ramp Modulation: Fade-in and Fade-out

The simple *RampModulator* produces a linearly increasing or decreasing output depending on the start and end values. It may be used to ramp up or down between any kinds of values – amplitudes, frequencies, etc. Fade-in and fade-out are common uses of this object. Portamento is a special circumstance and is handled with the *GlideModulator* instead. To set up the object, you give it the required information for counting time intervals.

For a fade-in modulation, start and stop are 0.0 and 1.0; here, the fade-in time is 1 second = 1000.0 mSec, and we supply the normal *processInfo.sampleRate*.

```
RampModulator fadeInModTor;


// ---     (start, stop, ramp time(mSec), sample rate)
fadeInModTor.startModulator(0.0, 1.0, 1000.0, processInfo.sampleRate);
```

For a fade-out modulation, start and stop are 1.0 and 0.0; here, the fade-in time is 5 seconds = 5000.0 mSec:

```
RampModulator fadeOutModTor;

// ---      (start, stop, ramp time(mSec), sample rate)
fadeOutModTor.startModulator(1.0, 0.0, 5000.0, processInfo.sampleRate);
```

To apply the fade-in/fade-out, you use two functions: one to get the modulation (ramp) value and the other to increment the clock. For block-processed modules like the LFO, you advance the clock by the block size; otherwise, you advance it by 1.0 (the default).

```
// --- get modulation multiplier
fadeInModValue = fadeInModTor.getNextModulationValue();
// --- bump the clock; here is for a LFO (block processed)

fadeInModulator.advanceClock(processInfo.samplesToProcess);
```

The resulting modulation value is a simple scalar multiplier that you apply to a signal. For the LFO output, you might write:

```
lfoOutput *= fadeInModValue;
```

6.7.1 Glide Modulation: Portamento

Portamento or glide modulation is a special case of pitch modulation. The user plays a note, which sounds as usual. Then, the next note is triggered, and the pitch glides up or down to the new note over a time-span the user selects. Each successive note glides up or down smoothly to the final pitch. Portamento may be applied as a linear shift or as a shift in semitones, as done in SynthLab. In addition, it may be applied with a constant time (e.g. 1000 mSec between each note, no matter how close or far apart they might be) or a constant rate (e.g. 1000 mSec/octave). The THX® constant time portamento chord is a famous example which plays in many theaters before a movie starts.

The *GlideModulator* object is a specialized version of the *RampModulator* that is designed to glide in semitones using the two MIDI note numbers, as described in the next section. All *ModuleCore* objects have a *GlideModulator* attached as a member, so it is ready to use without much work. This modulation is calculated on a per-block basis, as with the other low frequency modulators (LFOs and EGs). Using the *GlideModulator* only requires three function calls. The first initializes and starts the modulation; notice that the start and end MIDI notes are set as *double* data-types, and the glide time is in milliseconds. This function calculates and stores the distance between notes in semitones, named the *glideRange*, and an increment (step) value called *timerInc*.

```
bool startModulator(double startNote, double endNote,
                    double glideTime_mSec, double sampleRate);
```

To get the next glide modulation value, which is a pitch shift in semitones between the notes, you call the *getNextModulationValue* function, which implements a simple countdown timer to create the output.

```
double getNextModulationValue(uint32_t advanceClock = 1)
{
        double output = 0.0;
        if (timerActive)
        {
            // --- output
            output = countDownTimer*glideRange;
```

```
        countDownTimer -= advanceClock * timerInc;

        if (countDownTimer <= 0.0)
            timerActive = false;
    }
    return output;
}
```

The internal glide clock is advanced automatically by one tick during this function and may be advanced independently with a function. After each render call, we will need to advance the clock by the block size to ensure that the timing is correct.

```
void advanceClock(uint32_t ticks);
```

6.8 Pitch Calculation

Each MIDI note represents one semitone's musical distance. To calculate the number of semitones between two MIDI notes, you simply subtract the two note numbers. The equal temperament tuning equation calculates the oscillator pitch from a MIDI note number and a tuning reference for A4 (usually 440 *Hz*). Note also that the value 69 is the MIDI note number for A4.

$$pitch = (A4\_freq)\,2^{\left(\frac{NoteNum-69}{12}\right)} \tag{6.7}$$

To reverse the calculation and find a MIDI note number from a pitch in Hz, use Equation 6.2 and truncate the *NoteNum* value to an integer, which is the MIDI note number.

$$NoteNum = ceil\left(12 * \ln\left(\frac{pitch}{A4\_freq}\right) + 69\right) \tag{6.8}$$

6.8.1 *Oscillator* update *Methods: Pitch Modulation*

All SynthLab oscillators implement an *update* function that is nearly identical because the majority of the function involves pitch modulation. The pitch shift calculation creates a scalar value that you multiply with the MIDI note pitch value in *Hz*. The equation shows the relationship between semitones and pitch. Some prefer to implement the equation in cents rather than semitones – there is no mathematical difference in the end result; however you do need to formulate all shifts as either semitones or cents.

$$pitchshift_{semitones} = 2^{\left(\frac{pitchModSemitones}{12}\right)}$$
$$pitchshift_{cents} = 2^{\left(\frac{pitchModCents}{1200}\right)} \tag{6.9}$$

For our pitched oscillators, we will have numerous pitch shifts, which all need to be applied together. The good news is that you may simply add all the values in semitones (or cents), then only call the pitch shifting function once. You should memorize the relationships: 1 octave = 12 semitones and 1 semitone = 100 cents.

For pitched oscillators, we expose the following GUI controls and modulation inputs:

GUI Controls:

- octaveDetune
- coarseDetune (semitones)
- fineDetune (cents)
- unisonDetune (cents)

Modulation:

- bipolar pitch modulation (vibrato)
- glide modulation (portamento)
- MIDI pitch bend
- Global Tuning

The code for combining the modulation and GUI values, and calculating the pitch modulation value is shown below. First, we define the range of modulation in semitones. I chose one octave up and down; you may modify this value as you like.

```
const double kOscBipolarModRangeSemitones = 12.0;
```

The bipolar modulation value is scaled with the range and the intensity knob control.

```
double freqMod = processInfo.modulationInputs[kBipolarMod] *
                                kOscBipolarModRangeSemitones;
```

The glide modulation is handled with a separate object that does the calculation in semitones. Notice that there is a secondary pitch shift function that uses a lookup table rather than a power of two operation; it is commented out, and you can freely switch between the two functions to evaluate.

```
// --- do the portamento
double glideMod = glideModulator.getNextModulationValue();

// --- combine all sources in semitones
double currentPitchModSemitones = glideMod + fmodInput +
                            midiPitchBend + masterTuning +
                            parameters->octaveDetune * 12) +
                            parameters->coarseDetune) +
                            parameters->fineDetune / 100.0) +
                            parameters->unisonDetune / 100.0);

// --- lookup the pitch shift modifier (fraction)
//double pitchShift = pitchShiftTableLookup(currentPitchModSemitones);

// --- direct calculation version 2^(n/12) - equal temperament
double pitchShift = pow(2.0, currentPitchModSemitones / 12.0);
```

```
// --- calculate the modulated pitch value
double oscillatorFrequency = midiPitch*pitchShift;
```

The wavetable and virtual analog oscillators may be used for FM synthesis, in which case they must be able to generate negative frequencies and must be bounded to +/-Nyquist.

```
// --- BOUND the value to our range
boundValue(oscillatorFrequency, (-sampleRate/2.0), (+sampleRate/2.0));
```

The PCM sample and plucked string oscillators are <u>not</u> used for FM and are bounded to the lowest MIDI note (*OSC_FMIN* = ~8 Hz) and *OSC_FMAX* = 20,480 Hz. I use 20,480 as a top value in numerous objects; when the lower limit is set to 20 Hz, this produces ten octaves of pitch change, which has a connection to analog synths that used a 10V control voltage (CV) to modulate across ten octave ranges.

```
// --- BOUND the value to our range
boundValue(oscillatorFrequency, OSC _ FMIN, OSC _ FMAX);
```

At this point, we have the newly updated oscillator frequency. For the wavetable and virtual analog oscillators, this value is used to update the oscillator clock object that acts as the time-base. See Chapters 11 and 13 for the PCM sample and plucked string oscillator details.

```
// --- phase inc = fo/fs
oscClock.setFrequency(oscillatorFrequency, sampleRate);
```

6.9 Pulse-Width Modulation (PWM)

PWM is a bipolar modulation that operates on the pulse width (or duty cycle) of a square wave and usually modulates over half ½ the normal range: for example, from 5% to 50% or from 50% to 95%. This is due to the fact that the two half-range modulations sound identical to the ear. The *VAOscillator* is the only SynthLab oscillator that implements PWM. This is accomplished by simply adding half of the bipolar pulse width modulation (PWM) amplitude to the user's pulse width GUI control value. You can find an example in Section 10.9.4.

6.10 Phase Distortion

Invented and patented at the Casio Corporation, Phase Distortion (PD) is roughly in the same family as frequency modulation (FM) and phase modulation (PM) synths. A single index of modulation is used to modify the spectral content of the signal. In its simplest sense, PD alters the shape of the modulo counter's ramp, which results in a distorted waveform with a modified spectrum. In phase distortion, you speed up and slow down the time-base by changing the slope of the modulo counter. You might also imagine the modulo counter, which moves from 0.0 to 1.0, as being a phase value from 0.0 to 2π radians. The modulo counter wraps around at a point corresponding to the waveform's period T, which you may think of as the *x*-axis, as shown in Figure 6.4(a), with a slope of T/2π which is normalized to 1.0. In Figure 6.4(b), with a breakpoint placed at (0.5, 0.5), a pure sinusoid is generated. Figure 6.4(c) and (d) show how the counter output splits into two different slopes when the breakpoint is moved from the (0.5, 0.5) location.

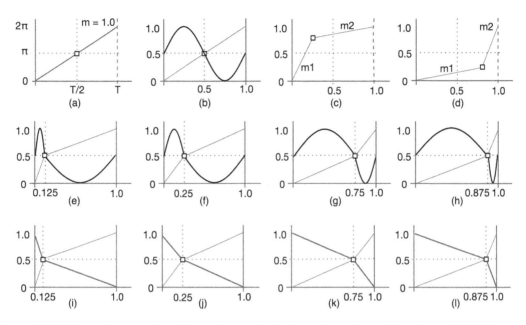

Figure 6.4 (a) The modulo counter with *x*-axis as period and *y*-axis as phase with a slope of 1.0, (b) a normal sinusoid lookup, (c) and (d) relocation of the breakpoint produces two slopes *m1* and *m2* while (e)–(f) show the distortion on a sinusoid and (i)–(l) show a ramp modified with phase distortion

In the most simple variation, you fix the *y*-breakpoint value at 0.5, which corresponds to the half-cycle point for most waveforms. Then you adjust the *x*-breakpoint value to apply the phase distortion as the modulo counter moves slower than normal (shallow slope) or faster than normal (steep slope). The distortion effects on a sinusoid and ramp waveform are shown in Figure 6.4(e)–(l).

The key to getting the proper result is understanding that the two-slope counter must always wrap around at the correct point so that the next cycle starts on the proper location of the first slope, *m1*. For single breakpoint phase distortion with an arbitrary breakpoint (x_{break}, y_{break}) producing two slopes *m1* and *m2*, the distorted modulo counter may be found with Equation 6.1.

$$distortedModCounter = \begin{cases} mcounter \leq x_{break} & (m1)(mcounter) \\ mcounter > x_{break} & (m2)(mcounter - x_{break}) + y_{break} \end{cases} \qquad (6.10)$$

You may also experiment with multiple breakpoints, or you may place discontinuities within the phase distortion curve. Aliasing can and will occur with phase distortion, and other options may be used to smooth over sharp breaks between the segment slopes. The SynthLab phase distortion function performs this simple one-breakpoint process. Modulating the shape value in time, which is the x_{break} variable here, can produce patches with a very nice sound.

```
double applyPhaseDistortion(double mcounter, double x_break,
                double y_break = 0.5)
```

```
{
    // --- limit to [0.1, 0.9] to prevent jagged slopes/aliasing
    mapDoubleValue(x_break, 0.0, 1.0, 0.1, 0.9);

    // --- calc 2 slopes
    double m1 = y_break / x_break;
    double m2 = (1.0 - y_break) / (1.0 - x_break);

    // --- can happen if breakpoint is (0.5, 0.5)
    if (m2 == m1) return mcounter;
    // --- apply distortion
    if (mcounter <= x_break)
        return m1*mcounter;
    else
        return (mcounter - x_break)*m2 + y_break;

    return mcounter;
}
```

6.11 Hard Sync

Hard sync is an old analog modulation type that was originally implemented with two oscillators. In much of the literature and industry jargon, these are named master and slave. In this text, they are named *reset oscillator* and *output oscillator*. The output oscillator is what the user hears and runs at a higher frequency than the reset oscillator, which runs at the MIDI note pitch. Each time the reset oscillator begins a new cycle, the output oscillator is reset to start over. Interestingly, this means that the reset oscillator's waveform is inconsequential as we only use its period to adjust the output oscillator. Figure 6.5(a) shows the hard sync sawtooth waveform, while Figure 6.5(b) shows the result with square waves, in which the hard sync acts as a duty cycle control. In the most basic hard sync case, the main oscillator is reset back to its starting point, which is −1.0 for Figure 6.5. Another option is to allow the user to adjust the reset point to begin the next cycle at a different value (or starting phase), as shown in Figure 6.5(c) and (d).

Once again, something that is simple in analog is full of problems when attempted digitally. Clearly, the discontinuity that is created will have aliased components, if not mitigated. For the virtual analog oscillators, this is possible to implement while rendering the main oscillator's waveform directly, though it is not simple. A different approach is employed in SynthLab for both the wavetable and the virtual analog oscillators; this involves crossfading the original main oscillator and the newly reset oscillator's two outputs for a short period of time, thereby smearing over the discontinuity in an attempt to lowpass filter it. This is shown in an exaggerated manner in Figure 6.6(a) for normal reset and in Figure 6.6(b) for resetting to a non-zero starting phase. This also means that for the duration of the crossfade window, we will need to have two oscillators (or modulo counters) running: one for the original signal and the other for the reset version. Another option is to center the crossfade window on the discontinuity, which requires synthesizing a portion of the waveform below −1.0.

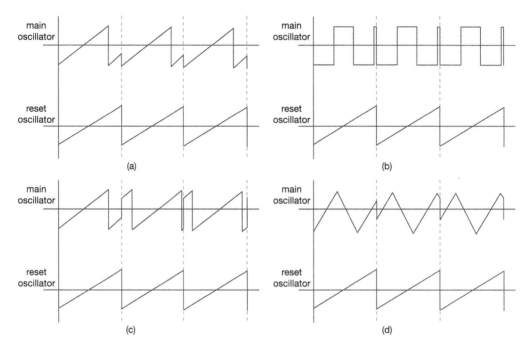

Figure 6.5 Hard sync with (a) ramp/sawtooth and (b) square-wave main oscillators, while (c) and (d) show the effect of moving the reset point for ramp and triangle waves; notice that the reset oscillator's waveform is not used other than as a resetting device

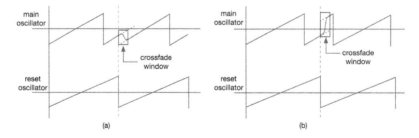

Figure 6.6 Crossfading to smear over a hard-sync discontinuity for (a) the normal reset and (b) reset to a non-zero starting phase

6.11.1 Hard Sync with a Virtual Primary Oscillator

Since the waveform of the primary oscillator is unimportant – only the reset signal is needed – in theory, we could hard sync an oscillator with an internal primary oscillator's time-base or, in other words, an invisible virtual primary oscillator that is grouped with the normal oscillator object. This is already implemented in the wavetable oscillator cores. The only GUI control required is the hard sync ratio control that operates on the range of [1.0, 4.0] – you may experiment with higher ratio values if you like as the mapping is easy to change.

To facilitate this operation, a hard sync C++ object called *Synchronizer* is supplied. This object contains two *SynthClock* objects, one for the virtual (imaginary) primary oscillator and the other for timing the crossfade, along with an *XFader* object for performing the crossfade operation. When the hard sync ratio is greater than one, the *Synchronizer* object's hard sync primary timebase is set to the new multiple of the current oscillator frequency:

```
// --- get the hard sync ratio, map to [1, 4]
hardSyncRatio = getModKnobValueLinear(
                        parameters->modKnobValue[MOD_KNOB_B],1.0, 4.0);

// --- set primary timebase
hardSyncronizer.setHardSyncFrequency(
                                oscillatorFrequency* hardSyncRatio);
```

You can check out the *Synchronizer* operation by examining the *WTOCore::renderHardSyncSample* function, which is called whenever the hard sync ratio is greater than 1.0. This function performs the following:

1   Check to see if primary clock has wrapped, indicating a new hard sync phase: if not wrapped, it calls the *renderSample* function as usual but uses the primary clock as the time-base
2   If a new hard sync phase starts, the crossfade clock begins, and the *Synchronizer* object performs the crossfade on the old output waveform and the newly synchronized waveform to blur over the discontinuity
3   When the crossfade is done, the function goes back to step 1 and starts monitoring the primary oscillator clock.

6.12 Filter Key Track Modulation

When filter key tracking is enabled, the filter's f_c value is set to match the MIDI pitch of the note that is playing or a frequency that is mathematically related to the MIDI pitch. For example, you may set the key track amount to +7 semitones, which would place the filter's f_c value a perfect fifth above the MIDI pitch. If the filter is self-oscillating, then the effect is one of harmonization. The modulation is simple to implement as it is a MIDI override of the user's f_c setting. There are numerous other options with this kind of modulation, including tracking slopes, center MIDI note values, and other advanced options. Key-track modulation usually requires two controls – one to enable the key-tracking and another that sets the distance either as a ratio or as an absolute offset, e.g. in semitones. The filter core objects include a dedicated on/off switch to enable/disable the function, and a mod knob that acts as a key-track offset control, ranging from −48 to +48 semitones or +/− four octaves. The key-track modulation is simple: when enabled, disregard the current GUI setting for the filter f_c, and replace it with the MIDI note pitch. Then offset this value in semitones using the normal pitch, shifting in semitones from Section 6.7. After that, update the filters in the normal manner. You can find an example in the filter core's *update* method:

```
// --- key tracking
if (parameters->enableKeyTrack)
{
```

```
        // --- get semitone offset
        ktFmodSemitones = getModKnobValueLinear(
            parameters->modKnobValue[FLT _ KEYTRACK], -48.0, +48.0);


        // --- reset current fc back to MIDI pitch
        fc = midiPitch;
}
```

The filter receives bipolar and unipolar modulation values from the LFO and EG sources, then the modulations are summed as normal, and the newly modulated filter f_c value is set:

```
// --- sum modulations
double fcModSSemis = bpFmodSemitones + egFmodSemitones +
                     ktFmodSemitones;


// --- multiply by pitch shift factor
fc *= pow(2.0, fcModSSemis / 12.0);
```

Bibliography

danphillips.com. "Wavestation Vector Mix Calculation." http://www.danphillips.com/wavestation/SYSEX/WSDevDoc.zip, Accessed October 14, 2020

Dodge, Charles & Jerse, Thomas. 1997. *Computer Music Synthesis, Composition and Performance*, Chap. 4. New York: Schirmer.

Junglieb, Stanley. 1986. *Prophet VS Digital Vector Synthesizer*. San Jose: Sequential Circuits, Inc.

MIDI Manufacturer's Association. 1999. *Downloadable Sounds Level 1*. https://www.midi.org/specifications-old/item/dls-level-1-specification, Accessed October 14, 2020

MIDI Manufacturer's Association. 1999. *Downloadable Sounds Level 2*. https://www.midi.org/specifications-old/item/dls-level-2-specification, Accessed October 14, 2020

Phillips, Dan. 1991. *Wavestation SR Reference Guide*. Tokyo: Korg Inc.

7 Envelope Generators and DCA

The Envelope Generator (EG) and Digitally Controlled Amplifier (DCA) are two common synth components found in most synth architectures. These two modules generate time-based amplitude change values. The EG renders a unipolar output value, which is applied as a modulation value to other modules. The DCA processes an input with gain and panning (left/right) multipliers; the SynthLab DCA processes stereo signals.

7.1 Envelope Generator Fundamentals

EGs are most commonly used to control the overall amplitude of the synthesized note-event – the time domain contour that the musician hears. Most EGs are documented with something like Figure 7.1(a), which shows an EG with attack, decay, sustain, and release (ADSR) segments. Some figures show the ADSR segments as lines, but they are usually curves; this is based not only on the early analog EG circuitry but also on how we perceive loudness. Some of the figures in this chapter show the EG with linear segments to make the figures simpler and aid in understanding, but remember that they will usually be curved in an exponential manner.

The attack segment is triggered from the note-on message, and the release segment is triggered from the note-off message. The message may be MIDI or a control voltage. There are several ways in which to specify the EG parameters. Figure 7.1(b) shows an EG that uses levels and rates, which is how the Yamaha DX7 EG is configured. The rate is simply the slope of the segment. Notice that the start level (L0) does not necessarily need to begin at 0.0, and the end level (L3) does not need to decay all the way to 0.0.

In most synths, the segments are specified as times, often in *mSec*. For the attack segment, it is the time from the start level (usually 0.0) to the maximum amplitude level (usually 1.0), and this makes sense. There is no sustain time setting, but there is a sustain level setting. The decay and release times, however, are not specified the way you might think.

A fundamental ramification of the decay and release times being referenced to full-scale is that the sustain level will alter the actual (perceived) decay and release times, as shown in Figure 7.1(d), in which the sustain level has been lowered, but the decay and release times have not changed.

The decay and release times are not the actual times you hear but the times it would take for the EG to decay or release from a full scale value of 1.0 all the way down to 0.0, as shown in Figure 7.1(c). This is independent of the curvature of the segments themselves.

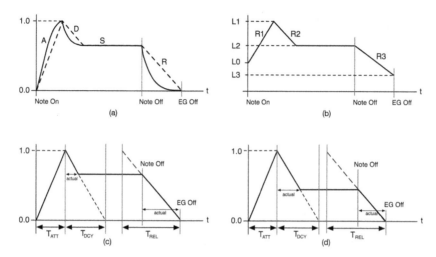

Figure 7.1 (a) ADSR envelope generator with linear (dashed) and exponential segments (b) specifying the EG using levels (L) and rates (R), and (c) the decay and release times are actually calculated from the full-scale value to zero and (d) changing the sustain level with all else constant changes the perceived decay and release times

In this case, you can see that the actual decay time the musician perceives has stretched a bit, while the actual release time has shrunk. If you think about it, this does make sense if the EG is controlling the overall amplitude of the note-event. For example, if the release time were fixed at, say, 1.0 second, then a loud note with a high sustain level and a quiet note with a low sustain level would have the same release time of 1.0 second, and that would not make sense to a musician playing the instrument. Playing quiet notes would have the same release times as loud ones. If you've played a piano, you know that is not the case: softly played notes decay faster because there isn't as much energy in the signal.

7.1.1 EG Contours

All of the EGs in Figure 7.1 consist of four segments, which are also called states: attack, decay, sustain, and release. There are several other variations that are useful in different applications. These include:

* AR: attack and release only, no sustain, as in Figure 7.2(a); the note may release and end long before the musician releases the key
* AHR: attack, hold and release; the hold portion is flat and usually at the maximum amplitude, as in Figure 7.2(b)
* DELAY: in some cases, such as in Figure 7.2(c), the attack state is delayed for some time before starting; this adds a "D" to the acronym, such as DAHR, and is simple to implement with a delay timer
* ADSLSR: attack, decay, slope, sustain, and release; the slope segment may move in the upwards or downwards direction – this is the SynthLab DX-EG object, which is similar to the EG used in the DX7; Figure 7.2(d) shows an upward slope version – notice that the slope segment is linear

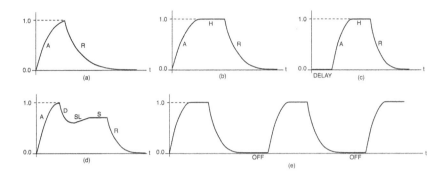

Figure 7.2 More EG contours including (a) AR, (b) AHR, (c) DAHR, (d) the SynthLab *DXEG* with linear slope segment (SL), and (e) the VCS3 re-triggering "trapezoidal" EG

- OFF: the VCS3 has an interesting "trapezoidal" (AHR) EG that includes an off-state and off-time; if the user sets the off-time to the maximum value, the EG behaves as normal, releases to zero, and is finished, but if the off-time is *less* than the maximum value, the EG stays off for that period of time, then retriggers itself for another sweep through the states, creating a self-retriggering EG; this is shown in Figure 7.2(e)

Other variations also exist, such as a double-attack EG (ADADSR), which can be useful in mimicking the lip-buzz attack of horn instruments, or the Casio CZ EG, which implements nine segments, including a double-release state after the note-off event occurs. The EG is rendered using a simple finite state machine, and it is easy to add or remove states or skip over states so that one algorithm may implement many of the contour variations.

7.1.2 EG Triggering and Note-On

EGs may be used as modulators for the various synth modules, including the output EG that controls the output amplifier and the filter EG, which modulates the filter cutoff frequency f_c. In almost all cases, the EG, no matter what its use as a modulator, is triggered to begin operation as a result of the MIDI note-on event. There are several modes of triggering and ways in which the EG can respond, dating back to early analog synths that were monophonic. When the user depresses a key, two signals are sent to the EG; these are called the trigger and gate, as shown in Figure 7.3(a). The trigger marks the note-on event, and the gate supplies the key hold time and the note-off event. Figure 7.3(b) shows an early variation in which the trigger and gate are combined into an s-trigger, which attempts to relay the same information about the note-event.

Suppose a musician plays a succession of notes, releasing each key before depressing the next. If this is done so quickly that the EG never fully releases, there are two ways in which the EG may respond. Figure 7.3(c) shows one variation in which the EG simply restarts from the last output level. Figure 7.3(d) shows another option in which the EG is forced to reset back to the starting point, even if the release period has not ended. This is called reset-to-zero (RTZ) or simply reset-mode, and it is clear that this mode will produce a more pronounced staccato sound, sometimes with audible clicks at the reset point.

7.1.3 Legato Mode

Now consider the case in which a musician plays a succession of notes but does not release each key just before depressing the next. On piano, this is called playing legato, which means that there is a smooth transition between notes as they blend into one another. Figure 7.4(a) shows the output for trigger/gate synths – for each new note-event, the EG returns to the attack state. But for s-trigger synths in Figure 7.4(b), there is no dedicated note-on signal, so the EG ignores the note-on events and never returns to the attack state, creating the legato playing style where notes blend smoothly together. On more modern synths, the s-trigger version is sometimes offered as an option called legato mode.

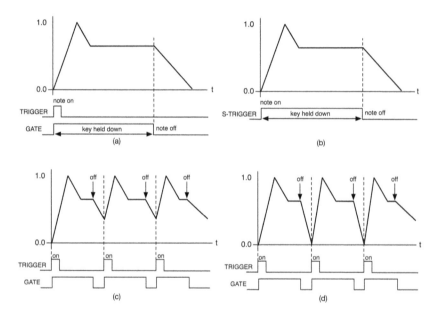

Figure 7.3 Early analog EGs with (a) trigger and gate signals, and (b) EG with s-trigger signal, (c) the EG restarts with each note on event from the previous output value and (d) the EG is reset back to the starting point with each note on event; the logic is shown as active-high but may be implemented as active-low as well

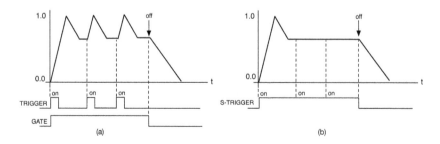

Figure 7.4 Legato playing with (a) a trigger/gate EG and (b) an s-trigger EG

7.1.4 EG Release and Note-Off

It should be evident by now that the EG and note-on and note-off events have a very close relationship. Additionally, when the EG is used to control the output amplifier, the note-event is only recognized as being complete when the EG's output value has decayed all the way to zero or its final end value, which the user may control on some EGs. This means that the EG plays a vital role in determining the state of each voice in a polyphonic synth. For a monophonic synth, the EG also has a special function with respect to legato mode operation, as outlined in Section 7.1.3. Notice that this means that the off-state needs to be included in the model.

7.1.4.1 Unconditional Release Mode

If the musician strikes a key and releases it quickly, before it has a chance to go from attack to decay to sustain, then we have a couple of options for handling this event. The majority of EGs will simply jump to the release state so the EG output decays from its value when the key is released, as shown in Figure 7.5(a) and (b) – notice that the EG never reaches peak amplitude. This behavior usually sounds natural because it is the way acoustic instruments usually function. Another option is called unconditional release mode; it is often paired with an AR or AHR EG contour. In unconditional mode, when the musician releases a key, the EG moves through all of its phases right through to the release and off phases, as shown in Figure 7.5(c). This allows a musician to hold down a chord and quickly release the notes, causing a volume swell without the need to keep the keys depressed.

7.1.5 EG Shutdown State

In addition to the four EG states of attack, decay, sustain, and release, there may be an additional state called shutdown. In shutdown mode, the EG descends from its current value right down to

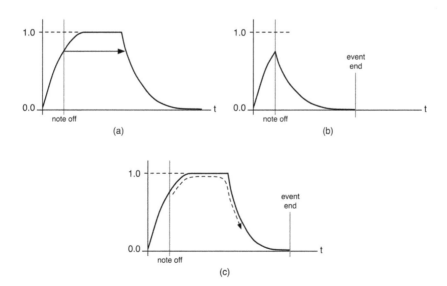

Figure 7.5 (a) The note-off event occurs before the EG reaches full amplitude and results in (b) a truncated version while (c) shows the unconditional release mode

0.0 over a very short period of time, in about a millisecond, and in a linear manner. You can see the shutdown phase in Figure 7.3(d) in reset-to-zero mode. It is also used during the voice-stealing operation to quickly shut down the voice that is being stolen. For voice-stealing, it is important that the shutdown take place fast enough that the musician does not discern a tactile response lag before the new voice and note are rendered.

7.2 EG Implementation: Finite State Machine

The ADSR EG can be modeled as a Finite State Machine (FSM) with the following states; the *DXEG* has an additional state called SLOPE that is between the decay and sustain states.

- OFF
- ATTACK
- DECAY
- SLOPE (*DXEG* only)
- SUSTAIN
- RELEASE
- SHUTDOWN

Figure 7.6 shows the state transition triggers in circles, which are either note-events or logic based on the EG output, crossing above or below some value. Figure 7.6(a) shows the standard ADSR, while Figure 7.6(b) shows one version of the *DXEG* with added slope state; in this case, the decay level L_{DCY} is below the sustain level. In the other variation, the decay level is above the sustain level, and the logic is reversed.

In C++ code, the FSM may be coded with a *switch-case* statement, a compound *if-else* statement, or a jump table if you are familiar with assembly languages. In SynthLab, the EGs are all implemented with *switch-case* statements. For example, the state transition logic from the attack to the decay state, using *switch-case* statements and a strongly typed *enum* for the state variable, would resemble the following code – note the check to see if the attack time is zero, in which case the FSM advances to the decay state, after setting the output to 1.0, which is the maximum EG output value:

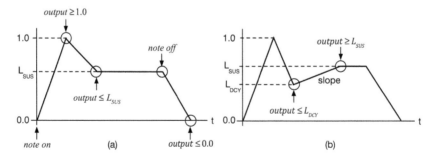

Figure 7.6 The circles show the state transition triggers for the (a) ADSR and (b) *DXEG* with added slope state; this EG may also have the decay level L_{DCY} set above the sustain level, and the transition trigger logic is inverted

```
case EGState::kAttack:
{
     // --- render value
     envelopeOutput = // <--- do the render here

     // --- check for next state
     if (envelopeOutput >= 1.0 || attackTime _ mSec <= 0.0)
     {
     // --- clamp to max value
          envelopeOutput = 1.0;

          // --- go to decay state
          state = EGState::kDecay;

          break;
     }
     break;
}
```

7.2.1 *EG Implementation: Note-On, Note-Off, and Shutdown*

The note-on and note-off messages play a special role in the EG's state, and these set up a few rules for the FSM.

7.2.1.1 *Note-On*

If a new note-on message arrives while the EG is OFF, it moves to the attack state and begins the EG render cycle. If a new note-on message arrives while the EG is running, the FSM has three options depending on the mode:

1   Normal mode: the EG moves back to the attack state and begins the render cycle from the current output value
2   Legato mode: the EG ignores the new note-on message (as the s-trigger would) and continues its render cycle
3   Reset-to-zero: the EG moves into its special emergency shutdown state (see Section 7.1.5) and descends to 0.0 rapidly

7.2.1.2 *Note-Off*

Handling of the note-off message depends on the EG conditionality.

1   An unconditional EG will ignore the note-off message and continue the EG render cycle, ending the EG render cycle only after the release state completes.
2   All other EG types will jump to the release state and begin decaying from that value down to 0.0 (or the user's selected release-end value), ending the EG render cycle

7.2.1.3 Shutdown

The shutdown state is special in that it may or may not be used, depending on the situation. There is no state transition trigger logic for this state. Shutdown is accomplished with a dedicated EG function call and is a result of either a note-off or a note-on message.

1   Reset-to-zero (monosynth): when enabled, new note-on messages force the EG into the shutdown state to create the jagged, click-y, instant-on sound
2   Voice steal (polysynth): in the event of a voice-stealing operation, the EG will go into the shutdown state to quickly end the note-event so the voice can be stolen and begin rendering a new note

The shutdown state uses a fast linear taper – this happens so quickly that no one will notice if it is linear or not. The taper uses a simple increment value, which represents a negative step that is subtracted from the output until it decays to 0.0. Knowing the sample rate, current output value, and shutdown time in milliseconds, the increment value is found as:

$$inc_{shutdown} = \frac{-(1000.0 * envelopeOutput)}{(t_{shutdown})(f_s)} \tag{7.1}$$

So, you can see that the shutdown operation is a special case, and it is always followed by a new note-on event. All of these states, rules, and transition logics are summed up in Figure 7.7, which shows the FSM diagram for the ADSR EG, including shutdown. The dotted lines show that the shutdown message may arrive any time after the EG has been started and will always result in the same state. Likewise, the note-off message may occur at any time after the EG begins rendering and results in a jump to the release state.

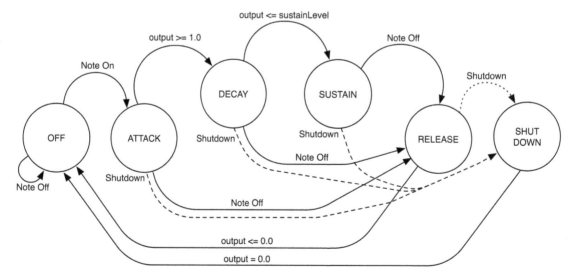

Figure 7.7 The FSM diagram for the ADSR EG with shutdown; this does not show the monosynth legato or reset-to-zero options to simplify the diagram

7.3 Digital EG Implementation: Rendering the Output

The last detail may be the most important: how do you render the lines or curves that make up the EG output with a digital system? There are several solutions, from simple to complex. I have a separate object for emulating an analog EG, so let's focus on a digital version first. Linear EGs are not especially useful for the output amplifier or the filter EG; however, they may be employed in FM operators, which use an embedded EG that is permanently connected to an oscillator's output. I use a method to convert the linear segments into exponential curves, and this allows the user to blend the linear and exponential curves together to generate any combination desired; this is the basis for the *DXEG* object, used exclusively for FM operators in SynthLab.

7.3.1 Linear and Exponential Steppers

A linear EG is easily rendered using simple counters with preset step sizes or increment values, as show in Figure 7.8(a). The counters usually move between off (0.0) and full-scale (1.0), but that is not a fixed rule; the counters may start at a non-zero value, and full scale does not necessarily need to be 1.0. In addition, some EGs allow the sustain level to be set below 0.0 as a negative number usually on the range of [−1.0, 0.0]. An exponential EG may be approximated using non-fixed counters whose increment values change by some pre-calculated amount, as shown in Figure 7.8(b). The Yamaha DX-7 EG is said to use this type of staggered counter system.

7.3.2 Linear EG

The equation that relates the attack, decay, slope, or release time in milliseconds to the step increment size is shown in Equation 7.2. This includes a *scale* variable that is +1.0 for the rising (upwards) segments and −1.0 for the downward segments (decay and release). However, you may adjust the *scale* to either expand or shrink the segment times or alter the minimum or maximum values. The DXEG features a slope segment that may move in the upward or downward direction depending on the decay level setting. Once that is known, the calculation is trivial.

$$scale = \begin{cases} 1.0 & upward \\ -1.0 & downward \end{cases}$$

$$egStepSize = scale\left(\frac{1000}{(f_s)(segTime\_mSec)}\right)$$

(7.2)

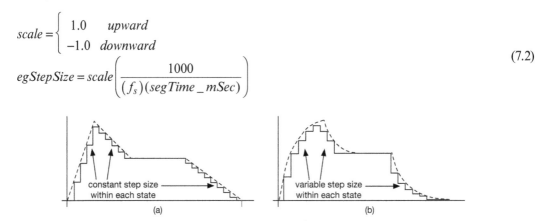

Figure 7.8 (a) Linear EG with constant step sizes within each state and (b) approximating an exponential EG with variable step sizes; the axes are unlabeled to show that the numerical limits of min and max are variable

7.3.3 Exponential EG from Linear EG

Converting the linear EG into an exponential one presents some challenges that might not be obvious at first glance. One simple option is to convert the linear values into decibel (dB) values with 0.0 dB as the maximum level – the top of the attack segment. This is easily accomplished with the standard dB equation and you can think of this as a linear to dB mapping. Now the problem is what to do with the linear EG value of 0.0 since you cannot calculate the *log* of a zero or negative value. If that value must be 0.0, then the value just before it needs to be very close to zero, or the user will hear a "step" as the EG shuts completely off. If you choose −60 dB for the last non-zero map value, the step is easily audible when used to modulate the output amp or filter. If you choose a small value like −96 dB or −120 dB, then the bottom section of the curve will be very flat and won't sound correct. Notice that slew limiting through a lowpass filter will have the same issue as well.

What we need is an exponential mapping equation that has its minimum and maximum values pinned down at 0.0 and 1.0. Fortunately, the MMA convex and concave transforms from Section 6.2 may be employed using the SynthLab functions that automatically fix the endpoints correctly – a bit more work than in the MMA documents. These functions allow you to choose to use a lookup table (LUT) instead of performing a *log10* or a *pow* function in C++ so you may experiment for the best CPU usage. The transforms and tables are designed on a range of [0.0, 1.0]. You simply call the mapping function to convert the values along the range that you need.

It is crucial that we maintain the special consideration that the decay and release times are specified from full-scale to zero, as discussed in Section 7.1, in which the sustain level plays a key role in the actual segment time perception. This means that we will only be using parts of the functions or tables, and not their entire ranges. In other words, for these segments, we need to operate on parts of the curves, not the entire curve. In order to make this work, we need a perfectly complementary function (or LUT) to ascertain the range of values so that we can sew together the segments properly. The concave and convex transforms (or tables) in Figure 7.9(a) and (b) may be used to find these values. Figure 7.9(c) shows the concept – the linear EG output is fed into either the convex or concave transform, depending on the state. The attack segment uses the convex transform, while the decay and release segments use the concave transform. Notice that the slope segment (SL) is kept linear for the *DXEGCore* that uses this method and that the attack segment does not use the entire range – it ends early, which is covered in Section 7.5 on analog EGs.

7.4 Biased EG Output

If you play an early analog synth or a faithful recreation, such as the Korg iPolysix® app, and you apply one of the EGs to the pitch modulation of the oscillators, something strange happens – the notes don't play in tune. This is because the pitch is only shifted positive from the attack state, and only goes back to 0.0 (no pitch shift) when the release state is complete. As shown in Figure 7.10(a), if the sustain level is not set to 0.0, then the pitch of the note will be sharp for the entire sustain duration of the note-event. While this might make an interesting harmonization effect with other oscillators, it is usually not exactly what is required. If you subtract from the sustain-level setting, then the EG is biased back down to 0.0 for the sustain portion, as shown in Figure 7.10(b). Here, you can see the importance of allowing a non-zero start or end point so that the note does not start or terminate flat in pitch with respect to the sustain portion, unless that is what the musician desires. The pitch and filter EGs in the Korg Wavestate® are set up this way, with minimum and maximum *y*-axis values of −100 to +100, or anything in between, corresponding to −1 and +1 for SynthLab's EGs.

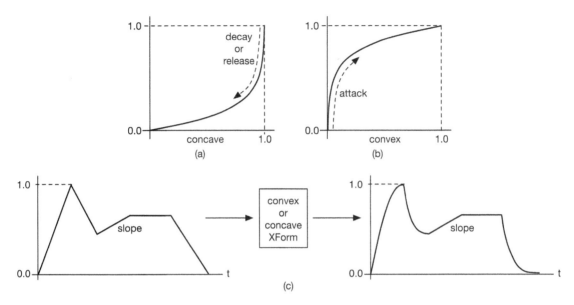

Figure 7.9 (a) The concave and (b) convex transforms are used to give contour to the linear segments, and (c) shows the overall concept; note that the slope segment is kept linear

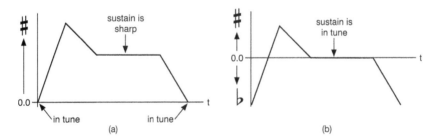

Figure 7.10 (a) When using the EG to modulate pitch, all of the portion above 0.0 is sharp, including the sustain segment, and (b) the biased EG pulls the sustain back in tune but causes the start and end of the note-event to be flat; adjustment of the start and end values mitigates this

7.5 Analog EG Emulation

The original analog EGs were always exponential in nature because they used one or more capacitors that charged for attack and discharged for decay and release. The attack, decay, and release knobs are implemented with variable resistors that set three different RC time constants, which control segment times. Ultimately, this is why the decay and release times are set from full scale to complete discharge, and it sounds correct to our ears that the sustain level influences these times. Figure 7.11 shows the underlying concept; in 7.11(a), the note-on event starts the capacitor C charging, while the note-off event causes the discharge. The *RC* time constants for ($R_{ATT}C$) and ($R_{REL}C$) set the attack and release times. The flat top that is normally formed during the charging process usually does not sound correct. In the Curtis CEM3310 EG chip (used in several older synth designs), the capacitor only charges to about 77% of the asymptote value, giving the attack

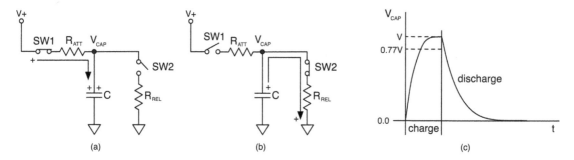

Figure 7.11 (a) SW1 closes for the note-on event, and the voltage source charges capacitor C through R_{ATT}, then (b) SW1 opens, and SW2 closes for the note-off event, which discharges the capacitor through R_{REL}; (c) shows the resulting event; note that V is the asymptotic charge voltage, and 0.77V is 77% of this value, used for the analog emulation

portion of the curve a more linear contour, as shown in Figure 7.11(c). More elaborate analog EG designs used multiple capacitors and resistors and electronic switches (transistors) to generate the EG voltage. Check out the schematic for the Oberheim SEM® module for an interesting two-capacitor EG circuit.

The equations for the charge and discharge time of an RC circuit are shown in Equation (7.3).

$$\begin{matrix} \text{charge} & \text{discharge} \\ Q = 1 - e^{-t/RC} & e^{-t/RC} \end{matrix} \qquad (7.3)$$

The RC term is called the time-constant and named τ. The capacitor's charge/discharge time is related to the time constant. A real-world non-ideal capacitor charges to about 98% at the time $t = 5\tau$. It takes the same amount of time to discharge to 2%. To model the CEM3310, we'll only let the capacitor charge to 77% and discharge from there as well. It charges to 77% of the total at the approximate time $t = 1.5\tau$. It discharges in about $t = 4.95\tau$. Normalizing the R and C values to 1.0, we obtain the Equation (7.4) for a 77% capacitor charge/discharge over a range $x = [0, 1]$ and $y = [0, 1]$.

$$\begin{matrix} \text{charge} & \text{discharge} \\ y = \dfrac{1}{0.77}\left(1 - e^{-1.5x}\right) & y = e^{-4.95x} \end{matrix} \qquad (7.4)$$

To implement an envelope generator with an exponential output, we will need to generate exponential curves based on e. This poses a fundamental problem: mathematical exponential functions do not discharge (decay) all the way down to 0.0 or charge all the way to 1.0. So, we need a way to not only generate an exponential approximation but also ensure that it advances smoothly across its thresholds.

7.5.1 Redmon's Analog EG Emulation

Nigel Redmon's implementation solves the exponential attack/decay issues and provides flexibility for many different curve shapes. It is also easy to modify to add more segments. Figure 7.12(a) shows a first order feedback structure with a single impulse as input and a feedback coefficient b

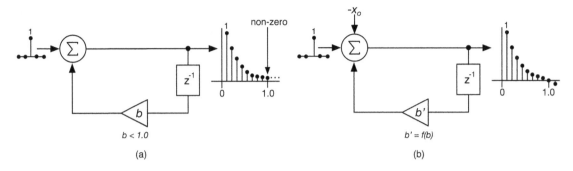

Figure 7.12 Attempting to generate a normalized exponential decay over the range of x = [0, 1] using (a) the first order feedback structure, we observe that the output does not decay to 0.0 and takes on a non-zero value at x = 1.0, while through (b) the addition of a negative bias signal and adjustment to the b coefficient (b'), we can achieve the proper decay curve and hit, then cross over the 0.0 value

that is slightly less than 1.0. The impulse will recirculate through the structure, being multiplied by b each time. It is evident that the output will never reach 0.0, though it will eventually become so small that it cannot be represented with a *float* or *double* data-type – this is called underflow and usually results in a de-normaled number that you see as *#DEN* when debugging. The idea behind Redmon's EG is to add a small offset -x_o, as shown in Figure 7.12(b). This tiny bias signal adds a small negative offset to the output value each time the impulse recirculates, eventually forcing the value to 0.0, then crossing it into negative territory. In order to achieve the same exponential curve, the b coefficient needs to be altered to make up for the added offset.

To find the value of the coefficient b, we need to know the RC time constant that we want to emulate. For the ADSR EG, there will be three different b values, one for each exponential state: b_{ATT}, b_{DCY}, and b_{REL}. For example, if we look at the analog attack and decay equations in (7.4), we see that the exponential functions inside are $e^{-1.5x}$ for the attack segment and $e^{-4.5x}$ for the decay and release segments. Looking at the decay/release exponential, we can calculate that at x = 1.0, which is where we would like the function to evaluate to 0.0, the function will return a non-zero value:

$$y(x) = e^{-4.5x}$$
$$y(1) = e^{-4.5} = 0.011109$$
(7.5)

For Redmon's EG, this value is the *Time Constant Overshoot* (TCO). To calculate and adjust the b coefficient in order to give the proper decay over the normalized range, use Redmon's equation (7.6).

$$t_s = \text{time in samples for attack, decay or release}$$
$$\alpha = \frac{-\ln\left[\dfrac{1+TCO}{TCO}\right]}{t_s}$$
$$b = e^{\alpha}$$
(7.6)

For example, to correct the exponential decay function in Equation (7.5), where the exponent is −4.5x, you evaluate it at x = 1 to produce 0.011109. Equation (7.7) shows what happens to the alpha value's numerator; it produces −4.511048, which produces a slightly *slower* decay time than −4.5 as applied to the exponential function. The addition of a small negative bias will then speed up the decay time so that hits 0.0 exactly in the time (in samples) required.

$$\alpha = \frac{-\ln\left[\dfrac{1+0.011109}{0.011109}\right]}{t_s} = \frac{-4.511048}{t_s} \tag{7.7}$$

$$b = e^{\alpha}$$

To find the bias value x_o, use Redmon's equation (7.8), where L_{SUS} is the sustain level on the range [0.0, 1.0].

$$x_0 = \begin{cases} attack & (1+TCO_{ATT})(1-b_{ATT}) \\ decay & (L_{SUS}-TCO_{DCY})(1-b_{DCY}) \\ release & (-TCO_{REL})(1-b_{REL}) \end{cases} \tag{7.8}$$

7.6 Synth Module: *EnvelopeGenerator*

Figure 7.13 shows the *EnvelopeGenerator* module, along with the three included module cores, and Table 7.1 lists the parameter structure and core information.

7.6.1 *LinearEGCore*

The linear EG is generally not useful as an amp EG, but it is set up for you to experiment with and to use as a starting point for your own EG ideas –the segments, timing calculations, and finite state machine operational code are present in the most minimal form possible. The *LinearEGCore* is available to download as an example EG core project for SynthLab-DM. Examine the code for this core to get started.

7.6.2 *AnalogEGCore*

The analog modeling EG core implements two EG contours: the traditional ADSR and attack-release (AR) modes. The AR mode has no sustain-level and is used as a starting point for experimenting with unconditional EGs. This EG implements Redmon's analog modeling equations (7.4)

Table 7.1 EnvelopeGenerator custom parameter structure and cores

Parameter Structure	Description
EGParameters	Used for all cores, includes additional DX controls

Included Core	Description
AnalogEGCore	Implements Redmon's analog modeling EG
DXEGCore	My variation on the Yamaha DX EG for FM synths
LinearEGCore	Ultra-simple linear EG to use as a starting point, Downloadable SynthLab-DM core project

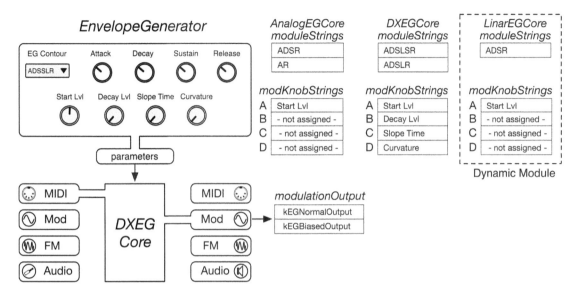

Figure 7.13 The *EnvelopeGenerator* module and the three included cores: DX-EG, analog EG, and linear EG; the module is shown with the *DXEGCore* selected

and (7.5) exactly; compare the C++ code with the equations. Notice that the calculation of attack, decay, and release time constants requires an *exp* operation so these are only updated when the user alters the GUI controls.

7.6.3 *DXEGCore*

The block diagram for the *DXEGCore* is shown in Figure 7.14. This EG has an added segment called "slope," as shown in Figure 7.9, and features a curvature control that uses the MMA concave and convex transforms to apply curvature to a linear EG FSM. The curvature control is a simple blending of the linear and transformed output values. The overall implementation follows a simple finite state machine design, as shown in Figure 7.7, but with the addition of the *slope* state, which is unaffected by the curvature control and remains linear. Examine the code for this core to see how the MMA transforms are applied, including the inverse transform versions.

The *DXEG* uses the simple calculations in Equation (7.2) to generate the various states, each of which has its own step-size, called the *egStepInc*. To simplify the object, the function *setStepInc* implements Equation (7.2) and is used to update the increment value each time the state changes.

7.7 EG Retrigger Modulation

The EG cores are modulation destinations for EG retrigger modulation. When retriggered, the EG will move directly back to the attack state and begin the FSM operation all over. Typically an LFO is attached as the modulation source. The retriggering operation occurs when a threshold is crossed. I made this a low-to-high crossing over the 0.5 unipolar middle value.

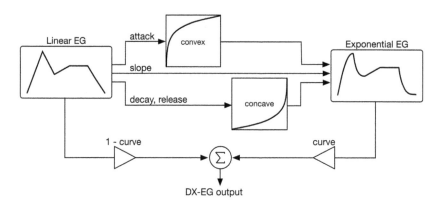

Figure 7.14 Conceptual block diagram of the *DXEG* with the curvature control; the concave and convex transforms are applied to the appropriate segments

7.8 EG Core Programming Notes

Section 7.8.1 through 7.8.6 list the main points for the five operational phases, plus constructor for the EG cores that subclass *ModuleCore* and override the same-named *SynthModule* virtual functions in Section 3.10. With the C++ files open, compare the programming notes and hints to the code that you see, and think about how each implements the FSM and deals with details like legato mode and shutdown. The EG cores all use a state-variable to keep track of their current EG segment. The *EGState* strongly typed enum is used for all cores and has enumeration strings for all possible states. If you want to add more states, such as a two-stage release, then modify this enumeration.

7.8.1 Construction Phase

All cores:

- The module strings are the EG contours, and their selection alters the FSM's state operation.
- Note the similarities and differences in the use of the mod knobs

7.8.2 Reset Phase

All cores:

- Reset the FSM state to *EGState ::kOff*
- Store sample rate, and calculate initial step values or coefficients
- Set the initial EG output value
- Clear the retriggering *noteOff* variable

Analog EG core:

- Calculates new time coefficients only if sample rate changes

```
// --- parameters
EGParameters* parameters =
        static _ cast<EGParameters*>(processInfo.moduleParameters);

// --- retain sample rate for update calculations
sampleRate = processInfo.sampleRate;

// --- reset the state
envelopeOutput = parameters->startLevel;
state = EGState::kOff;

noteOff = false; // for retriggering EG
```

7.8.3 Note On Phase

DX EG and linear EG:

* Calculates the linear attack step size, then subtracts it from the output variable to effectively "back up" the EG by one click; this is used to make the initial attack state produce a perfect value of 0.0 or the user's start level

All cores:

* Set FSM state to *EGState::kAttack*
* Use mod knob A to set the start level, which is the initial output value
* Calculate velocity-to-attack, and note number-to-decay scaling values with a simple linear coefficient
* Notice the way in which legato mode is handled – the EG does not reset its output value when in legato mode

```
if (parameters->velocityToAttackScaling)
    attackTimeScalar = 1.0 - processInfo.noteEvent.midiNoteVelocity / 127.0;
else
    attackTimeScalar = 1.0;

if (parameters->noteNumberToDecayScaling)
    decayTimeScalar = 1.0 - processInfo.noteEvent.midiNoteNumber / 127.0;
else
    decayTimeScalar = 1.0;
```

7.8.4 Update Phase

All cores:

* Recalculate the step sizes or time constant coefficients according to GUI parameter changes
* Note that there is no real-time modulation input; the MIDI velocity and note number are only applied during the note-on phase

- When the MIDI sustain pedal is depressed, and the CC value is greater than 63, a sustain override flag is set, along with a release pending flag
- When the sustain pedal is released, the *update* function calls the note-off handler if the release is pending
- Notice how the retriggering modulation operates, crossing the threshold from low to high

```
else if(!noteOff)// process retriggering
{
    double retrig = processInfo.
                    modulationInputs->getModValue(kTriggerMod);

    if (retrig > 0.5 && !retriggered)
    {
        // --- reset
        envelopeOutput = parameters->startLevel;

        // --- go to the attack state
        state = EGState::kAttack;

        retriggered = true;
    }
    else if (retrig < 0.5 && retriggered)
    {
        retriggered = false;
    }
}
```

7.8.5 Render Phase

All cores:

- Steps through the finite state machine implemented with switch/case statements and uses the *EGState* and the known attack, decay, and sustain levels to trigger movement into the next state
- Output values are written into the *modulationOutput* array slots
- The for-loop only writes output values for the first iteration but runs all iterations to advance the state machine properly; this is especially important if the number of samples to render is less than the normal block size

DX core:

- Notice the way in which the MMA convex and concave, and their reverse functions are used to apply curvature to the state segments, except *EGState::kSlope*, which remains linear

```
// --- decode the state
switch (state)
{
    case EGState::kOff:
    {
        // --- if not legato, reset to start level
        if (!parameters->legatoMode)
            envelopeOutput = parameters->startLevel;

        break;
    }

    case EGState::kAttack:
    etc...
```

7.8.5.1 DX Core Decay and Release

The DX core decay and release states operate the same way for the linear output, simply adding the new *stepInc* to the current value. However, we need to make sure we follow the rules for decaying from full scale, which involves only using a section of the normalized concave transform and is accomplished with a mapping function. This requires using the opposite transform to find the point at which the decay level hits the transform curve. Once the point is found, the section of the transform curve, as shown in dotted boxes in Figure 7.15, needs to map to the same part of the EG's curved segment, which is dependent on both the levels and the times involved. The mapping function effectively shrinks or expands the curve sections to stretch them into place.

7.8.6 Note Off Phase

All cores:

- EGs are the only modules that implement meaningful note-off handlers because of their contribution to the note-event life cycle in Section 4.1

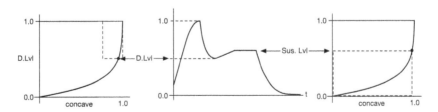

Figure 7.15 The decay and release portions of the EG curve need to be mapped to the correction sections of the normalized concave transform

- Notice how the sustain override flag will bypass the note-off handler if the sustain pedal is depressed
- All cores move the FSM into the *EGState::kRelease* state

7.9 The Digitally Controlled Amplifier (DCA)

The digitally controlled amplifier (DCA) is the digital equivalent of the analog voltage controlled amplifier (VCA), and it is the simplest of the synth modules, using basic calculations for gain (dB to raw) and panning (see pan modulation in Section 6.2.2). The DCA sits at the output of the voice architecture and controls the time domain contour of the note-event. The DCA is hard-wired to the amp EG that sets the note life cycle as this EG is responsible for reporting the end-of-note event. This object is so basic and simple that it does not use module cores. There is only one DCA object. The DCA needs to calculate the overall gain and panning of the voice output. Since the oscillators are pan-able, SynthLab does not implement a GUI control for pan – notice that, for it to work properly, there would need to be a GUI pan control for every voice. However, the pan functionality does play a role in two different ways: for unison mode, three of the four detuned voices are panned according to a simple scheme. You can see this code in the *SynthEngine::update* function, in which the panning and detuning are set for unison mode operation. The DCA pan operation is also a modulation destination, and you may connect an LFO or EG to source the pan modulation routing. All voices will pan alike, but they will begin the panning at note-on time, so staggering the note-events will produce quite a dizzying display of the pan function.

7.9.1 DCA EG Modulation Intensity

The DCA has a tiny GUI parameter structure, and the SynthLab projects only expose one control: the EG intensity. The EG intensity is interesting because it is a bipolar intensity value applied to the EG, whose output is unipolar in nature. This is a special modulation because of the way in which it operates. The EG mod intensity control defaults to a value of 1.0 so that the amp EG and DCA will work in the normal fashion. Reducing the intensity value scales the output and reduces it, like a volume control. When the intensity control is at 0.0, the DCA is silent. When the intensity control goes negative, rather than inverting the phase of the audio signal, we invert the EG control signal itself, simply by adding 1.0 to the value. This inverts the operation in an interesting way. Figure 7.17(a) and (b) show how the EG intensity control operates with a positive or negative polarity. For the inverted version, loud becomes quiet, and quiet becomes loud, with the note-event ending at maximum volume.

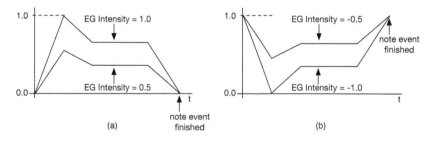

Figure 7.16 (a) The EG intensity acts as a simple gain control when positive, but (b) when negative, it inverts the unipolar signal

7.9.2 DCA Note On Phase

When the user strikes a MIDI key, the controller sends a velocity value that translates into how much force was used to strike the key. The velocity value is converted to a raw value, as described in Section 6.2's MIDI velocity modulation equations, and uses a built-in function. The MIDI velocity arrives in the note-event structure.

```
bool DCA::doNoteOn(MIDINoteEvent& noteEvent)
{
    // --- store our MIDI velocity
    midiVelocityGain = mmaMIDItoAtten(noteEvent.midiNoteVelocity);

    etc...
```

7.9.3 DCA Update Phase

The DCA update phase is the only interesting operation as it applies the amp, EG, and panning modulation values. The amp modulation control creates the tremolo effect and must connect to a LFO's unipolar-from-max output value in order to operate intuitively. The update function is shown below in its entirety. Examine the code, and notice how the EG intensity control is handled.

```
// --- apply Max Down modulator
double ampMod = doUnipolarModulationFromMax(
                modulationInput->getModValue(kMaxDownAmpMod), 0.0, 1.0);
ampMod *= parameters->ampModIntensity;

// --- EG modulation
double egMod = parameters->ampEGIntensity * modulationInput->getModValue(kEGMod);

// --- flip EG output
if (parameters->ampEGIntensity < 0.0)
    egMod += 1.0;
```

The DCA also has built-in support for MIDI CC #7 (volume):

```
// --- support for MIDI Volume CC
double midiVolumeGain = mmaMIDItoAtten(midiInputData->getCCMIDIData(VOLUME_CC07));
```

The final gain calculation is just a combination of all of these, along with the original velocity-based gain value.

```
// --- calculate the final raw gain value
// multiply the various gains together
gainRaw = midiVelocityGain * egMod * ampMod;

// --- apply final output gain
if (parameters->gainValue_dB > kMinAbsoluteGain_dB)
    gainRaw *= pow(10.0, parameters->gainValue_dB / 20.0);
```

```
else
    gainRaw = 0.0; // OFF
```

The pan modulation uses the *panValue* as the center of operation. This value is 0.0, except for the unison mode, where the value is preset according to the unison mode scheme. Pan modulation is described in Section 6.2.2.

```
// --- now process pan modifiers
double panTotal = panValue + (parameters->panModIntensity *
                                modulationInput->getModValue(kPanMod));

// --- limit in case pan control is biased
boundValueBipolar(panTotal);

// --- equal power calculation in synthfunction.h
calculatePanValues(panTotal, panLeftGain, panRightGain);
```

7.10 Exercises

7.10.1 *SynthLab-DM: Pre-Release state*

The linear EG is used as the example dynamic module for the EG object. Download the sample code, then compile and install the DLL into the SynthLab-DM project of your choice, following the instructions in Section 5.2.2. Select the linear EG core to use for the output amp EG and filter EG, and pay attention to how it sounds. Next, add a second release state modifying the FSM code and adding a new *EGState::kPreRelease*, and use one of the mod knobs to adjust the pre-release time and another to set the pre-release level. Implement the required code in the methods corresponding to the operational phases.

7.10.2 *Stand-Alone Module Exercise: More Contours*

Add a stand-alone EG object to a plugin of your own design, and write the code to integrate it into your system, remembering the five operational phases. You may choose any of the cores as a starting point. Add the GUI controls, then make sure you can update and render the EG values properly. Next, modify the core by adding more EG contours – the stock objects only implement two contours each, so you have plenty of free module strings to add more contours. Notice how the additional contours change the FSM operation. You may need to add more states to the *EGState* enumeration.

7.10.3 *Stand-Alone Module Exercise: Unconditional Release*

Review the way the unconditional release EG operates when the musician triggers a complete cycle of EG states with a press and release of a key. Add unconditional release operation to your modified stand-alone module. What changes need to occur in the note-off handler?

7.10.4 *Advanced Module Core: Yamaha and Casio CZ EGs*

Figure 7.17(a) and (b) show the EG contours for the Yamaha EX and Casio CZ series synths, respectively. Both feature multiple decay and release segments. Implement one or both EGs using

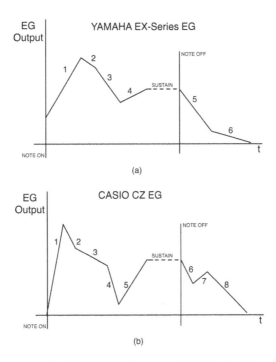

Figure 7.17 Two more EG contours for the (a) Yamaha EX and (b) Casio CZ series synths; the contours are shown as linear here for simplicity; most segments are curved

a stand-alone module core object in your own project or in any of the downloadable SynthLab projects. Think about the challenges with the larger finite state machines and whether you intend to implement curvature on some or all of the EG segments. Notice that the decay and release segments may move in the up or down direction, with the exception of the last release segment, which decays downward to 0.0 or the release level.

Bibliography

digichip.com. "CEM3310 Voltage Controlled Envelope Generator Datasheet." https://www.digchip.com/datasheets/parts/datasheet/922/CEM3310-pdf.php, Accessed October 14, 2020

Hurtig, Brent, Ed. 1984. *Synthesizer Basics*, pp. 29–35. Winona: Hal Leonard Corporation Korg, Inc. 1997. *Triton Music Workstation Basic Guide*. Tokyo: Korg Inc. manuals.lib. "Casio CZ-1000 Operation Manual." https://www.manualslib.com/manual/1160175/Casio-Cz-1000.html, Accessed October 14, 2020

Redmon, Nigel. "Envelope Generators Part 2." http://www.earlevel.com/main/2013/06/02/envelope-generators-adsr-part-2/, Accessed October 14, 2020

Yamaha, Inc. 1983. *DX7 User's Manual*. Tokyo: Yamaha Inc.

8 Low Frequency Oscillators

Low Frequency Oscillators (LFOs) belong to the render-group of synth building blocks as they render an output without processing an input signal. LFOs are used as modulation sources that generate relatively slow-moving values used to modulate the parameters of a destination object. Since these oscillators are not used for audio frequencies, they do not suffer from aliasing issues and can be generated with extremely simple equations. They are sometimes called *trivial oscillators*. The requirements for LFOs and pitched oscillators are summarized as follows:

LFO Requirements:

- Frequency range: 0.02 Hz–20.0 Hz (though this is highly variable)
- Constructed from simple equations, lookup tables, or piecewise functions
- Aliasing not a consideration since these are not used for audio output
- For block processing, LFO samples are only generated once per block prior to modulation

Pitched Oscillator Requirements:

- Frequency range: 20 Hz–20,480 Hz (10 octaves)
- Constructed from tables or band-limiting algorithms; direct form and other traditional DSP algorithms have issues which make them unsuitable
- Should not alias, but if aliasing is present, then it must be as inaudible as possible or masked by other harmonic components
- For block processing, samples are generated on each sample interval to fill the block

8.1 Noise Oscillators and Generators

Noise oscillators are unique in that they are used in both LFOs and pitched oscillators. These oscillators do not have a fundamental oscillator frequency f_o like the others. They may be calculated with random number generators. The *NoiseGenerator* produces white, Gaussian white, and pink noise. You can add more noise types as well, and there are numerous variations. The output of the *NoiseGenerator* is always on the range [−1.0, +1.0].

White noise is the result of a truly random number and has a flat spectrum indicating constant amplitude across all frequency components, as shown in Figure 8.1(a). The name "white" corresponds to white light, which includes equal contributions from all the visible color frequencies – also known as the color spectrum.

Gaussian white noise (also called additive Gaussian white noise or *AGW*) likewise has a flat frequency response, as shown in Figure 8.1(a). The difference is in the variance of the sample amplitudes. In white noise, there is an equal probability that any sample will lie anywhere in the range

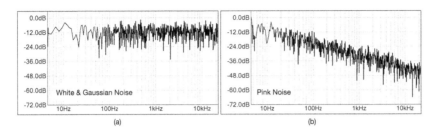

Figure 8.1 The frequency spectra of (a) white and (b) pink noise; FFT length is 131,072 points

of [−1.0, +1.0] – each output is random and uncorrelated to the previous outputs, and over time, averaging the sample values results in a zero mean. Gaussian white noise also has a zero mean when averaged over time. The difference lies in the Gaussian sample value variance, which follows a bell-shaped curve called the *standard distribution*. This means that an output sample has a higher probability of being near the extreme (center) +/−1.0 than of being near the minimum value around 0.0.

Pink noise has a spectrum that rolls off at −3 dB/octave or −10 dB/decade, as shown in Figure 8.1(b). There are numerous approaches to the digital design of the shallow filter, which is simpler in analog. Paul Kellet's "economy" method involves a simple, three-coefficient lowpass filter on white noise. This pinking filter code is detailed in the SynthLab documentation and the firstpr.com reference.

There are several methods of generating the random noise signals. The Standard Library object called *std::default_random_engine* simplifies the creation of white and Gaussian white noise significantly.

```
std::default _ random _ engine defaultGeneratorEngine;
```

Gaussian (normal distribution with mean = 0, variance = 1):

```
std::normal _ distribution<double> normalDistribution(mean, variance);
gaussianWN = normalDistribution(defaultGeneratorEngine);
```

White (random distribution on interval [−1, +1]):

```
std::uniform _ real _ distribution<double> randomDisribution(-1.0, 1.0);
whiteNoise = randomDisribution(defaultGeneratorEngine);
```

Pink (filtered white noise):

```
pinkNoise = doPinkingFilter(doWhiteNoise());
pinkNoise *= 0.25; // filter gain is > 1
```

8.2 Oscillator Clocking

All non-noise oscillators require a time-base that is directly linked to the system sample rate. Most SynthLab oscillators will use the same time-base, which consists of a modulo counter named *mcounter*. This is also known as a phase accumulator, but I use modulo counter exclusively here. A modulo counter starts from 0.0, then begins counting upwards at a rate corresponding to the oscillator's frequency. The counter step-size is called the phase increment (*phaseInc*) and is applied once per sample period. When the modulo counter crosses above the value 1.0 by some amount Δ, the clock rolls over and begins counting upward again, starting from the Δ value. Figure 8.2(a)

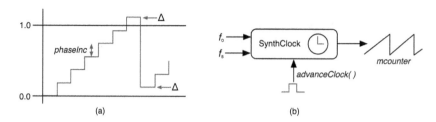

Figure 8.2 (a) The modulo counter steps upward by the *phaseInc* on each sample period until the counter crosses 1.0 and wraps to the same offset, and (b) the block diagram form of the *SynthClock* object

demonstrates this concept: the *phaseInc* is the step-size, and the counter rolls over to the offset level Δ. The *phaseInc* calculation is blissfully simple and requires no trig function calls – it is simply the ratio of the desired frequency of oscillation f_o and the sample rate f_s.

$$phaseInc = \frac{f_o}{f_s} \tag{8.1}$$

8.2.1 The SynthClock Object

To handle the modulo counter operation, I have included a simple C++ object called *SynthClock*. Figure 8.2(b) shows a conceptual block diagram of the *SynthClock* object. You use the *setFrequency* function to apply f_o, f_s to calculate the *phaseInc*, and the *advanceClock* function to increment the time-base. The functions *wrapClock* and *advanceWrapClock* are used for the wrapping operation.

8.2.2 Reversing Time and Oscillator Scanning

All of the SynthLab oscillators can be designed to run forward or backwards, the latter a requirement for FM synthesis that also allows interesting waveform generation. To run an oscillator backwards, you simply negate the *phaseInc* parameter so that it counts down rather than up. The *SynthClock* object will take care of wrapping the *mcounter* in the opposite direction. You can generate numerous new waveforms from your existing ones quite easily. One concept is called *scanning*; this is when you alternate the forward and reverse directions each time the *mcounter* wrap occurs in either direction. This produces back-to-back waveform cycles, as shown in Figure 8.9, for the sine and triangle scanned waves. These were popular for early wavetable pitched oscillators as the scan reversal operation is simple to implement. You can also change the direction at different points in the waveform cycle or follow more complex patterns to create distinctive waveforms.

8.3 LFO Waveforms and Rendering Equations

The SynthLab's default LFO core produces nine different waveforms, as shown in Figures 8.3 and 8.4. The calculations for each waveform are listed to the right, while the name and constant enumeration strings are to the left.

8.3.1 Fundamental Waveforms

The first set of waveforms consists of the most common LFOs you will find in most synths. These include ramp up, ramp down, and triangle waveforms. These are all calculated directly from the *SynthClock's mcounter*, using simple equations. The ramp up waveform is used as the basis for the others.

8.3.2 Exponential Waveforms

The default *LFOCore* also synthesizes exponential versions of the three basic waveforms. The MMA concave transform *concaveXForm* is used to apply the exponential curve shaping across the input and output ranges [−1.0, +1.0]. The key to using these transforms is applying them to the correct parameter, which varies from one waveform to the next and is shown for these waveforms in Figures 8.3 and 8.4.

8.3.3 Sinusoidal Approximations

For the LFO sine waveform, we could use a high-resolution lookup table, but that might be over-kill for our LFO, which is only rendering one output sample per block of rendered samples. There are numerous sinusoidal approximations, ranging from simple to relatively complex. The sinusoids they produce are visually and, for most people, audibly identical, but the Fourier spectra reveal the harmonic distortion components. The parabolic sine approximation is nearly distortion free and so clean that it can even be used as a pitched oscillator if desired. Figure 8.5 shows the spectra and equations for each.

8.3.4 Random Sample and Hold

The noise generator is commonly used to sample the random output and hold the value for some period of time. This requires the noise generator, a register to hold the output value, and a *Timer*

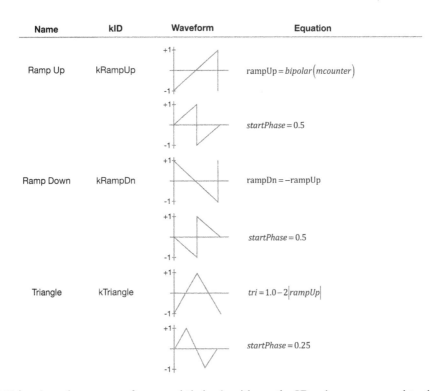

Name	kID	Waveform	Equation
Ramp Up	kRampUp		$rampUp = bipolar(mcounter)$
			$startPhase = 0.5$
Ramp Down	kRampDn		$rampDn = -rampUp$
			$startPhase = 0.5$
Triangle	kTriangle		$tri = 1.0 - 2|rampUp|$
			$startPhase = 0.25$

Figure 8.3 Triangle and ramp waveforms and their algorithms; the ID values correspond to the waveform selector in SynthLab

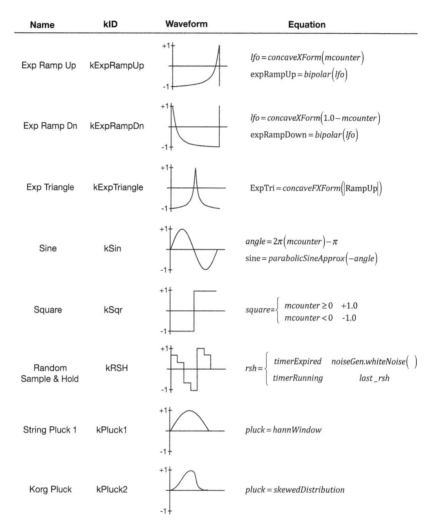

Name	kID	Waveform	Equation
Exp Ramp Up	kExpRampUp		$lfo = concaveXForm(mcounter)$ $expRampUp = bipolar(lfo)$
Exp Ramp Dn	kExpRampDn		$lfo = concaveXForm(1.0 - mcounter)$ $expRampDown = bipolar(lfo)$
Exp Triangle	kExpTriangle		$ExpTri = concaveFXForm(|RampUp|)$
Sine	kSin		$angle = 2\pi(mcounter) - \pi$ $sine = parabolicSineApprox(-angle)$
Square	kSqr		$square = \begin{cases} mcounter \geq 0 & +1.0 \\ mcounter < 0 & -1.0 \end{cases}$
Random Sample & Hold	kRSH		$rsh = \begin{cases} timerExpired & noiseGen.whiteNoise(\ ) \\ timerRunning & last\_rsh \end{cases}$
String Pluck 1	kPluck1		$pluck = hannWindow$
Korg Pluck	kPluck2		$pluck = skewedDistribution$

Figure 8.4 Exponential, sinusoidal, square, random, and pluck waveforms and their algorithms

object to trigger the sampling operation. For the common sample and hold LFO, the timer is set to expire after N sample periods related to the LFO frequency's period $T = 1/f_o$. This produces a waveform with random amplitude values and a constant hold time. In another variation, you ignore the LFO frequency and reset the timer with a random hold time for each trigger. This produces both random amplitudes and random hold time intervals. These LFO block diagrams are shown in Figure 8.6.

8.3.5 Stepped (Quantized) Waveforms

The stepped or quantized LFO waveforms are also sample and hold types, but they can be implemented without timers. One option is to use the quantization formula on the *mcounter* value

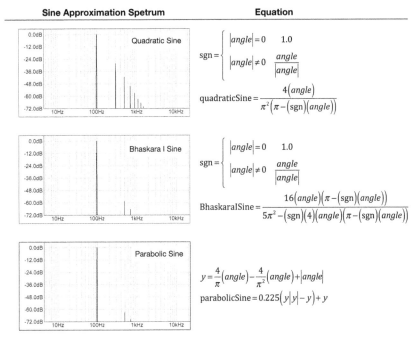

Figure 8.5 Frequency spectra and equations for three popular sinusoidal approximations: quadratic, Bhaskara I, and parabolic, with f_o = 100 Hz

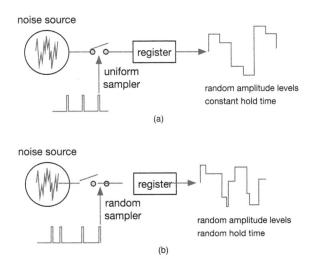

Figure 8.6 Random sample and hold LFOs with (a) random amplitude and constant hold time, and (b) random amplitude and random hold times

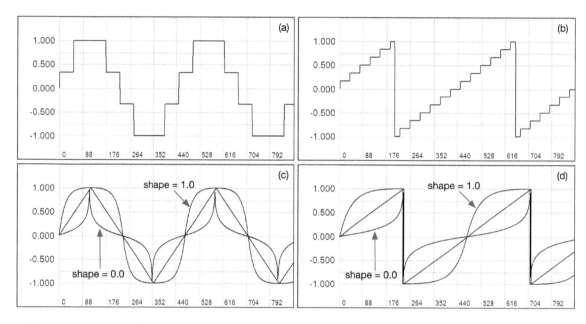

Figure 8.7 Stepped LFO waveform examples: (a) three-step sine, (b) six-step triangle, and shaped LFO waveforms (c) triangle and (d) ramp up with shape control = (0.0, 0.5, 1.0)

to produce the steps; this technique uses the same bit-crusher algorithm that appears in my FX plugin book. Another option is to use the mapping functions in *synthfunctions.h*, which map double values to unsigned integers, and vice versa. This first quantizes the LFO output value as an *unsigned integer*, then remaps it back to a *double* value. The quantization occurs on the LFO's final bipolar output value, prior to attenuation and other processing. In the SynthLab LFO, the stepper value is an integer that dictates the total number of steps across the output amplitude range; note that −1.0 is not counted as a step. Figure 8.7(a) and (b) show two waveforms processed at different quantization levels *(QL)*. Quantizing the square wave has no effect as it is always a one-step waveform. Quantizing the random sample and hold waveform will produce variations on the sample and hold that can be quite interesting.

8.3.6 One-Sided (Unipolar) Waveforms

There are a few unipolar LFO waveforms, including Korg's "pluck" wave. Here, the idea is to simulate a plucked string, which goes sharp and then comes back into tune very quickly at the attack of the note; the note never goes flat during the plucking process. The waveform resembles a leaning or skewed window function in Figure 8.4.

8.4 Render Modes

There are three common render modes for the LFO: one-shot, free-run, and synchronized (sync). The one-shot LFO renders one cycle of the waveform and then stops, either holding the last output or forcing the last output to zero. The free-run LFO starts running on the first note-on event, then runs forever, never resetting the LFO. In sync mode, the LFO is phase-reset and restarted on each new note-on event.

8.5 Waveform Shaping

One common LFO parameter that varies widely in implementation is a *shape* control, which alters some aspect of the LFO's time-domain signal. A simple technique is to blend the output of two different LFO waveforms, A and B, using the shape control to mix them in different ratios, producing a range of hybrid waveforms. If one of the signals is a sinusoid, then the shape control will behave in a similar manner to a lowpass filter. Another method is to use waveshaping on the LFO output or the modulo counter value to bend the segments. For the SynthLab LFO cores, when the modulation knob is above 0.5, the reverse concave transform is applied, while the normal concave transform is applied when the control is below 0.5. This produces a shape control that is sometimes called a curve or curvature control. Figure 8.7(c) and (d) show how the shape control affects the curvature of two different waveforms. When shape = 0.5, no curvature is applied.

8.6 Delay and Fade-in Times

There are two more common LFO parameters: delay time and fade-in time. The delay time specifies how long it will take the LFO to start generating non-zero samples. The fade-in time uses a linear amplitude ramp to fade the LFO from an amplitude of 0.0 to 1.0. For SynthLab, both times are given in milliseconds. The implementations are easy: for the delay time, use a *Timer* object that is reset at note-on and set to expire at the user's delay time setting. For fade-in, use a *RampModulator* object to generate a linear ramp of values from [0.0, +1.0] over the user's fade-in time period, then scale the output with the ramp.

8.7 Starting Phase

To adjust the starting phase of the LFO, you add a phase offset to the modulo counter so that it starts at a non-zero location. An offset of 0.5 produces a shift of 180 degrees. You may want to experiment with the LFO starting phase as it applies to the triangle and ramp waveforms. If you examine Figure 8.3, you will see that the triangle and ramp waveforms start and end at non-zero locations. When used in one-shot mode, the LFO may start or end abruptly. In addition, when trying to blend LFOs with the sinusoidal waveform, there will be phase issues as the sine always starts and ends on 0.0. Figure 8.3 shows how to adjust the starting phase of the SynthLab LFO triangle and ramp waveforms to make them symmetrical, starting and ending at 0.0.

8.8 DC Offset

You may also offset the LFO waveform with a constant value called a DC offset. To do this, you simply add or subtract a static value to the LFO's output. Notice that you may use it to convert one-sided LFO waveforms into bipolar versions. You need to decide how to handle values outside of the normalized bipolar range [−1.0, +1.0].

8.9 *SynthLFO* and Cores

The *SynthLFO* and its core objects are shown in block form in Figure 8.8. The custom module strings are the LFO waveform strings, and the mod knobs are chosen for the most common operations.

8.9.1 *LFO Controls, Modulations, and Features*

The LFO frequency and output controls are self-explanatory. The step control quantizes the output when its value is two or greater and works as an interesting arpeggiator when connected to modulate an oscillator's pitch. The BPM sync is a special feature and locks the LFO rate to a specified musical duration using the host's BPM value and the BPM sync modulation in Section 6.4. Table 8.1 lists the cores and their functionality.

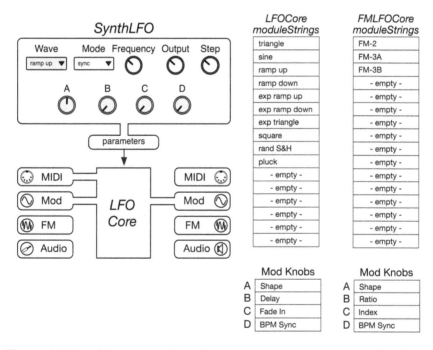

Figure 8.8 The *SynthLFO* and its two cores block diagrams, module strings, and mod knobs

Table 8.1 LFO cores and their special modulation capabilities (*) downloadable dynamic module projects

Parameter Structure	Description
LFOParameters	Every possible parameter for both cores

Core	Features
*LFOCore**	Classic LFO waveforms, including the one-sided pluck waveform, based on the Korg Wavstate LFO
*FMLFOCore**	Creates FM LFO waveforms using phase modulation (see Section 16.6)

8.10 LFO Core Programming Notes

With the C++ files open, compare the programming notes with the code that you see, starting with the class descriptions of each core. The LFO cores use the *SynthClock* as their time-base. The normal core implements the waveform equations in Figures 8.3 and 8.4. The LFO core implements two FM algorithms: carrier and modulator in series, and a modulator – modulator – carrier version. Compare the code to the details in Section 16.6.

The cores require two registers: one to store the current output value for one-shot mode, which holds the last value indefinitely, and another for the random sample and hold value. There is also a *renderComplete* flag for the one-shot operation. Table 8.2 lists the *LFOCore* member objects and their LFO function. See the C++ documentation for object details.

Sections 8.10.1 through 8.10.4 summarize the five operational phases, plus the constructor for the *LFOCore*. Make sure to examine the code while digesting their operational phase details. The *FMLFOCore* only differs in the render operation.

8.10.1 Construction Phase

The LFO core constructors are super simple as they only expose the module string and mod knob labels.

- The module strings are the waveform names, and their index values map to the GUI control selection values

8.10.2 Reset and Note-On Phases

The reset and note-on operations are nearly identical. The only real difference is that the note-on function branches according to the free-run mode status and does not reset timers for this state. Setting up the timers is straightforward – note the use of MAX constants:

```
delay_mSec = getModKnobValueLinear(parameters->modKnobValue[LFO_DELAY],
                                    0.0, MAX_LFO_DELAY_MSEC);
delayTimer.setExpireSamples(msecToSamples(sampleRate, delay_mSec));

fadeIn_mSec = getModKnobValueLinear(
   parameters->modKnobValue[LFO_FADE_IN], 0.0, MAX_LFO_FADEIN_MSEC);

fadeInModulator.startModulator(0.0, 1.0, fadeIn_mSec,
                                    processInfo.sampleRate);
```

Table 8.2 LFOCore member objects

LFO Functionality	C++ Object	Member Name/Notes
Time-base	*SynthClock*	*lfoClock*
Noise Generation	*NoiseGenerator*	*noiseGen*
Sample & Hold	*Timer*	*sampleHoldTimer*
Delay	*Timer*	*delayTimer*
Fade-In	*RampModulator*	*fadeInModulator*
Pluck Waveforms	*BasicLookupTables*	*lookupTables*

For sync mode, the phases are adjusted to produce symmetrical waveforms starting and ending at 0.0.

```
if (parameters->waveform == LFOWaveform::kTriangle)
    lfoClock.addPhaseOffset(0.25);


if (parameters->waveform == LFOWaveform::kRampUp ||
    parameters->waveform == LFOWaveform::kRampDown)
        lfoClock.addPhaseOffset(0.5);
```

8.10.3 Update Phase

The LFO core update functions are quite simple as this is a basic modulator.

- BPM sync uses the *getTimeFromTempo* function and is detailed in Section 6.5. The *frequency_Hz* parameter is the sync target
- Bipolar linear FM is applied to the *frequency_Hz* parameter to calculate the final LFO frequency and is detailed in Section 6.4 using the pre-calculated modulation range
- The SynthClock member is updated with the new oscillator frequency

```
modValue =
    processInfo.modulationInputs[kFrequencyMod]*LFO _ HALF _ RANGE;

modulatedFreq _ Hz = parameters->frequency _ Hz + modValue;

// --- update the phase inc from the frequency
lfoClock.setFrequency(newFrequency _ Hz, sampleRate);
```

8.10.4 Render Phase

The block diagram in Figure 8.8 shows that the LFO accepts incoming MIDI and modulation values, and writes its output into the *modulationOutputs* array. There are two outputs defined: normal and inverted. The render operation is made up of five steps:

1. Check delay timer; if not expired, set output = 0.0 and return
2. Check one-shot mode: call the *lfoClock->wrapClock* method, and check the return value; if wrapped, then the one-shot cycle is completed; set the flag and return the final LFO value
3. Decode the *parameters->waveform* enumeration and render the waveform according to the calculations in Figures 8.3 and 8.4. Partial code listing:

```
if (parameters->waveform == LFOWaveform::kSin)
{
    outputValue = parabolicSine(-(lfoClock.mcounter*kTwoPi - kPi));
}
else if (parameters->waveform == LFOWaveform::kRampUp)
    outputValue = bipolar(lfoClock.mcounter);
```

```
else if (parameters->waveform == LFOWaveform::kExpRampUp)
    outputValue = bipolar(concaveXForm(lfoClock.mcounter));
else if (parameters->waveform == LFOWaveform::kTriangle)
    outputValue = 1.0 - 2.0*fabs(bipolar(lfoClock.mcounter));
```

etc...

4   Apply post-render processing to output value

- Step quantize: see Section 6.1.3
- Shape: use the concave transform functions to modulate according to distance above/below center value of 0.5

```
if (parameters->modKnobValue[LFO _ SHAPE]) >= 0.5)
    shapeOut = bipolarConvexXForm(outputValue);
else
    shapeOut = bipolarConcaveXForm(outputValue);
```

Next, use split-bipolar transform on the mod knob value (see Section 6.1), then blend in some amount of the curved waveform, along with the normal output:

```
// --- split bipolar for multiplier
double shape = splitBipolar(parameters->modKnobValue[LFO _ SHAPE]);

outputValue = shape*shapeOut + (1.0 - shape)*outputValue;
```

- Apply fade-in modulation: this is standard fade-in ramp modulation detailed in Section 6.1.4

5   Write normal and inverted outputs into modOutputs

```
processInfo.modulationOutputs[kLFONormalOutput] = outputValue;
processInfo.modulationOutputs[kLFOInvertedOutput] = -outputValue;
```

8.11 Exercises

8.11.1 SynthLab-DM: The Pluck Waveform

Implement the basic string pluck waveform in Figure 8.4. The simple version uses a Hann windowing function to produce the one-sided waveform. For the Hann window, you can use the *BasicLookupTables* object already declared in the *LFOCore*. First, you need to add the *kPluck* enumeration item to the existing definition in the *lfocore.h* class definition file.

```
enum class LFOWaveform { kTriangle, kSin, . . . , kRSH, kPluck };
```

The lookup table does all the work, and there are no parameters on the pluck waveform to manipulate. In the *render()* function, you need to decode the LFO waveform and set the output variable using the lookup table object. See Appendix A for *BasicLookupTables* details.

```
// --- use hann table; can experiment
```

```
else if (parameters->waveform == LFOWaveform::kPluck)
    outputValue = lookupTables->readHannTableWithNormIndex(lfoClock.
    mcounter);
```

8.11.2 SynthLab-DM: Korg Pluck Waveform

While the Hann window works reasonably well in short-duration one-shot mode, the Korg version is more realistic for stringed instrument emulation. Notice that the Korg waveform is a bent or leaning bell curve that may be fashioned in a variety of manners. Research "skewed distribution," and formulate your own version of the Korg pluck waveform. Is there a parameter you can vary to easily change the skew? If so, you could re-purpose a mod knob to allow user adjustment.

8.11.3 SynthLab-DM: Mod Knob Shape to DC Offset Control

For this exercise, you change the function of the shape control to add or remove a DC offset instead. The shape control defaults to a value of 0.5 so we can set that as the no-offset value, then increase in the positive or negative direction using the *splitBipolar* function (see *synthfunctions.h*). When the user moves the control above 0.5, you apply a positive DC offset, and when the control is below 0.5, you apply a negative DC offset.

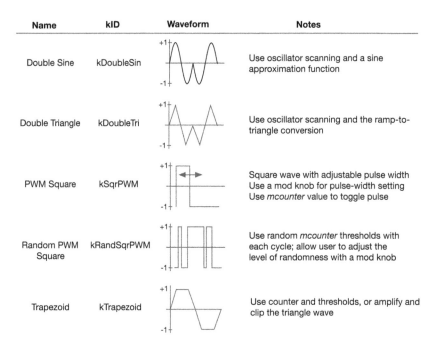

Name	kID	Waveform	Notes
Double Sine	kDoubleSin		Use oscillator scanning and a sine approximation function
Double Triangle	kDoubleTri		Use oscillator scanning and the ramp-to-triangle conversion
PWM Square	kSqrPWM		Square wave with adjustable pulse width Use a mod knob for pulse-width setting Use *mcounter* value to toggle pulse
Random PWM Square	kRandSqrPWM		Use random *mcounter* thresholds with each cycle; allow user to adjust the level of randomness with a mod knob
Trapezoid	kTrapezoid		Use counter and thresholds, or amplify and clip the triangle wave

Figure 8.9 Additional LFO waveforms for your custom object

8.11.4 Advanced Module: Create a Novel LFOCore

Finally, make your own *LFOCore* object using the existing object as a basic template, and keep the normal modulations. For your personal *LFOCore*, add the new LFO waveforms from Figure 8.9, and implement any four mod knob parameters you wish, starting with the suggested modifiers.

Mod Knob A: starting phase
Mod Knob B: pulse-width (for square PWM)
Mod Knob C: DC offset
Mod Knob D: BPM Sync (keep existing)

Bibliography

Korg.com. "Wavestate Owner's Manual." https://www.korg.com/us/support/download/product/0/840/, Accessed October 14, 2020

firstpr.com. "DSP generation of Pink (1/f) Noise." http://www.firstpr.com.au/dsp/pink-noise/, Accessed October 14, 2020

9   Wavetable Oscillators

Wavetable oscillators are pitched oscillators that cycle through a lookup table to generate a waveform. These are some of the earliest of the digital oscillators designed for audio use, having been around since the 1960s. Chowning's FM synthesis required wavetable oscillators as they are inherently stable and can produce the same sequence of output values over and over. Wavetables were used in the first hybrid synths, such as the Sequential Circuits Prophet VS, as well as fully digital synths, like the Korg M1 and Yamaha DX7. Wavetable synthesis seems to come and go in popularity, but right now it is very hot – this may be due to the appearance of more morphing wavetable synths and tools that allow us to develop scores of wavetables at a time from algorithms or found-sounds.

9.1 Wavetable Fundamentals: Table Lookup

The traditional wavetable is a pre-calculated array of length N that contains one cycle, minus one sample, of some waveform. The length is typically a power of two, but that is not strictly required. The oscillator uses a pointer or an index value to access samples stored in the table. In the most primitive form shown in Figure 9.1(a), the oscillator outputs these values directly, skipping through the table at a lookup interval called *wtPhaseInc*, which is an integer. More advanced versions use floating point increment values and interpolation to calculate in-between values, as shown in Figure 9.1(c).

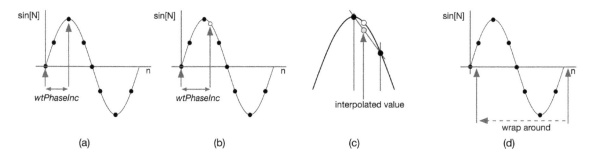

Figure 9.1 Reading an $N = 8$ point wavetable with (a) integer lookup and (b) floating point lookup with (c) linear interpolation and (d) the read index wraps around to the start of the table when the added phase increment pushes the lookup point past the table's ending index

When the table index or pointer passes the last sample in the array by some amount Δ, it wraps back around to the top of the array with an offset of Δ and continues marching through the buffer, as shown in Figure 9.1(d). This is simply a scaled version of the modulo counter time-base we use for the LFO and the other pitched oscillators, and we can use the same basic clocking functionality. The wavetable phase increment value is simply the modulo counter value multiplied by the table size N.

$$wtPhaseInc = N\frac{f_o}{f_s} \tag{9.1}$$

When the *wtPhaseInc* value is much less than one, you interpolate multiple values between a pair of points, then move to the next pair. When the *wtPhaseInc* is much greater than one, you skip over multiple table cells and interpolate only between the last set – the number depends on the order of interpolation.

9.1.1 Wavetable Aliasing

There are two sources of aliasing: first, the wavetable may have been pre-computed with aliasing components already included. For example, sampling the trivial ramp LFO will produce aliasing in the resulting wavetable because the original signal was already aliased. Second, when the *wtPhaseInc* is very much greater than one, the index is making large skips through the table, causing it to appear under-sampled. In practice, if the table contains typical musical sounds with harmonics that decay rapidly or exponentially, then the aliasing will be subtle or perhaps masked by other harmonic components. Interestingly, to avoid large *wtPhaseInc* values, as the oscillator frequency increases, the table length should decrease.

9.1.2 Band-Limited Tables via the Fourier Series

An early approach to preventing aliasing involved pre-calculating the tables as band-limited Fourier series sums. These Fourier series summations have been in the literature for almost two centuries and allow you to easily generate a table of any length, filled with a preset number of harmonics and in harmonic ratios that generate the desired waveforms. The goal here is to synthesize waveforms that do not alias because their spectra are band-limited to the Nyquist frequency. The Fourier series representations for three common synth waveforms are shown in Figure 9.3. Notice that, for a wavetable, we only need a single cycle of the waveform so that $f_o = 1$ Hz, and k represents the harmonic number. If you want the fundamental plus 64 harmonics, k would vary from 1 to 64. To calculate the maximum number of harmonics below Nyquist for a given pitch, use Equation (9.2).

$$numHarmonics = \frac{f_s}{2(pitchHz)} \tag{9.2}$$

Figure 9.2 shows the 88-note keyboard with a few pitches and number of harmonics below Nyquist for $f_s = 44.1$ kHz. There are 128 MIDI notes in total; MIDI note 0 has the pitch of a C, 8.1758 Hz, while MIDI note 127's pitch is a G, 12.5438535 kHz. Equation (9.2) also shows that for any harmonic signal above ½ Nyquist can only contain a single harmonic component, or aliasing will occur. As you play successively higher notes, the waveform gets closer and closer to being a pure sinusoid.

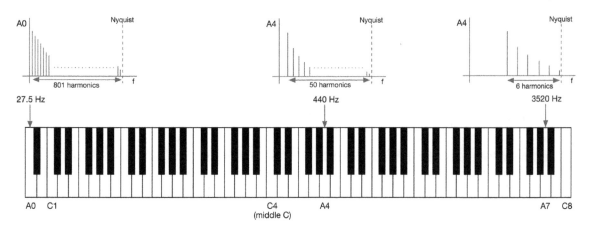

Figure 9.2 The 88-note piano keyboard starts at A0 (MIDI note 21), with 801 harmonics, and ends at C8 (MIDI note 108), with 5 harmonics; f_s = 44.1 kHz and A0, A4, and A7 are shown

Waveform	Fouier Series Formula
Ramp Up Sawtooth	$$Y(n)_{SAW} = \sum_{k=1}^{\infty} (-1)^{k+1} \frac{1}{k} \sin(k\omega nT)$$ $$= \left[\sin(\omega nT) - \frac{1}{2}\sin(2\omega nT) + \frac{1}{3}\sin(3\omega nT) - \frac{1}{4}\sin(4\omega nT) + ... \right]$$
Triangle	$$Y(n)_{TRI} = \sum_{k=0}^{\infty} (-1)^{k} \frac{1}{(2k+1)^2} \sin((2k+1)\omega nT)$$ $$= \left[\sin(\omega nT) - \frac{1}{9}\sin(3\omega nT) + \frac{1}{25}\sin(5\omega nT) - \frac{1}{49}\sin(7\omega nT) + ... \right]$$
Square	$$Y(n)_{SQUARE} = \sum_{k=0}^{\infty} \frac{1}{(2k+1)} \sin((2k+1)\omega nT)$$ $$= \left[\sin(\omega nT) + \frac{1}{3}\sin(3\omega nT) + \frac{1}{5}\sin(5\omega nT) + \frac{1}{7}\sin(7\omega nT) + ... \right]$$

(9.3)

To generate wavetables on-demand or during synth instantiation, you implement the additive Fourier series equations (9.3) by sampling one cycle minus one sample of the desired waveform. For example, to synthesize the sawtooth waveform into an array with some number of harmonics (*numHarmonics*) and array length of *tableLength*, you would write this (*kPi* is the pi constant):

```
for (int i = 0; i < tableLength; i++)
{
    // --- sawtooth: += (-1)^g+1(1/g)sin(wnT)
    for (int g = 1; g <= numHarmonics; g++)
```

```
{
        double n = double(g);
        double phi = 2.0*kPi*i*g / tableLength;
        sawTable[i] += pow(-1.0, (g + 1.0)) * (1.0/g) * sin(phi);
    }
}
```

In practice, these summations usually result in values greater than 1.0, so you need to normalize the array after synthesis. Notice that there is no parameter for sample rate in the accumulation equation. The sample rate is only required to calculate the maximum number of harmonics. Figure 9.3(a) and (b) show a ramp up (sawtooth) waveform synthesized with 14 harmonics, plus the fundamental; the number of ripples in the waveform and the number of harmonic spikes in the spectrum are the same (15). The harmonic envelope is shown in the dotted line and is correct for this waveform. The waveform in Figure 9.3(c) looks more like an analog sawtooth, with most of the ripples smoothed over, except the bumps at the top and bottom of the discontinuity.

The waveform and spectrum in Figure 9.3(c) and (d) are the result of applying the Lanczos correction function. The ripples in the time domain plot are at a maximum in the area immediately around the waveform discontinuity. Although discovered by Wibraham in 1848, this became known as the Gibbs Phenomenon (Hewitt & Hewitt). Lanczsos derived a method for smoothing the ripples in the time domain with the application of correction factors called σ factors. These are calculated using a $sin(x)/x$ or *sinc* function, as shown in Equation (9.4). We will revisit Lanczos when we discuss virtual analog oscillators.

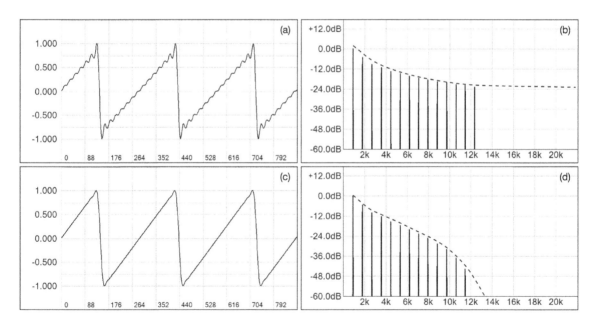

Figure 9.3 (a) Waveform and (b) spectrum of a sawtooth synthesized with 14 harmonics plus the fundamental and (c) the Lanczos corrected waveform and (d) resulting spectrum; the harmonic envelope is shown with a dotted line

$$\sigma_N = \frac{n\pi}{M} \quad \sigma_N = \frac{\sin(\sigma_N)}{\sigma_N} \tag{9.4}$$

M = number of harmonics
n = harmonic number
σ_n = Lanczos sigma for harmonic n

Adding the correction factors to the C++ code is not difficult; you simply multiply the factor to scale the *sin()* function. To add Lanczos correction to the previous code, you just add the factor calculation inside the inner loop.

```
// --- Lanczos Sigma Factor
double x = g*kPi/nHarms;
double sigma = sin(x)/x;
sawTable[i] += pow(-1.0, (g + 1.0))*(1.0/g) * sigma * sin(phi);
```

9.1.3 Multi-Wavetables

With the exception of the sine or cosine waveforms, which include only a fundamental and no harmonics, we cannot simply use one table for the entire range of MIDI notes without aliasing. This means that we will need multiple tables spread across the keyboard with various numbers of harmonics for a given target waveform/spectrum. In the earliest wavetable synths, when memory was expensive and limited, designers typically used either one table per octave or one table per minor third (four tables per octave). The other notes were interpolated between the tables, with the table limits at the top note, so interpolation was only performed to lower the pitch, and the *wtPhaseInc* value was less than 1.0. The 1986 Sequential Circuits Prophet VS had nine wavetables spread across the keyboard, as shown in Figure 9.4(a). Later, placing tables at minor third intervals became the industry standard.

With cheap memory today, we may ask: how many tables do we need to cover every MIDI note such that each has exactly the maximum number of harmonics below Nyquist? The answer depends on the table lengths, which also dictate the number of harmonics we may calculate with the Discrete Fourier Transform (DFT). If we hold the table lengths constant at $N = 256$ and $f_s = 44.1$ kHz, then there are 54 individual tables needed to cover every note. The first table is valid for the first 53 MIDI notes. Then, there is a single table for each note up to number 100. The last few tables are shared across several notes; the last table with only a single harmonic component will cover MIDI notes 125–127. My wavetable oscillator uses this approach and requires a set of tables to cover every note. The wavetable data source is set up so you may invent your own variations; if you like, you can just use one table across the entire keyboard, but be prepared for crispy aliasing.

9.1.4 Generating Interesting Tables

While the Fourier synthesis equations work for simple waveforms, harmonically rich and interesting waveforms require more work. Many of the wavetables in the Sequential Circuits Prophet VS were designed in the frequency domain first, then generated with additive Fourier synthesis. Today, we have numerous tools to allow the development of a practically unlimited number of

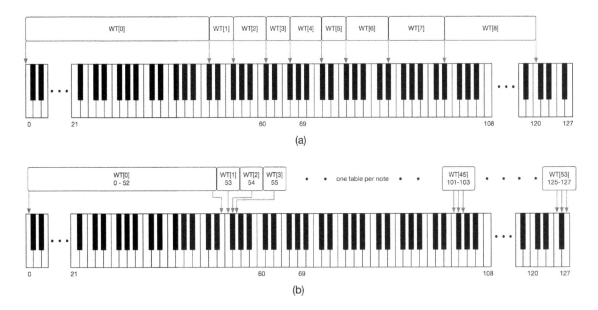

Figure 9.4 (a) Wavetable spacing in the Prophet VS and (b) modern wavetable synth using 54 high-resolution tables such that every note has every harmonic up to Nyquist

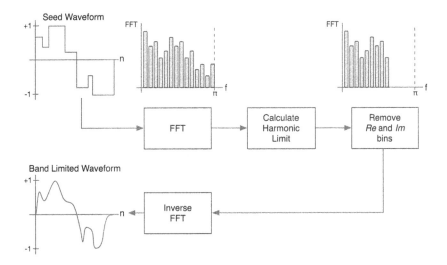

Figure 9.5 Flowchart of a system to generate band limited wavetables from a seed table; the process is repeated as many times as you need

interesting and harmonically rich waveforms. Figure 9.5 shows the flowchart for a typical sound development tool that starts with a seed waveform that is alias-free up to Nyquist. The FFT is taken and the harmonic limit calculated from the desired note pitch and the sample rate. Bins above the limit are zeroed in the real (*Re*) and imaginary (*Im*) FFT arrays. The inverse FFT produces the band-limited waveform. Note that this method of filtering via bin removal will not work for filtering a continuous stream of data blocks, but for our single waveform, it is fine.

9.2 Wavetable Objects and Database

When using closely spaced, dense multi-wavetables and multiple voices, the sheer number of tables can grow out of control. When we implement morphing wavetable oscillator cores, we will need sets of wavetables to morph across. The SynthLab wavetable objects are stored in a database. Any wavetable core may create and add tables to the database, which has no maximum limit. All wavetable oscillators can share these wavetables. Simple interfaces are implemented so that you are not restricted to the SynthLab tables, and you may freely invent your own table readers and generators. The database is shared across all wavetable oscillators using the *std::shared_ptr*.

9.2.1 Static and Dynamic Wavetables

Ultimately, the wavetable is accessed as an array of *float* or *double* values. Static wavetables are prefabricated prior to runtime. They may be compiled into the plugin with a header (.h) file or as a binary resource. They may also be read at run-time out of a binary file that is stored in a known location. Dynamic wavetables are synthesized at run-time and may need to be re-synthesized if the sample rate changes. Some software synth plugins and apps that require large numbers of tables will synthesize them using the algorithm in Section 9.1.4 at startup, populating internal tables or storing them on disc.

9.2.1.1 *StaticWavetable and DynamicWavetable Structures*

The *StaticWavetable* structure is designed for statically declared wavetables. It is also designed to work with my TableMaker software, which generates wavetable sets that cover every MIDI note with non-aliasing harmonic content. The *StaticWavetable* structure includes pointers to either an array of *doubles* or an array of 64-bit unsigned integers or *uint64_t*. When creating the tables and storing arrays in header files or as binary data, the 64-bit *double* values are encoded directly as binary data. When writing to the file as hex encoded values, we get the maximum resolution of the data without needing the scores of digits that make up the fractional part when writing a *double* value as a hex-string. This becomes more important if you use TableMaker, which can also write binary files of data, including the ability to encrypt the tables. In addition, this structure holds a pointer to an array of *double* values so that you may use traditional C++ arrays of doubles as the wavetables. Both pointers are declared as *const* and always point to statically declared tables that do not need to be deleted.

The *DynamicWavetable* structure is identical to the static version in everything except for the fact that it holds a pointer to an array of double values that is not declared as *const*. Both structures contain additional information that aids in reading the tables. All SynthLab wavetables have power-of-two table lengths, and therefore, we may wire-and the updated read location to perform the circular buffer table wrap.

```
// --- StaticWavetable
const uint64_t*  uTable;
```

```
const double* dTable;
// --- DynamicWavetable
double* table = nullptr;

// --- common to both
uint32 _ t tableLength = kDefaultWaveTableLength;
uint32 _ t wrapMask = kDefaultWaveTableLength - 1;
doubleoutputComp = 1.0; // --- output scaling factor
doubletableFs = 44100.0;
const char* waveformName;
```

The *tableFs* is the sample rate used to synthesize the table. It is not used in any of the objects in SynthLab but is there if you need it. The waveform name is optional, but it is used in SynthLab to populate the dynamic waveform lists.

9.3 Wavetable Sources and Database

The *IWavetableSource* interface is used to create a C++ class that provides access to a set of wavetable structures. You can think of a "wavetable source" as all of the information needed to synthesize <u>one</u> waveform across the range of MIDI notes. This interface allows you to implement your wavetables however you wish and is one of the central design patterns in SynthLab. There are four wavetable source objects included as examples in Table 9.1, and studying these will help you see how the *IWavetableSource* interface is implemented.

The sine and drum sources shown in Figure 9.6(a) store only one table, which is used for all MIDI notes. The sine source interpolates the single table across the range of pitches while the drum source implements pitch-less tables, giving you two examples of simple but useful kinds of wavetables. The static and dynamic table sources each include an array of 128 *SynthLabWavetable* structures, one for each MIDI note, as shown in Figure 9.6(b), and you can see that the wavetable structures may point to the same table of data: for example, the first 53 structures all point to the same table because it contains the maximum number of harmonics below Nyquist. The tables are all read and interpolated the same way, so these sources differentiate between different kinds of tables. The engine's wavetable database, shown in Figure 9.6(c), consists of a set of wavetable sources indexed with unique names.

Table 9.1 The built-in *IWavetableSource* C++ objects and descriptions

IWavetableSource Object	Description
DynamicTableSource	Stores dynamically created tables and is used in the example module core that synthesizes parabola and triangle waveforms at startup; there is one table per octave of MIDI notes
StaticTableSource	Stores the static hex encoded wavetables that *TableMaker* produces, with each MIDI note table getting its own table that will not alias
DrumWTSource	A special static wavetable source for pitch-less tables, such as drums or sound effects
SineTableSource	Stores a single static sinusoidal table of *double* values that is used for all MIDI notes

The morphing core accesses tables in banks, shown with the dotted line in Figure 9.6(d), but it is important to understand that the bank is a conceptual idea that is simply a set of unique waveform names presented to the user as a single string (name). The *SynthLabBankSet* is a structure that contains an array of *SynthLabWavetables*, and it is only used to store tables and initialize the wavetable database with a set of tables in one function call. Once the tables are registered, the database treats them like any other wavetable and is not aware that they are grouped as a bank.

The *WavetableDatabase* is created in the *SynthEngine* and shared across all *SynthVoices* and their wavetable oscillators. The database is a *std::map* that stores *IWavetableSource* pointers via unique key strings. Your wavetable core object may query the database for table sources, and it may create and add new table sources at construction time. This means you are free to code your own object that exposes the *IWavetableSource* interface functions in Table 9.2 and add it to the database. You do not need to use my objects or my structures; you only need to provide the interface to your own implementation. The database uses unique name strings corresponding to the core module strings. SynthLab fills the GUI waveform selectors with these unique strings any time a new core object is loaded.

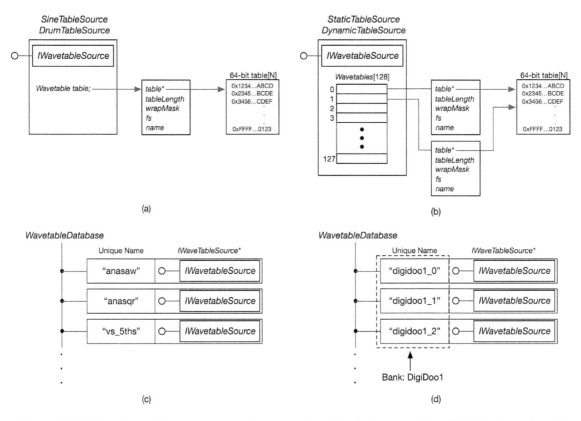

Figure 9.6 (a) The sine and drum sources only store and read a single wavetable, while (b) the static and dynamic sources each store an array of wavetables, one per MIDI note, while (c) the *Wavetable-Database* contains a dictionary of *IWavetableSource* pointers whose keys are unique strings that name the waveforms; (d) a wavetable bank is a name given to a set of wavetables used for wavetable morphing

Table 9.2 The *IWavetableSource* interface

IWavetableSource Function	Argument	Description
selectTable	midiNoteNumber	Instructs the object to select a table and store it for rendering notes; the table is selected with the MIDI note number
readWaveTable	*readIndex*, which is a normalized value	Reads the wavetable using a *double* read index with an integer and fractional part; interpolation is used to find the value located between samples
getWaveTableLength	None	Returns the length of the currently selected wavetable
getWaveformName	None	Returns the waveform name for GUI

9.3.1 *Reading/Interpolating the Wavetable*

The *IWavetableSource* object needs to implement the *readWaveTable* function. As an example, the *SineTableSource* version is shown here. It performs the following:

- Calculate the read location as $N(f_o/f_s)$ where N is the table length in samples
- Use the *modf* function to split the read location into an integer and fractional part (*intPart* and *fracPart* respectively)
- The *intPart* is the index of the first sample to read
- Increment the *intPart* by one, then do the circular wrap with the mask to find the second sample to read
- Read both samples and perform linear interpolation that is the *fracPart* distance between them, producing the output value
- The output value is scaled using information saved with each table; this is to help you normalize the loudness of the wavetables, if needed.

```
// --- read and interpolate, return the audio sample
virtual double readWaveTable(double oscClockIndex)
{
    // --- two samples from table
    double wtData[2] = { 0.0, 0.0 };

    // --- location = N(fo/fs)
    double wtReadLoc = sineWavetable.tableLength * oscClockIndex;

    // --- split the fractional index into int.frac parts
    double intPart = 0.0;
    double fracPart = modf(wtReadLoc, &intPart);
    uint32_t readIndex = (uint32_t) intPart;
    uint32_t nextReadIndex =
                        (readIndex + 1) & sineWavetable.wrapMask;

    // --- two table reads
```

```
wtData[0] = sineWavetable.dTable[readIndex];
wtData[1] = sineWavetable.dTable[nextReadIndex];
// --- interpolate the output (0.0 and 1.0 set the distance)
double output = doLinearInterpolation(0.0, 1.0,
                                      wtData[0],
                                      wtData[1],
                                      fracPart);
// --- scale as needed
return sineWavetable.outputComp * output;
}
```

9.4 *WTOscillator* and Cores

Figure 9.7 shows the WTOscillator module, along with three of the five module cores.

Table 9.3 lists the GUI parameter structure and core descriptions. The *IWavetableSource* object performs the reading and interpolation. The oscillator cores are designed to generate distinctly different types of waveforms and demonstrate different kinds of tables, including one-shot and pitch-less tables. The *MorphWTCore* is a special variation and is used for wavetable morphing in Section 15.2. It registers sets of wavetables stored as banks and exposes bank names rather than waveform names. However, the same mechanism is used for the database storage and wavetable read/interpolate operations.

9.4.1 *Wavetable Oscillator Controls, Modulations. and Features*

Table 9.4 lists the module controls common to all cores and the GUI calculation section or equations. The coarse tuning and fine-tuning operate in semitones and cents, respectively, and are part of the pitch modulation update calculation, while the pan and output controls are common to almost all other oscillators and allow blending of the quad oscillator render block. Table 9.5 lists the cores and their special functionality.

Table 9.3 WTOscillator custom parameter structure and cores: (*) downloadable SynthLab-DM core project (*) downloadable dynamic module projects

Parameter Structure	Description
WTOscParameters	Used for all cores; includes all oscillator parameters
Example Core	**Description**
ClassicWTCore	16 waveforms based on analog and other classic table waveforms; demonstrates typical wavetable looping
MorphWTCore	The morphing oscillators in Section 15.2 use banks of waveforms instead of individual tables. This core demonstrates how to create and use these sets (banks) of waveforms for the morphing oscillators
*FourierWTCore**	Wavetables generated with Fourier synthesis to demonstrate dynamically created wavetables whose contents change if the sample rate changes
*DrumWTCore**	One-shot wavetables with single drum sounds mapped across all keys using PCM samples of classic electronic drums
SFXWTCore	Bonus core of sound effects taken from PCM samples, demonstrating how to use pitch-less, one-shot wavetables

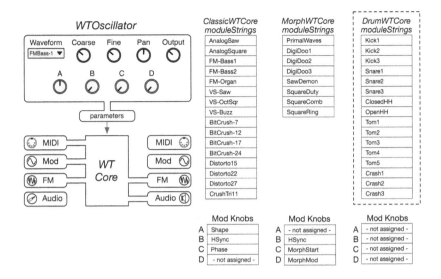

Figure 9.7 The *WTOscillator* and the three included cores: classic, morphing, and drums; two special bonus cores are also included for Fourier synthesis and sound effects

Table 9.4 Module controls shared across cores

Module Control	Description	GUI Calculation (Section)
Coarse	Coarse tuning in semitones	Pitch modulation (6.7.1)
Fine	Fine-tuning in cents	Pitch modulation (6.7.1)
Pan	Left/Right pan	Constant power panning (6.2.2)
Output	Output level in dB	dB to raw: $10^{(dB/20)}$

Table 9.5 Wavetable cores and their special modulation capabilities

Core	Features and Special Modulations (Section)
ClassicWTCore	Self hard-sync modulation (6.9.1)
FourierWTCore	Shape modulation with phase distortion (6.8)
	Phase offset that moves initial wavetable read index
MorphWTCore	Self hard-sync modulation (6.9.1)
	Waveform morphing modulation (15.2) with morph start and morph intensity controls
DrumWTCore	Bare minimum implementation without modulation; best place to start
SFXWTCore	when examining the core code

9.5 Wavetable Core Programming Notes

With the C++ files open, compare the programming notes with the code that you see, starting with the class descriptions of each core. The wavetable core objects all use the same time-base, implemented with a *SynthClock* modulo counter that is reset and advanced with each note-event.

The cores that support self hard-sync modulation include a *Synchronizer* object to help implement that function. All cores except the morphing core include a member that acts as the selected wavetable source. The morphing core includes an array of two wavetable sources, which it interpolates between to create the wave morphing effect. Sections 9.5.1 through 9.5.5 summarize the five operational phases, plus the constructor for the wavetable cores. Make sure to examine the code while digesting their operational phase details.

9.5.1 Construction Phase

All cores:

- The module strings are the waveform names, and their index values map to the GUI control selection values; the strings will be used to query the database for the selected waveform
- The mod knobs are not used in the drum and sound effect cores
- The cores demonstrate multiple was to assign module strings, from string literals to bank array names (morphing core)

9.5.2 Reset Phase

All cores:

- Reset clocks and synchronizer
- Query database for tables and register if not found; this minimizes the number of tables required for operation
- Each core demonstrates a different way to add tables and recall their name strings

Fourier WT core:

- Recalculate the wavetables when the sample rate changes

To query the database for an *IWavetableSource* pointer, use the *wavetableDatabase* interface pointer and the unique name string:

processInfo.wavetableDatabase->getTableSource("FMBass-1");

If the function returns *nullptr*, you can add the table using a table source and name string. This code uses an old-fashioned pointer and the *new* operator rather than shared pointers; this is a requirement of the dynamic module core loading system, which must implement an API interface that does not use the standard template library (*std::*) or other third-party libraries that may corrupt the heap when calling functions and passing pointers across the thunk layer.

```
StaticTableSource* wt = new StaticTableSource;
wt->addSynthLabTableSet(&fmbass1 _ TableSet);
```

processInfo.wavetableDatabase->addTableSource("FMBass-1", wt);

9.5.3 *Note-On Phase*

The note-event begins with a note-on handler that is both similar and quite simple across the cores:

- Store MIDI pitch (except drum and SFX cores)
- Reset the SynthClock modulo counter member to either 0.0 (all cores) or the starting phase point (classic, morphing, and Fourier cores); notice how the mod knob C value is used to calculate the phase offset for the cores that support it
- NOTE: there is nothing to do in the note-off phase

```
// --- parameters
midiPitch = processInfo.noteEvent.midiPitch;

// --- reset to new start phase
if(processInfo.unisonStartPhase > 0.0)
    oscClock.reset(processInfo.unisonStartPhase / 360.0);
else
    oscClock.reset(parameters->modKnobValue[MOD _ KNOB _ C]);
```

9.5.4 *Update Phase*

The pitched core update phases follow the same four steps that you will find on the other pitched oscillators. The *update* function's main goal here is to have the correct wavetable selected and the correct interface pointer stored for the render phase that will immediately follow.

1 Calculate the pitch modulation value based on GUI controls and pitch modulation sources
2 Select the wavetable source based on the user's waveform selection string; the morphing core selects two sources
3 Select the wavetable based on the final modulated pitch value
4 Set up hard synchronizer, shape, or other modulation variables

The classic core wavetable selection code follows, starting with the final oscillator frequency calculation that sets the oscillator time-base – this is identical across all pitched oscillators that use the *SynthClock* time-base object.

```
// --- calculate the modulated pitch value
double oscillatorFrequency = midiPitch*pitchShift;

// --- BOUND the value to our range
boundValue(oscillatorFrequency, WT _ OSC _ MIN, WT _ OSC _ MAX);

// --- phase inc = fo/fs
oscClock.setFrequency(oscillatorFrequency, sampleRate);
```

The next step is to select the table source using the user's GUI selection index value, which corresponds to the GUI control that holds the 16 waveform strings. The old-fashioned *const char** is used due to the same dynamic core and thunk issues, as described in the previous section.

```
// --- select the wavetable source
const char* wave = coreData.moduleStrings[parameters->wavetableIndex];
```

```
selectedTableSource =
            processInfo.wavetableDatabase->getTableSource(wave);
```

Finally, the exact table is selected based on the MIDI note number of the modulated pitch value. Check the morphing core code to see how it selects two tables based on the morphing index, as detailed in Section 15.4.3.

```
// --- select table
uint32 _ t midiNote = midiNoteNumberFromOscFrequency(oscillatorFrequency);
```

```
selectedTableSource->selectTable(midiNote);
```

The rest of the update phase involves only simple gain and pan calculations or storing mod knob values for later.

9.5.5 Render Phase

All pitched oscillators must render samples one block at a time and write stereo audio data to their output buffers. A simple *for-loop* sets up the block render operation. All wavetable cores use a separate *renderSample* function so you can easily modify them without changing the for-loop code. The drum and sound effect cores have the minimum implementation, and both operate in one-shot mode so the oscillator only renders the table once, then outputs zeros thereafter. The *SynthClock* time-base *advanceWrapClock* function returns true if the modulo counter has wrapped, indicating that the one-shot event is complete. The drum and sound effect cores store this value.

```
double DrumWTCore::renderSample(SynthClock& clock)
{
    // --- read source
    double oscOutput =
        selectedTableSource->readWaveTable(clock.mcounter);

    // --- advance and wrap clock; save wrap notice for one-shot
    oneShotDone = clock.advanceWrapClock();

    return oscOutput;
}
```

The other three cores implement the same function plus an additional method for the self hard-sync operation; make sure you compare the hard-sync function with the code and modulation description in Section 6.9. First, the buffers are accessed, and the for-loop is set up:

```
float* leftOutBuffer = processInfo.outputBuffers[LEFT _ CHANNEL];
float* rightOutBuffer = processInfo.outputBuffers[RIGHT _ CHANNEL];
```

```
for (uint32 _ t i = 0; i < processInfo.samplesToProcess; i++)
{
```

Next, the hard sync ratio value is checked, and the corresponding function calls are made. These oscillators use phase distortion for shape modulation so the oscillator shape parameter is a function argument:

```
// --- render the saw
double oscOutput = 0.0;
if (parameters->hardSyncRatio > 1.0)
    oscOutput = renderHardSyncSample(oscClock,
                                parameters->oscillatorShape);
else
    oscOutput = renderSample(oscClock,
                                parameters->oscillatorShape);
```

Lastly, gain and panning are applied; notice that the glide modulator is advanced outside the loop as it is a granulized, slow-moving modulation source.

```
// --- scale by gain control
oscOutput *= outputAmplitude;

// --- write to output buffers
leftOutBuffer[i] = oscOutput * panLeftGain;
rightOutBuffer[i] = oscOutput * panRightGain;
}

// --- advance the glide modulator
glideModulator->advanceClock(processInfo.samplesToProcess);
```

9.6 Exercises

9.6.1 SynthLab-WT_{DM} Drum Core: Mod knob D to Reverse Playback

Mod knob D is unassigned in the all of the wavetable cores. Download the drum core sample dynamic module code, then compile and load it to test. When you are satisfied that it generates drum sounds correctly, add functionality such that when mod knob D has a value that is greater than 0.5, the tables play in reverse. HINT: the *SynthClock* time-base is fully capable of running backwards.

9.6.2 SynthLab-WT_{DM}: Pan Modulation

The classic wavetable core implements shape modulation as its unique modulation destination and is set up in the modulation matrix. Set up a dynamic module project that implements the classic wavetable core, then change the module name so you can differentiate between them in the SynthLab-WT_{DM} project. Test the shape modulation using an LFO as the modulation source and the OSC1, 2, 3, or 4 "mod" destinations. Next, alter the code to replace the shape modulation with pan modulation, using the existing panning code as a basis. Test the pan modulation with the same LFO. Shape and pan are both examples of bipolar modulation destinations.

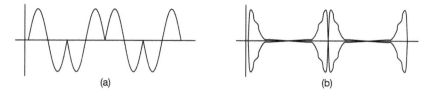

Figure 9.8 Wave scanning may be used with simple waveforms (a) or more complex one-shot drum tables (b) to produce new sounds

9.6.3 SynthLab-WT$_{DM}$: Modify the Wavetable Source

The *DrumWTSource* C++ object implements the pitch-less, one-shot drum wavetable sources. Examine the drum core's constructor, and note the first few lines where the tables are added to the source with *addWavetable*. Trace this code into the *DrumWTSource*, and you will see that each table is stored as a separate waveform that is mapped across the keyboard. Alter the source so that the drum tables map chromatically to the first 16 MIDI keys, starting with middle C (60).

9.6.4 Advanced Module: Create a Wave Scanning Oscillator

Wave scanning is a wavetable variation that generates a new and interesting set of sounds from the existing tables without needing to create or modify new tables. It works by reversing the wavetable read direction each time the read index wraps around the table boundary. This forwards-backwards-forwards scanning motion produces a kind of double-waveform where every other waveform is reversed in time, as shown in Figure 9.8(a). A more complex table, such as the one-shot drum tables in Figure 9.8(b), usually results in very strange and interesting sounds. Note that this operation can cause kinks or discontinuities in the output waveform that may produce aliasing components. Create your own novel wavetable core that implements wave scanning in the table source. Use mod knobs to control aspects of the scanning, such as the re-scan threshold index – the table index that signifies the direction reversal.

Bibliography

Hewitt, Edmund & Hewitt, Robert. 1979. "The Gibbs-Wilbraham Phenomenon: An Episode in Fourier Analysis." *Archive for History of Exact Sciences*, vol. 21, no. 2, pp. 129–160. New York: Springer.

Kleimola, Jari. 2005. "Design and Implementation of a Software Sound Synthesizer," Master's Thesis, Supervised by Välimäki, Vesa. Helsinki University of Technology. http://lib.tkk.fi/Dipl/2005/urn007886.pdf, Accessed October 14, 2020

Lanczsos, C. 2010. *Applied Analysis*. New York: Dover.

Moore, Richard. 1990. *Elements of Computer Music*, Chap. 3. Eaglewood Cliffs: Prentice-Hall.

Moorer, James. 1976. "The Synthesis of Complex Audio Spectra by Means of Discrete Summation Formulae." *Journal of the Audio Engineering Society*, vol. 24, no. 9, pp. 717–727.

Roads, Curtis. 1996. *The Computer Music Tutorial*, Chap. 3. Cambridge: The MIT Press.

Stilson, Tim & Smith, Julius O. 1996. "Alias-Free Digital Synthesis of Classic Analog Waveforms." Proceedings of the 1996 International Computer Music Conference.

10 Virtual Analog Oscillators

Virtual Analog (VA) oscillators are interestingly named. They have nothing to do with analog circuits, components, block diagrams, or signal flow. They do not model the physical characteristics of any kind of analog oscillatory system, like pendulums or springs with attached masses. Analog oscillators have no Nyquist limit and cannot alias. Their waveform shapes look identical to those of trivial oscillators, no matter what the frequency of oscillation. One of the goals for VA oscillators is to preserve that perfect shape as much as possible. The applications of VA oscillators tend to take two directions. One is to retain the perfect analog oscillator waveform and harmonic spectrum with either no aliasing or with aliased components so low in amplitude that they are either inaudible or masked by other non-aliased components. Another direction is to create waveforms that are cheap to render on low-CPU and memory-starved devices, such as mobile phones, tablets, and toys/games. In these cases, aliasing is allowed, even if it is audible, because of the tradeoff in CPU and memory savings.

10.1 VA Oscillator Fundamentals

VA oscillator analysis starts with the notion that discontinuities in a waveform are the primary cause of aliasing. The trivial ramp LFO waveform exhibits massive aliasing, as shown in Figure 10.1(a) and (b). The lower limit for the plot in Figure 10.1(b) is −96 dB, the theoretical noise floor for 16-bit PCM digital audio, while it is −60 dB in Figure 10.1(a), which is used throughout the text. Lowering the measurement floor reveals more aliasing, though aliased spectral amplitudes below −60 dB are extremely suppressed, and I usually use −60 dB as a ballpark threshold on the tolerable aliasing amplitudes.

Figure 10.1(c) and (d) show the same trivial oscillator output whose waveform has been altered in the time domain to suppress the aliased components. The VA oscillator attempts to filter the aliased components out by manipulating the points around the discontinuity.

10.1.1 Saw and Square Continuities

Traditionally, a discontinuity in a function is a point in the domain where the function instantaneously jumps from one value to another, with no time or space between the level shift. Some say that the function takes on both values at once. But according to a less rigorous definition, a discontinuous edge is a place where two geometrical entities – lines or curves – meet up. It can also describe a single function that contains a glitch. Types of discontinuity are named "continuities" as they relate to how continuous a function may be. In Figure 10.2(a), you see a smooth and continuous

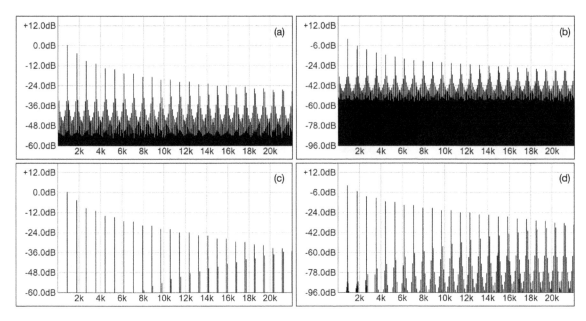

Figure 10.1 A trivial sawtooth waveform spectrum with (a) −60 dB and (b) −96 dB lower limits, and a VA oscillator spectrum with (c) −60 dB and (d) −96 dB lower limits

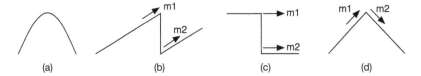

Figure 10.2 (a) A smooth continuous function, (b) a ramp discontinuity, and (c) square discontinuity both have similar mathematical traits – identical slopes on each side of the edge, while the triangle in (d) has two different slopes on each side of the discontinuity

function. The sawtooth and square discontinuities have the same slopes (*m1* and *m2*) on either side of the discontinuity and are said to be *C1* continuous (the 1 stands for first derivative or slope). The triangle in Figure 10.2(d) is not *C1* continuous.

If we limit the discussion to the C1 continuity, we can use some clever math to adjust the points around the discontinuity so as to smooth over the offending edge of a trivial oscillator. We applied a naïve version of this idea with the linear crossfading technique for hard sync in Section 6.10, smoothing over a discontinuity to reduce aliasing. There are a few approaches to VA oscillator design. Perhaps the earliest attempt is Lane's distorted and filtered sinusoids, which was followed up by Stilson and Smith's Band Limited Impulse Train (BLIT) method.

10.2 Band Limited Impulse Train (BLIT)

The idea behind BLIT is to generate a softened or rounded discontinuity that would have resulted in lowpass filtering an impulse and then produce a stream of filtered impulses. Equation

(10.1) produces a stream of *sinc* function-shaped pulses, as shown in Figure 10.3(a). If you invert every other *sinc* pulse, you arrive at the bipolar BLIT waveform of Figure 10.3(b). With the pulse train established, synthesizing the three basic waveforms of sawtooth, square, and triangle are all performed with integration (these are fundamental relationships you can find in many math and engineering texts), as shown in Figure 10.3(c). The integration is performed in the digital domain using reverse Euler or bilinear integrators.

$$y(n) = \frac{M}{P} Sinc_M \left[\frac{M}{P} n \right]$$
$$Sinc_M(x) \triangleq \frac{\sin(\pi x)}{M \sin(\pi x / M)} \tag{10.1}$$

BLIT has problems that make it one of the more difficult algorithms to implement. First is the generation of the BLIT sequence itself. Using the *sinc* function requires two calls to the *sin* function. Another idea is to sample a sum of windowed *sinc* functions and store them in a set of tables corresponding to different fractional shifts of the impulse. This is necessary because the period of the desired waveform may not be an integer multiple of the sample rate. Thus, the tables would need to be interpolated at runtime. This is known as BLIT-SWS. A larger issue is that the band-limited impulses overlap, and the tail of one must be mixed with the head of the next. This requires knowing when the next discontinuity is going to occur as well as look-ahead information. This can be problematic because we would like to have zero delay in synthesizing the waveform. The band-limited impulse has to be generated for each discontinuity, so, as the frequency becomes higher, the CPU usage increases. As Andy Leary points out, another issue with these methods is that the integration steps in BLIT and BLIT-SWS introduce an unwanted and undesirable DC offset into the signal at oscillator startup time.

10.3 Band Limited Step (BLEP)

Eli Brandt improved on the idea by performing the integration on a single *sinc* function in Figure 10.4(a), then storing that pre-integrated waveform in Figure 10.4(b). This removes the

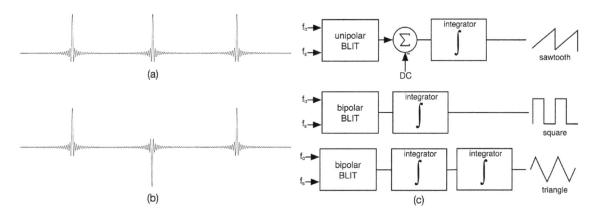

Figure 10.3 (a) Unipolar and (b) bipolar BLIT signals, and (c) algorithms for converting them into traditional waveforms

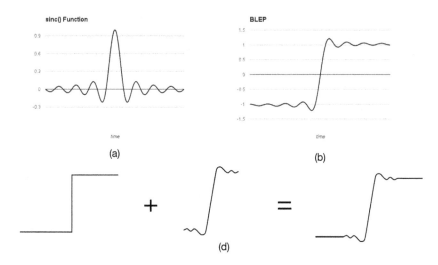

Figure 10.4 (a) A *sinc* function and (b) its integration produces a wavy step; (c) to use the BLEP, superimpose it on top of the discontinuity; notice that only a small section of the BLEP waveform is used

requirement for integration on the fly. This is called a Band Limited stEP function or BLEP. In this method, there is no generation of an impulse train. Instead, you start with a trivial oscillator, then use the stored BLEP waveform to make corrections to points that are on either side of the discontinuity. One way to imagine this is to take a piece of the BLEP step edge and superimpose it on the offending discontinuity, as shown in Figure 10.4(c). You can see that only a small piece of the BLEP function has been applied to the step edge; in practice, you will only need to alter a few points on each side so you don't need the complete BLEP. This also preserves that perfect analog shape for most of the waveform. In my BLEP oscillators, I allow correction of one, two, or four points on each side of the discontinuity, depending on the oscillator's frequency.

For implementation, a preferable solution to superimposing the BLEP edge involves windowing the *sinc* pulse to a certain width, performing the integration, and subtracting out the unit step to create a residual signal of correction factors that are simply added or subtracted from the waveform. The windowing is performed on the *sinc* function zero-crossing boundaries. Figure 10.5 shows two different windowed *sinc* functions; in Figure 10.5(a), only the center pulse of the *sinc* function is windowed and integrated. This produces a residual for correcting one sample on each side of the discontinuity. In Figure 10.5(b), the windowed *sinc* function is widened to include the next lobe zero-crossings. This produces a residual for correcting up to four samples on each side of the discontinuity (when doubling the window size while keeping the same table length, the zero crossings fall on two-sample boundaries).

10.3.1 Using the BLEP Residual

Figure 10.6 shows the idea behind the residual method, starting with the isolated rising edge of a trivial square-wave oscillator in 10.6(a) and deciding to alter two points on each side of the discontinuity. Lining up the residual so its discontinuity is on top of the trivial oscillator discontinuity is shown in Figure 10.6(b). The arrows line up exactly with the sample locations, and the residual

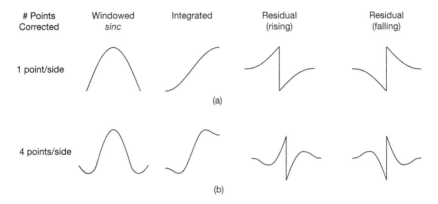

Figure 10.5 Two sets of windowed BLEP waveforms, where (a) the central pulse is truncated and windowed and (b) the central pulse is combined with the next pair of zero-crossings to form a wider windowed function; the integrated windowed signals, and the rising and falling residuals are shown for each case

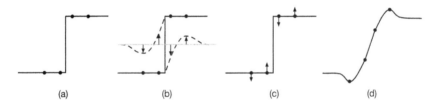

Figure 10.6 (a) A rising discontinuous edge showing the two samples on each side (b) superimposing the residual over the discontinuous edge (c) adjusting these four points based on the residual and (d) the BLEP corrected discontinuity

curve shows how much to alter each point in Figure 10.6(c). After only four points have been altered, we arrive at Figure 10.6(d), which mimics the result of superimposing the BLEP edge onto the waveform, as shown in Figure 10.4(c).

10.3.1.1 Strategy: One Large BLEP Table

In BLEP table-based approaches, you store the BLEP residual and use it accordingly. One strategy that I use for the SynthLab-VA project involves storing a single, finely sampled version of the BLEP residual in a 4,096-point table. There are two sets of tables: one for the correction of one point per side and the other for the correction of one, two, three, or four points per side of the discontinuity. They are generated with two different window widths. Within the second set of tables are more tables, all the same length but processed with different windows during table creation. Figure 10.5 uses simple rectangular windowing of the BLEP central pulse and its side pulses. But there are numerous other windows that may be used. The *sythconstants.h* file includes these tables:

- A single table using rectangular windowing on the central *sinc* pulse, which allows for the correction of one point per side; the table is named *dBLEPTable*

- Seven (7) tables for correcting one to four points per side, with the window name coded in the table name, e.g. *dBLEPTable_8_HANN* for the Hanning window and *dBLEPTable_8_BLKHAR* for the Blackman-Harris window

10.3.1.2 Strategy: Many Small BLEP Tables

Another approach involves storing many small tables of residual samples. In 2009, Andy Leary and Charlie Bright of Korg Research and Development were awarded US Patent 7,589,272, assigned to Korg, Inc. for *Bandlimited Digital Synthesis of Analog Waveforms*, which describes both a method for generating the band-limited signals with BLEP and a method for hard-syncing two oscillators with discontinuous waveforms. This patent describes an implementation in a hardware format with shift registers and accumulators (there is no code in the patent), and is certainly worth reading and experimenting.

Instead of consuming memory for large, finely sampled tables, another approach may be taken, noting that, at any given time, you are only correcting a handful of points around the edge – why store gigantic tables to process only a few points? Suppose you want to correct two points per side of the discontinuous edge. Instead of one giant table, you can implement a set of very small tables of only four points each, two points per side. Then, you can use interpolation between the tables to generate the missing data you would normally get with a large table. This approach saves memory but requires inter-table interpolation. As a point of reference, the BLEP functions in SynthLab will allow you to interpolate the 4,096-point table if you like – I've found that interpolation is inaudible because the table is so finely sampled. You can find much more information about optimal table sizing and BLEP approaches in Pekonen et al. (2011)

10.3.2 BLEP Correction Calculation

Regardless of whether you are using a single large table or many small tables, one common problem exists: you need to know how far away you are from the edge of the discontinuity, and this implies that you need to look ahead when evaluating the modulo counter's value. Once you have that edge distance, you can look up the correction value however you wish. The Leary-Bright patent demonstrates short transversal delay lines to facilitate looking ahead in the signal. Since we are using C++, we have another option:

Monitor the value of the trivial oscillator output (the modulo counter), and detect when you are one, two, three, or four samples away from the edge – this is possible because you know the clock's *phaseInc* value: for example, if the current modulo counter plus the *phaseInc* is greater than 1.0, then you know you are within one sample of the discontinuity. In Figure 10.7(a), you can see how this works diagrammatically. The discontinuous edge occurs in the center when the modulo counter rolls over from 1.0 back to 0.0, and the distance from the point on the left side is $t(-)$, while that on the right is $t(+)$.

There is a final issue involved that is inescapable: the oscillator's desired frequency. It is simple to calculate the number of points per waveform cycle, which will then determine how many points per *side* of a discontinuity we may correct. This may be BLEP's main drawback for high fidelity synthesis. Therefore, we need to follow the rules in Table 10.1, correcting either one, two, or four points per side.

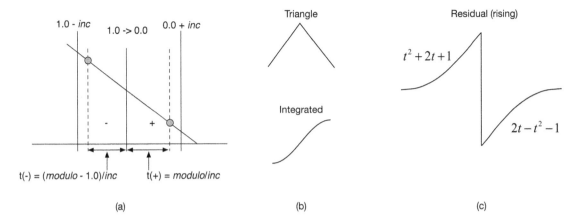

Figure 10.7 (a) Geometrically determining the distance from the discontinuity to points on either side of the edge; (b) a triangle pulse integrates to a smooth sigmoid, similar to that of Figure 10.5(a); and (c) the BLEP rising edge residual is approximated with two second order polynomials, one for each side of the edge

Table 10.1 Number of BLEP correction points per side versus oscillator frequency

Oscillator Frequency	Number of Points Corrected per Side
$f_o < f_s/8$ (1/4 Nyquist)	4
$f_o < f_s/4$ (1/2 Nyquist)	2
$f_o > f_s/8$	1

10.4 Polynomial BLEP Approximation

Välimäki proposes implementing the BLEP residual by approximating the original *sinc* function with a polynomial and names it *PolyBLEP*. Different polynomials of different orders may be chosen, but a simple solution is to use a unipolar triangular pulse, shown in Figure 10.7(b); this is the linear approximation of the windowed *sinc* pulse in Figure 10.5(a). Integrating this triangle produces the sigmoid (*s*-shaped) curve in Figure 10.7(b), which can be expressed in closed form and thus requires no table. Subtracting out the perfect step and then converting to bipolar results in the following two-part residual, shown in Figure 10.7(c). Equation 10.2 shows the polynomials used to compute each of the curves in Figure 10.7(c). The independent variable is *t* (time) as this was Välimäki's notation. For our purpose, *t* is the distance from a point to the discontinuous edge.

$$PolyBLEP(t) = \begin{cases} t^2 + 2t + 1 & -1 \le t \le 0 \\ 2t - t^2 - 1 & 0 < t \le 1 \end{cases} \tag{10.2}$$

The one-point-per-side *PolyBLEP* produces only a tiny bit more aliasing than you see in Figure 10.1(c), so when only correcting one point per side, it comes close enough to the rectangular-windowed *sinc* pulse that I use it for the *VAOscillator* core object. For two or more points per side, I use the wider windowed tables instead.

10.5 Choosing the BLEP *sinc* Source

Interestingly, using the perfect *sinc* pulse as the basis for the BLEP correction does not necessarily produce the best results. There are numerous factors and tradeoffs involved. One approach involves trying different windows on the ideal *sinc* pulse, while another involves starting with traditional FIR lowpass filter design and then varying design parameters, such as pass-band ripple, stop-band attenuation, or transition width. The results of variations upon these approaches can be found in Otalvara et al. (2016), in which the psychoacoustic masking curves are used as evaluation criteria for determining the audibility of aliased components, with preservation of harmonic envelope and significant aliasing reduction acting as the dual design targets.

SynthLab includes a set of windowed sinc pulses, as listed in Section 10.3.1.1. If we focus only on four points per side correction, we may glean insight from the full range spectral plots in Figure 10.8. The majority of aliasing occurs below the −60 dB line. In addition, we observe that there is a tradeoff between preserving harmonic envelope and aliasing; the Hann windowed spectrum has the least aliasing but the poorest preservation of harmonic envelope. Where have we seen this before?

10.5.1 BLEP and Lanczos

Compare the plots in Figure 10.8(c) and (d) to the Lanczos sigma corrected Bandlimited wavetable in Figure 9.3(c) and (d). Notice also how the Lanczos sawtooth waveform (9.3c) has small wavy

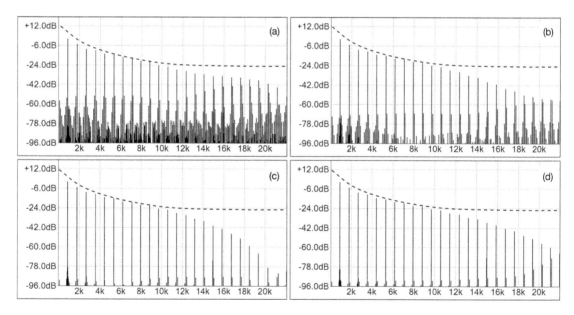

Figure 10.8 Sawtooth waveforms using 8-point BLEP correction with (a) rectangular (b) triangular (c) Hamming and (d) Blackman-Harris windowed *sinc* BLEP residuals; the dotted line represents the harmonic envelope of a perfect sawtooth waveform; note the location of the −60dB level

humps just before and just after the discontinuity, and a flat "perfect" waveform between. In the frequency domain, we observe the same issue with the lack of harmonic envelope preservation. It appears that BLEP and Lanczos may be related. In 2016, Singh and Pirkle (2016) proved that BLEP correction is mathematically identical to Lanczos sigma correction. All along, we've really been trying to convert a trivial waveform into an equivalent, band-limited, Lanczos sigma corrected waveform. The fundamental difference is that, for BLEP, the correction is on-the-fly as the waveform is being rendered, whereas Lanczos applies to pre-calculated wavetables.

10.6 Other VA Algorithms

A drawback with BLEP is that technically, it will only adequately correct a waveform with a *C1* continuity, which, for synthesizers, is generally sawtooth (ramp) and square wave, but even in non-C1 cases, you can still obtain a massive reduction in aliasing in other trivial oscillators using *PolyBLEP* alone. There are more approaches to synthesizing the traditional waveforms without Fourier wavetables including Lane's original distorted sinewaves and Välimäki's Differentiated Parabolic Waveform (DPW) algorithm.

10.6.1 Differentiated Parabolic Waveform (DPW) Oscillators

Välimäki (2005) observed that differentiating a parabolic waveform produced an output that was similar in shape to a trivial sawtooth but with greatly reduced aliasing. Squaring a ramp or sawtooth waveform generates a parabolic waveform. Differentiating it produces the parabolic waveform. The DPW oscillator algorithms synthesize the sawtooth and triangle waveforms but tend to produce more aliasing than BLEP, and I do not use them for high-quality synthesis. One advantage is that the triangle wave is available since the algorithm does not depend on continuity type.

10.7 BLEP Square Wave

Since the square wave has a *C1* continuity, we are also able to use BLEP to correct its edges and produce alias suppressed waveforms. The only thing you need to keep track of is the direction of the discontinuity (rising or falling). The fundamental issue that makes this difficult occurs when you use an extreme pulse width setting. If the frequency of oscillation rises high enough, the edges come within a sample interval of one another. At a 1% pulse width, this occurs at about 2 kHz for a 44.1 kHz sample rate. This would require using BLEP at least twice since we have overlapping BLEP transition regions. For BLEP with a wider transition region, it becomes tricky since there are more points to overlap. These may need to be corrected more than twice.

But there is another way to generate square waves using a synth programming trick that was used on older digital synths that did not offer a PWM square wave oscillator. The sum-of-saws method uses two sawtooth waveforms to synthesize a square wave with an adjustable duty cycle. The idea, shown in Figure 10.9(a), consists of summing two sawtooth waveforms together where one waveform has been inverted and phase shifted. Because the waveforms consist of straight lines (ramps), they will sum to 1.0 or −1.0, depending on the crossover point between them, as shown in Figure 10.9(b). And, with the modulo counter approach, shifting the phase means simply adding an offset between 0.0 and 1.0 to the existing value, then wrapping as needed.

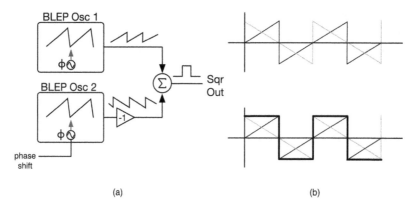

Figure 10.9 (a) Two sawtooth waveforms are combined to generate a square wave (b) shows how the ramps add or subtract to produce values of −1.0 or +1.0

10.8 *VAOscillator* and Core

The *VAOscillator* is shown in block diagram form in Figure 10.10(a), while Figure 10.10(b) shows the SynthLab diagram and the one and only *VAOCore*. The custom module strings are the three output waveform names, and the mod knobs are chosen for mixing the waveforms and applying pulse-width for the square wave output. Unlike the other oscillators, the *VAOscillator* and core are designed to render two waveforms at once, saw and square; then, the user may mix them in any ratio with the *WaveMix* mod knob. This is actually borrowed from the Oberheimm SEM®, which allowed mixing of square and sawtooth waveforms only.

Table 10.2 lists the GUI parameter structure and core description. Notice that the VA oscillator and core are the simplest of the oscillator objects; their five operational phases and functions are the simplest of those in SynthLab.

10.8.1 *VA Oscillator Controls, Modulations, and Features*

Table 10.3 lists the module controls common to all cores and the GUI calculation section or equations. The coarse tuning and fine-tuning operate in semitones and cents, respectively, and are part of the pitch modulation update calculation, while the pan and output controls are common to almost all other oscillators and allow blending of the quad oscillator render block.

10.9 VA Core Programming Notes

With the C++ files open, compare the programming notes with the code that you see, starting with the class description of the core. As with the wavetable oscillator, the VA core uses the same time-base, implemented with a *SynthClock* modulo counter that is reset and advanced with each note-event. Sections 10.9.1 through 10.9.5 summarize the five operational phases, plus constructor for the wavetable cores. Make sure to examine the code while digesting their operational phase details. The VA core is blissfully simple because it is purely algorithmic and does not require tables, files, databases, or other external components for rendering its output. This makes it a very lean object and ideal for use in mobile devices.

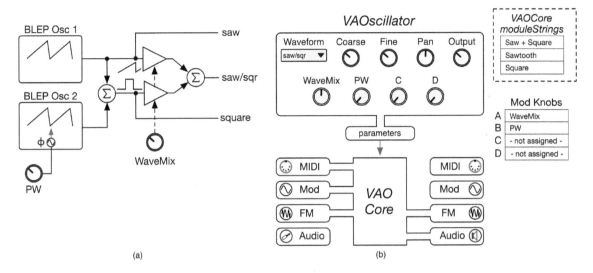

Figure 10.10 The *VAOscillator* (a) internal block diagram and (b) SynthLab diagram; there is only one core, which is also available for download as a SynthLab-DM project

Table 10.2 *VAOscillator* custom parameter structure and cores: (*) downloadable SynthLab-DM core project

Parameter Structure	Description
VAOscParameters	Includes the pulse-width parameter that is exclusive to the VA oscillator
Example Core	Description & Special Features
*VAOCore**	Simple VA oscillator core that demonstrates the sum-of-saws method for generating square waves and uses the Blackaman-Harris windowed BLEP table. This is the only oscillator that features pulse-width modulation, which is used as its unique osc mod.

Table 10.3 *VAOscillator* module controls

Module Control	Description	GUI Calculation (Section)
Coarse	Coarse tuning in semitones	Pitch modulation (6.7.1)
Fine	Fine-tuning in cents	Pitch modulation (6.7.1)
Pan	Left/Right pan	Constant power panning (6.2.2)
Output	Output level in dB	dB to raw: $10^{(dB/20)}$

10.9.1 Construction Phase

- The module strings are the waveform names, and their index values map to the GUI control selection values; the strings will be used to query the database for the selected waveform
- The mod knobs implement the wave mixing and pulse width

10.9.2 *Reset & Note On Phases*

The only detail here involves the starting phase for the sawtooth versus square wave, which is also repeated in the note-on handler. The SynthLab-VA project implements four of these oscillators, and the waveform starting-phase is important if the user mixes different waveforms. To phase align the saw and square waveforms, you need to offset the sawtooth by half a period so the first output sample is 0.0 in the center of the ramp, which is accomplished by offsetting the *SynthClock's* starting point.

```
if (parameters->waveform == VAWaveform::kSawtooth)
    oscClock.reset(0.5); // --- 0.5 for saw
else
    oscClock.reset(0.0);
```

10.9.3 *Note-On Phase*

The note-event begins with the note-on handler that is both similar and quite simple across the cores:

- Store MIDI pitch (except drum and SFX cores)
- Reset the *SynthClock* modulo counter member to either 0.0 (all cores) or the starting phase point (classic, morphing, and Fourier cores); notice how the mod knob C value is used to calculate the phase offset for the cores that support it
- NOTE: there is nothing to do in the note-off phase

10.9.4 *Update Phase*

The VA core update phase is simpler than the rest as there are no table or sample selections, just a simple update of the oscillator time-base that is identical to the other oscillators.

1   Calculate the pitch modulation value based on GUI controls and pitch modulation sources (Section 6.8.1)
2   Set the oscillator time-base with the new frequency
3   Calculate the output gain and pan
4   Store the pulse-width for the render phase

What is interesting here is the pulse width control since the *VAOscillator* is the only SynthLab oscillator that is capable of PWM. The core stores a *pulseWidth* variable for the render operation and recalculates it during the update phase, starting with getting the value from the mod knob – the percent is converted to a fraction.

```
// --- pulse width from ModKnob
//    note the way this works 0.0 -> 50% PW 1.0 -> 95% PW
pulseWidth = getModKnobValueLinear(
                parameters->modKnobValue[MOD _ KNOB _ B], 0.5, 0.95);
```

Next, the bipolar modulation value is acquired from the *kUniqueMod* input value.

```
// --- this value is modulated and then bound
double pwModulator =
            processInfo.modulationInputs->getModValue(kUniqueMod);
```

To use this value effectively, call the bipolar modulation function and cut the return value in half so that bipolar modulation will revolve around the center point that the user chooses with the mod knob. Lastly, the value is bounded to 5% and 95% (feel free to modify these limits).

```
pulseWidth += 0.5 * doBipolarModulation(pwModulator, 0.5, 0.95);
```

```
// --- bound it
boundValue(pulseWidth, 0.5, 0.95);
```

10.9.5 Render Phase

The VA core renders both the sawtooth and square wave at the same time, using the same function, then outputs the desired waveform or blends with the wave mix control for the saw/square combination waveform. The *VAOCore* uses two helper functions for rendering, each producing one sample per sample interval. The *renderSquareSample* uses the sum of saws method, calling the *renderSawtoothSample* twice and returning the sawtooth value via a pass by reference output parameter.

```
double renderSawtoothSample(SynthClock& clock);
double renderSquareSample(SynthClock& clock, double pulseWidth_Pct,
                          double& sawtoothSample);
```

The *renderSawtoothSample* function consists of three parts. First, check the oscillator frequency, and determine the maximum points per side to adjust; see Table 10.1.

```
double pointsPerSide = 0;
if (clock.frequency_Hz <= sampleRate / 8.0) // Fs/8 = Nyquist/4
    pointsPerSide = 4;
else if (clock.frequency_Hz <= sampleRate / 4.0) // Fs/4 = Nyquist/2
    pointsPerSide = 2;
else // Nyquist
    pointsPerSide = 1;
```

Next, create the trivial oscillator output, and call the BLEP function, which returns the BLEP correction factor.

```
double sawOut = bipolar(clock.mcounter); // create triv saw
double blepCorrection = 0.0;
```

```
// --- get the correction factor
blepCorrection = doBLEP_N(4096,                    /* BLEP table length */
                          clock.mcounter,     /* mod count */
                          fabs(clock.phaseInc),
                          1.0,                /* edge height = 1.0 */
                          false,              /* falling edge */
```

```
                        pointsPerSide,   /* N points per side */
                        false);          /* no interpolation */
```

Lastly, add the correction factor to the trivial sawtooth value and advance the clock time-base.

```
// --- add the correction factor
sawOut += blepCorrection;

// --- setup for next sample
clock.advanceWrapClock();
```

The *renderSquareSample* function calls the sawtooth render function twice. Notice the use of the *SynthClock::saveState* and *restoreState* functions, which are used to provide the temporary phase offset needed for the current *pulseWidth* value.

```
// --- sum-of-saws method
// --- set first sawtooth output
sawtoothSample = renderSawtoothSample(clock);

// --- save clock state
clock.saveState();

// --- phase shift on second oscillator
clock.addPhaseOffset(pulseWidth);

// --- generate 2nd saw
double saw2 = renderSawtoothSample(clock);

// --- subtract = 180 out of phase
double squareOut = 0.5*sawtoothSample - 0.5*saw2;

// --- restore original clock state
clock.restoreState();

return squareOut;
```

The DC correction function uses my formula for adjusting the DC offset based on the pulse width; as the pulse width becomes wider at the top, the DC offset needs to shift downward to make up for the added area under the curve. This may also be accomplished with a high-pass filter.

```
// --- apply DC correction
double dcCorrection = 1.0 / pulseWidth;

// --- modfiy for less than 50%
if (pulseWidth < 0.5)
    dcCorrection = 1.0 / (1.0 - pulseWidth);
```

```
// --- apply correction
squareOut *= dcCorrection;
```

The *render* function first acquires the output buffers, like the other oscillators, then sets up the block processing loop:

```
float* leftOutBuffer = processInfo.outputBuffers[LEFT_CHANNEL];
float* rightOutBuffer = processInfo.outputBuffers[RIGHT_CHANNEL];

// --- render square and saw at same time
for (uint32_t i = 0; i < processInfo.samplesToProcess; i++)
```

The loop code calls the rendering function that produces both outputs, which are output or linearly blended according to the user's waveform selection.

```
double oscOutput = 0.0;
// --- render both saw and square always, choose output with param
double sawOutput = 0.0;
double sqrOutput = renderSquareSample(oscClock, sawOutput);

if (parameters->waveform == VAWaveform::kSawAndSquare)
{
    // --- blend with mod knob
    double mix = parameters->modKnobValue[VAO_WAVE_MIX];

    oscOutput = sawOutput*mix + sqrOutput*(1.0 - mix);
}
else if (parameters->waveform == VAWaveform::kSawtooth)
    oscOutput = sawOutput;
else if (parameters->waveform == VAWaveform::kSquare)
    oscOutput = sqrOutput;

// --- scale
oscOutput *= outputAmplitude;

// --- write to output buffers
leftOutBuffer[i] = oscOutput * panLeftGain;
rightOutBuffer[i] = oscOutput * panRightGain;
```

10.10 Exercises

10.10.1 SynthLab-VA$_{DM}$: Mod Knob C to Shape Control

You can create a simple oscillator shape control with one of the spare mod knobs using the phase distortion shaping technique (Section 6.9) utilized in the wavetable cores. Add a waveform shape control that applies phase distortion to generate different sounds. Apply the phase distortion to the synth clock *mcounter* value prior to use. How does this affect the BLEP correction's ability to suppress aliasing?

10.10.2 SynthLab-VA$_{DM}$: Shape Modulation

The VA oscillator's unique modulation capability produces PWM; however, this only applies to the square waveform. Modify the core code to implement shape modulation when the user has selected the sawtooth-only waveform.

10.10.3 Advanced Module: Implement Välimäki's DPW

Download the Välimäki's DPW algorithms for generating sawtooth and triangle waves. Implement the algorithm as your own dynamic module core.

Bibliography

arizona.edu. 2020. "Continuity." http://www-isl.ece.arizona.edu/ACIS-docs/HTM/DATA/ACIS/FCG/03MATH/0003.HTM, Accessed October 14, 2020

Brandt, Eli. 2001. "Hard Sync without Aliasing." Proceedings of the International Computer Music Conference, Havana, Cuba.

Dattorro, Jon. 2003. "Effect Design Part 3 Oscillators: Sinusoidal and Pseudonoise." *Journal of the Audio Engineering Society*, vol. 50, no. 3. pp. 115–146.

Kleimola, Jari &Välimäki, Vesa. 2012. "Reducing Aliasing from Synthetic Audio Signals using Polynomial Transition Regions." *IEEE Signal Processing Letters*, vol. 19, no. 2.

Lane, J., et al. 1997. "Modeling Analog Synthesis with DSPs." *Computer Music Journal*, vol. 21, no. 4, pp. 23–41.

Leary, Andrew & Bright, Charles. 2009. "Bandlimited Digital Synthesis of Analog Waveforms." United States Patent 7,589,272.

Moore, Richard. 1990. *Elements of Computer Music*. Eaglewood Cliffs: Prentice-Hall.

Moorer, James. 1976. "The Synthesis of Complex Audio Spectra by Means of Discrete Summation Formulae." *Journal of the Audio Engineering Society*, vol. 24, no. 9, pp. 717–727.

Nam, Juhan & Välimäki, Vesa, Abel, Jonathan & Smith, Julius O. 2010. "Efficient Antialiasing Oscillator Algorithms using Low-Order Fractional Delay Filters." *IEEE Transactions on Audio, Speech and Language Processing*, vol. 18, no. 4. pp. 733–785.

Otalvara, Francisco, Behura, Samarth & Pirkle, Will. 2016. "Perceptually Alias-Free Waveform Generation using the Bandlimited Step Method and Genetic Algorithm." Presented at the 141th Audio Engineering Society Convention, New York.

Pekonen, Jussi, Lazzarini, Victor, Timoney, Joseph, Kleimola, Jari & Välimäki, Vesa. 2011. "Discrete-Time Modeling of the Moog Sawtooth Waveform." EURADISP *Journal on Advances in Signal Processing*, Article ID 10.1155/2011/785103.

Singh, Akhil & Pirkle, Will. 2016. "The Relationship between the Bandlimited Step Method (BLEP), Gibbs Phenomenon, and Lanczos Sigma Correction." Presented at the 141th Audio Engineering Society Convention, New York.

Stilson, Tim & Smith, Julius O. 1996. "Alias-Free Digital Synthesis of Classic Analog Waveforms." Proceedings of the 1996 International Computer Music Conference.

Välimäki, Vesa. 2005. "Discrete-Time Synthesis of the Sawtooth Waveform with Reduced Aliasing." *IEEE Signal Processing Letters*, vol. 12, no. 3, pp. 214–217.

Välimäki, Vesa & Huovilainen, Antti. 2006. "Oscillator and Filter Algorithms for Virtual Analog Synthesis." *Computer Music Journal*, vol. 30, no. 2, pp. 19–31, Cambridge: MIT Press.

Välimäki, Vesa, Nam, Juhan, Abel, Jonathan & Smith, Julius O. 2010. "Alias-Suppressed Oscillators Based on Differential Polynomial Waveforms." *IEEE Transactions on Audio, Speech and Language Processing*, vol. 18, no. 4, pp. 786–798

11 PCM Sample Playback Oscillators

Early sampler instruments were capable of recording sounds – single musical tones (note-events) from acoustic instruments, short audio clips, or sound effects – and playing them back with the ability to speed up or slow down the playback so as to generate proper musical pitches when desired. This idea led to sample playback synthesizers, which played banks of pre-recorded musical instrument sounds or sound effects. Due to confusion regarding the terms "sample" and "wave" and "wave file," I use the term "PCM sample" to specifically refer to a recorded event that is not a wavetable. PCM stands for Pulse Code Modulation, the technique of encoding voltage levels as numbers. In contrast to the early samplers, the newer sample playback synths used sets of samples called "multi-samples," made of recordings of note-events at different pitches across the range of an acoustic instrument. These PCM samples were mapped to different keys on the keyboard and followed a paradigm similar to the wavetable synths, in which a single PCM sample is used for a range of playback notes via interpolation. Typically, intervals of a minor third or octave were used.

11.1 PCM Sample Playback Modes

Figure 11.1 shows the four commonly used playback modes: one-shot; loop; transient plus loop; and transient, loop, and release. Pitch-less PCM samples are designed to playback at the speed they were recorded, while the pitched versions are designed to map to the keyboard with proper musical note playback. As in the wavetable, when PCM sample data is read out using an increment value greater than one, aliasing may occur. Early samplers had no way of generating alias-free multi-samples from a single recording, so the effect of aliasing is sometimes associated with them and is sometimes seen not as a problem but rather as a kind of personality of the device.

11.1.1 One-shot Mode

In one-shot mode, shown in Figure 11.1(a), the PCM data is played from beginning to end exactly once, and then playback stops, even if the key is still being held. Latching one-shot allows the user to trigger the playback with a single press and release of a key or button. One-shot PCM samples are usually used for drum hits or sound effects and may or may not be pitched.

11.1.2 Loop Mode

In looping mode, shown in Figure 11.1(b), the entire PCM sample is looped from beginning to end and then repeated. These loops are often pitch-less, implementing drum beats or background pads. When using loops of musical material, playback at speeds other than normal often sounds artificial.

11.1.3 Transient + Loop Mode

Figure 11.1(c) depicts the transient plus loop operation and is the most common mode for PCM sample playback synths. In this mode, the PCM sample recording contains the initial transient sound plus a section of the waveform containing the steady state portion that is looped, while the key is held. When the key is released, the sustain loop continues, and an artificial release envelope is applied via the DCA and its EG. This is the most common kind of PCM sample playback as it has been used in numerous synths, like the Korg M1 and Kurzweil K2000/2500. The Legacy PCM core object implements 16 sets of these multi-samples to generate its 16 different waveforms.

11.1.4 Transient + Loop then Release Mode

Figure 11.1(d) shows the transient plus loop then release mode in which the transient and release portions of the waveform are preserved, with the transient loop section positioned between them. This allows a very accurate synthesis of the original instrument waveform that includes both the attack and the release information. The release portion may also be further shaped with the DCA and EG.

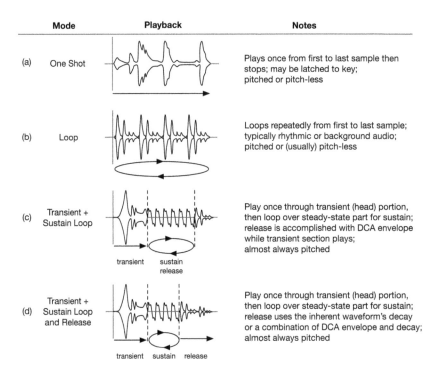

Figure 11.1 The four common modes of PCM sample playback include (a) one-shot; (b) loop; (c) transient plus loop; and (d) transient, loop, and release

11.2 PCM Sample Storage

PCM samples are usually much longer than the few hundred or thousand sample points of a wavetable, and this may be problematic. Unlike the wavetables that can be compiled into the synth, PCM samples are almost always packaged in a separate file or set of files; this necessitates the opening and parsing of the files in order to populate buffers for playback. One simple way to package the PCM samples is in a "wave" file (with the extension *.wav*). This is especially attractive since the wave file format includes the ability to store one or more sample loop points along with the audio data. However, it also exposes the raw material to the user, who may then copy or move the data into another device. Typically, only one PCM sample is stored in a wave file, so this generates numerous files to maintain. For this text, the wave file format works well and will allow you endless experimentation with PCM samples, which you can buy, get for free, or even generate yourself.

11.2.1 Packaging Samples in Wave (.wav) Files

The wave file format was conceived to store more information than just the audio data and relevant information about it, such as channel count, number of samples, and samples per data word. The wave file format consists of chunks of information named riff-chunks, along with the raw audio data encoded as bytes. Audio samples may be encoded as 8-, 16-, or 24-bit integers, or 32- or 64-bit floating point values.

In particular, the wave file format also includes the option to store the

1   Sample period ($T = 1/f_s$)
2   Loop count (may have more than one loop, though we use single-loop files exclusively)
3   Starting and ending sample indexes for each loop in the file
4   SMPTE time code information
5   MIDI Unity Note
6   MIDI Pitch Fraction

11.2.1.1 MIDI Unity Note Information

In addition to being able to store multiple loop points, the wave file format also includes the MIDI unity note and MIDI pitch fraction, which are important for PCM samples. The MIDI unity note represents the MIDI note number of the pitch that will occur if the PCM samples are read out with a phase increment of 1.0 – in other words, the note that was originally recorded for the sample. If the pitch of the note is not a standard MIDI pitch (e.g. instruments that do not use Western intonation, such as sitar), then the MIDI pitch fraction may contain the additional pitch offset information.

In the past, it was common for professional sample and loop generating companies to encode the MIDI unity note information in the wave file, making it simple to decode and calculate the phase increment lookup value. More recently, this paradigm has been mostly ignored, with the note number and name encoded into the name of the wave file, e.g. *flute_A#4.wav*. Clearly, encoding the unity note like this is problematic as there is no standard whatsoever. However, searching for the note string within the filename is not unreasonable, and the Mellotron ® PCM samples in the Mellotron core are encoded this way.

11.2.2 Calculating the PCM Phase Increment

For pitch-less samples and loops, the phase increment is simply set to 1.0, and the loop or sample will play at the same rate and pitch, no matter which key is used to trigger the event. To mimic the early samplers, the pitch can be adjusted for interesting effects, but for musical pitches to be accurate, the original pitch of the sample must be known either from the embedded unity note number or from a lookup table once the filename has been decoded. The phase increment value (called the playback ratio) may be calculated in two different manners. Equation (11.1) uses the MIDI note number:

$$phaseInc = 2^{\frac{M-U}{12}}$$

M = MIDI note number of note being played   (11.1)
U = MIDI unity note number

To avoid the power-of-two operation, Equation (11.2) can be derived easily, using the equivalent length of a wavetable with the same MIDI unity note pitch.

$$phaseInc = \frac{f_o}{f_U}$$

f_o = frequency of note being played   (11.2)
f_U = frequency of unity note (original sample pitch)

11.2.3 Multi-Samples and the Keyboard

Multi-samples are generated for multiple pitches across the keyboard and are distributed across the range of notes in a similar manner to the wavetables in Figure 9.4. These include but are not limited to:

1   One PCM sample per octave
2   One PCM sample per minor third interval (four samples per octave)
3   One PCM sample per note

For the Mellotron samples used in the *MellotronCore*, the original keyboard had a limited range of 35 keys from G2 to F5, so the samples in that set are likewise limited in range.

11.3 Loading PCM Samples

The early PCM sample-based synths usually incorporated ROM (read only memory) chips, with samples that were permanently burned into them. These devices, and the method of encoding the audio information in them, were proprietary and part of an embedded audio system specific to each manufacturer. To offer more PCM samples for the user after the unit was purchased, some manufacturers made expansion cards with still more ROM, which could be inserted into dedicated hardware ports on the synth. Later, PCM samples were distributed on CD-ROM and loaded via SCSI data ports onto synths that had this capability. The ability to load new sample sets is attractive for end users, while disc or CD-ROM-based storage is attractive for the manufacturers as they have control over distribution. However there is one sticky point that needs to be addressed, no matter what sample delivery system is used: when should this new, non-factory data be read and loaded into ROM? There are two basic options:

1   Pre-load the data into RAM (random access memory) when the synth starts up or when a new expansion card, hard disc, or CD-ROM is attached
2   Load the PCM data from hard disc or CD-ROM on-the-fly as the user depresses each key

If the PCM sample data is loaded all at once and placed into RAM, the synth engine and synth voices will have instant access to the data via simple pointers or table index values, and the PCM oscillators will begin rendering their outputs immediately. However, if the synth loads significant amounts of data, this forces the user to wait for the data to load. In addition, this is not memory-efficient since many samples may be loaded into memory but never actually played. In the all-at-once paradigm, the user must wait for the data to load, but the programming code is very simple for both reading the data into RAM and rendering the audio output.

On the other hand, if the data is loaded from a disc as the user plays the notes, you need to create a file input stream from the disc and begin accessing the data, which is far too slow for real-time operation. But processing threads can be used to allow each note-event to optimize the parallelism inherent in polyphonic playing, and data can be read in chunks. In this on-demand system, multiple threads can be used for more efficiency, but the code will be much more complex because it will need to include: setting up and waiting for disc access, creating a worker thread to fetch data from the disc, and synchronizing that thread so it does not interfere with the synth's native processing threads.

In the on-demand paradigm, the time it takes to access the disc and begin fetching data to render is prohibitive and will cause a noticeable tactile and audible delay. This brings up a third, hybrid option that combines both ideas. At load-time, you only read out the first chunk (say, 4096 samples) of each PCM sample, and you save that in RAM. This significantly reduces the load time and memory required. Then, when the user plays a note, you begin reading from that data in RAM for the beginning of the note-event and launch the thread that performs disc accesses for the rest of the data. From that point on, the code involves synchronizing the disc accesses and fetching chunks of data as needed for the rendering operation. Clearly, this is a significant coding challenge and involves heuristic problems, such as switching PCM sample sets on-the-fly while notes are being held.

11.3.1 Data Brick Files

Another way to package the samples sets is in one giant contiguous data "brick" file that contains all of the sample information, loop points, etc. but is compacted into a sequential data file. This hides the data from the user and even with simple encryption techniques can make the data very difficult to steal. In the hybrid approach, the brick file might contain an array of just the starting portions of the waveforms. For educational purposes, I am delivering the data in wave files stuffed into folders. However, if you would like to experiment with using the brick files or reading samples on-demand, you can find tools to extract the wave samples and loop points at www.willpirkle.com/synth-tools.

11.3.2 Sample Slicing

In sample slicing, you start with a wave file that contains multiple musical events. Then, an algorithm is used that finds the transient edges of these musical events and creates slice points.

The wave file can then encode these multiple loop points or else be split into individual wave files, each containing a slice. These loops can then be mapped to the keyboard or touch-screen display, and the user plays the loops as if they were musical notes. The methods for finding the transient edges involves math that is interesting and deep. Usually, multiple methods are used, including finding time-based transients and locating energy or spectral bursts that indicate a transient edge. A free, open-source library of tools named *aubio* is available at https://github.com/aubio/aubio and includes a command line utility called *aubiocut* that detects transient edges in a wave file, then slices it into a set of smaller wave files. You have control over several factors used in the detection operation. The wave files are named according to the time location of the starting slice. The *Wave-Folder* object in the next section can decode the *aubio* filenames to create sets of pitch-less loops that can be mapped to the keyboard and is included as the *WaveSliceCore*.

11.3.3 *PCMSample and WaveFolder C++ Objects*

To facilitate PCM sample loading and rendering, I've designed two helper objects that do most of the work. The *PCMSample* object is used to open a wave file and extract its information, and works for both Windows and MacOS. The audio data is loaded and stored in an array of floating point values. The *PCMSample* object also parses and saves the loop start and end points, and the MIDI unity note number. The object works with mono or stereo uncompressed 8-, 16-, or 24-bit integer wave files as well as 32- and 64-bit floating-point files – in all cases, the final data is available in 32-bit floating-point form only, which is also the synth's preferred audio data type. Each wave file will have its own associated *PCMSample* object.

In the SynthLab-PCM synth, each set of multi-samples that generates one waveform is stored in its own directory, as shown in Figure 11.2(a). The name of the directory is the name of the selected sample in SynthLab (though that is easy to change). At startup, the PCM samples are loaded from the wave files and stored in *PCMSample* objects, organized in an array of 128 slots, each corresponding to the MIDI note number for that sample's pitch. Each SynthLab PCM core object implements an instrument with up to 16 patches. You can see that for the Mellotron, there is one wave file per note for all 35 keys on the instrument, from G2 through F5, as shown in Figure 11.3(b). Each file is extracted into a dynamically created *PCMSample* object whose pointer is stored in the array. Since the sample set is incomplete for all 128 MIDI notes, the bottom G2 data is used for all notes below it, while the F5 data is used for all keys above it. Another option would be to simply not render the notes outside the original range, but that may confuse the user. For the legacy core samples, there are missing samples at the top and bottom of the range as well as within the existing samples that are placed on minor-third boundaries from A1 through C4, as shown in Figure 11.3(c). All of the legacy samples are designed for bass sounds – thus the limited range – and were taken from free samples appearing in *Future Music* and *Computer Music* magazines. In addition to the member functions in Table 11.1, the *PCMSample* object also stores information as member variables, including:

numChannels: number of audio channels; SynthLab supports mono or stereo files
loopCount: number of loops in the file; SynthLab only parses the first loop
loopStartIndex: starting index of loop (absolute index)
loopEndIndex: ending index of loop (absolute index)
unityMIDINote: MIDI note number for unity note

Table 11.1 The *PCMSample* object's functions

PCMSample Function	Argument	Description
loadPCMSample	filePath	Opens, decodes, and extracts the audio data from a wave file located at the *filePath* argument; also extracts loop and unity note information
getSampleBuffer	None	Returns a *const float* (read-only) pointer to the audio data array for rendering
setPitchless	_pitchlessSample	Sets the pitch-less sample flag on the object, forces read phase increment to 1.0 always

The *WaveFolder* object extracts all of the PCM samples from the wave files present in a patch folder and builds the array of pointers to the corresponding *PCMSample* objects. The MIDI unity note number may be encoded in the wave file or may exist as character strings in the file names, as shown in Figure 11.2(a). In the latter case, the *WaveFolder* object will attempt to intelligently extract the note number from the file name (names with both "#" and "b" are supported) and will embed the corresponding MIDI note number in the *PCMSample* object. Once all the files have been parsed, the *WaveFolder* object will perform a second pass over the array of pointers, copying each pointer to fill the slots that may be missing due to incomplete sample sets. This simplifies the note rendering operation, giving us access to each sample using the MIDI note number as the array look-up index. The *WaveFolder* object has only two main functions: the constructor, which stores the outer directory, and the sample folder (e.g. M300 Brass in Figure 11.2). Once constructed, the *IPCMSampleSource* object calls the *parseFolder* method to extract and set up the 128 *PCMSample* pointers in Figure 11.2. The prototype and variable descriptions are below; notice the flag that indicates a folder of *aubiocut* wave slices from Section 11.3.2.

```
parseFolder(PCMSample** sampleSet, /* pointer to array of pointers */
            bool pitchlessLoops,  /* pitchless loop flag */
            bool aubioSlices)   /* aubio slices flag */
```

The details of the folder parsing are in the function and perform the operations in Figure 11.2. For *aubiocut* pitch-less loops, the *WaveFolder* is set up to map these loop slices to the C-major scale notes (all white keys), starting with middle-C (MIDI note 60) and mapping upwards. You may easily modify this code for your own mappings.

11.4 PCM Sources and Database

The *IPCMSampleSource* interface is used to create a C++ class that provides access to a set of PCM multi-samples arranged in an array. You can think of a "sample source" as all of the information needed to synthesize one PCM multi-sample across the range of MIDI notes. This interface allows you to implement your PCM sample sources however you wish and is one of the central design patterns in SynthLab. As long as your sample source object implements the interface functions, it will work seamlessly with the PCM core objects. The *SynthLabPCMSource* object exposes this *IPCMSampleSource*, and you may use it as an example to design your own. Figure 11.3(a) shows the arrangement of *IPCMSampleSource* objects in the database. This is identical to the *WavetableDatabase* construction and follows the same paradigm.

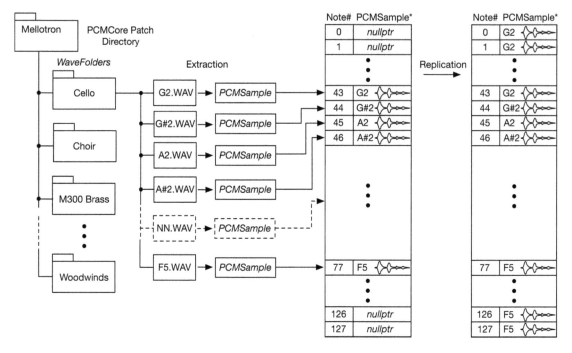

Figure 11.2 The Mellotron core directory contains subdirectories for each patch, which, in turn, contains a set of wave files; each of these is extracted into a *PCMSample* object and stored in an array of pointers in an *IPCMSampleSource* object

The *PCMSampleDatabase* is created in the *SynthEngine* and shared across all *SynthVoices* and their PCM oscillators. The database is a *std::map* that stores *IPCMSampleSource* pointers via unique key strings. Your PCM core object may query the database for sample sources, and it may create and add new PCM sample sources at construction time. The database uses unique name strings because, ultimately, the user will need to select the waveform from a list of unique names. SynthLab fills the GUI waveform selectors with these unique strings any time a new core object is loaded. Table 11.2 lists the *IPCMSampleSource* functions and their descriptions.

11.4.1 Reading/Interpolating the PCM Sample

The *IPCMSampleSource* object implements the *readSample* function that does the work in reading and linearly interpolating the audio samples. This code is actually quite simple. The SynthLab sample playback oscillator cores are the only oscillators that do not use the *SynthClock* object for a time-base. Instead, the sample phase index value is calculated and stored along with a read index. The *IPCMSampleSource* performs the read and interpolate operation, then updates the read index and returns it to the core for storage via pass-by-reference:

```
PCMSampleOutput readSample(double& readIndex, double inc)
```

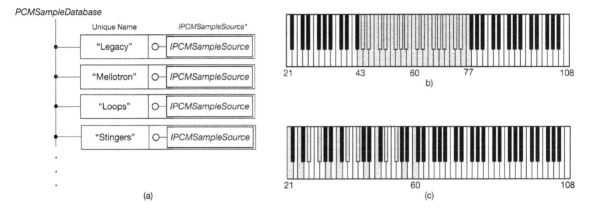

Figure 11.3 (a) The sample sources are arranged in a database and accessed via a unique name string; (b) the shaded keys show the included wave files for the Mellotron, sampled on every note from G2 through F5, while the (c) legacy files include samples on minor third boundaries from A1 through C4

Table 11.2 The *IPCMSampleSource* interface

IPCMSampleSource Function	Argument	Description
selectSample	oscFrequency	Selects a *PCMSample* object based on the oscillator frequency and the MIDI unity note frequency in Equation (11.2)
readSample	readIndex inc	Reads the PCM data using a read- *readIndex* and increment (*inc*) value, then returns the output data in a structure
setSampleLoopMode	SampleLoopMode	Sets the loop mode: *one-shot, loop,* or *sustain*
deleteSamples	None	Used during destruction

The code for finding the fractional sample location is identical to that of the wavetable oscillator cores, and the only real difference is the data source that provides the sample values. The PCM oscillator cores output into a very simple structure that contains the audio data (mono or stereo) and an active channel count.

```
struct PCMSampleOutput
{
    double audioOutput[STEREO_CHANNELS] = { 0.0, 0.0 };
    uint32_t numActiveChannels = 0;
};
```

For a single channel wave file, the read code is below; the variable called *selectedSample* is an *IP-CMSampleSource** that is parsed when the user chooses a new PCM sample patch. This interface is used to access the data in the sample buffer via the *getSampleBuffer* function. The linear interpolation uses the fractional part (thus, the first arguments, 0 and 1) and the two adjacent samples from the buffer.

```
// --- split the fractional index into int.frac parts
double dIntPart = 0.0;
double fracPart = modf(readIndex, &dIntPart);
uint32_t nReadIndex = (uint32_t)dIntPart;

// --- mono file
if (selectedSample->numChannels == 1)
{
    // --- check for end of file (theoretically won't happen)
    int nReadIndexNext = nReadIndex + 1 >
        selectedSample->sampleCount - 1 ? 0 : nReadIndex + 1;

    // interpolate between the two
    output.audioOutput[LEFT_CHANNEL] =
            doLinearInterpolation(0, 1,
            selectedSample->getSampleBuffer()[nReadIndex],
            selectedSample->getSampleBuffer()[nReadIndexNext],
            fracPart);
    output.audioOutput[RIGHT_CHANNEL] =
                                    output.audioOutput[LEFT_CHANNEL];
    readIndex += inc;
}
```

11.4.2 *Looping the PCM Sample*

Looping the PCM sample is a bit more involved than the wavetable. First, the sample loop type is identified which sets the looping logic. For one-shot samples, once the end is reached, the *readIndex* variable is set to −1, which indicates that the loop is finished, and the output will be silent after that. For ordinary loops from start to end, once the *readIndex* crosses the end point, it is wrapped back to the head of the buffer. For transient plus loop, when the loop end point is crossed, you wrap back to the loop start point. That logic is fairly simple, and you may find the details in the *SynthLabPCMSource::readSample* method.

11.5 *PCMOscillator* and Cores

The *PCMOscillator* and core objects are shown in block form in Figure 11.4. There are three cores for you to use as examples or for modification. The legacy core contains the original samples from the first edition of the book, with transient plus loop and MIDI notes embedded in the wave files. The Mellotron core's samples are free and available at https://sonicbloom.net/en/free-sb-mellotron-samples/; note that they are set up as long (five- to eight-second) one-shot waveforms, and embed the note name and number in the filename. The wave slice core uses multiple sources for loops and *aubiocut* to slice them up – see the readme.txt file in each folder for information about the free loop source URL and notes about slicing.

Table 11.3 lists the GUI parameter structure and core descriptions.

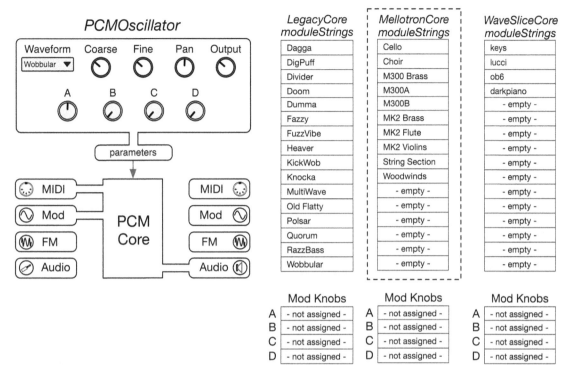

Figure 11.4 The *PCMOscillator* block diagram and module strings; none of the mod knobs are assigned in these cores

Table 11.3 *PCMOscillator* custom parameter structure and cores: (*) downloadable SynthLab-DM core project

Parameter Structure	Description
PCMOscParameters	Used for all cores, includes all oscillator parameters

Example Core	Description
LegacyCore	16 samples on minor third intervals covering the lower half of the keyboard, mainly for bass sounds
MellotronCore	Long Mellotron samples, one per note across the original keyboard range
*WaveSliceCore**	Demonstrates mapping wave-slices to individual keys to create a slicer-rompler style instrument; *aubiocut* was used to create the individual wave slice *.wav* files

11.5.1 PCM Oscillator Controls, Modulations, and Features

Table 11.4 lists the module controls common to all cores and the GUI calculation section or equations. The coarse tuning and fine-tuning operate in semitones and cents, respectively, and are part of the pitch modulation update calculation, while the pan and output controls are common

Table 11.4 Module controls shared across cores

Module Control	Description	GUI Calculation (Section)
Coarse	Coarse tuning in semitones	Pitch modulation (6.7.1)
Fine	Fine-tuning in cents	Pitch modulation (6.7.1)
Pan	Left/Right pan	Constant power panning (6.2.2)
Output	Output level in dB	dB to raw: $10^{(dB/20)}$

to almost all other oscillators and allow blending of the quad oscillator render block. The PCM oscillator cores do not have any mod knob mappings, so you are free to experiment. The PCM core unique modulation is pan modulation (Section 6.2.2).

11.6 PCM Core Programming Notes

With the C++ files open, compare the programming notes with the code you see, starting with the class descriptions of each core. The PCM cores do not use the *SynthClock* as their time-base; instead, they keep track of their own *phaseInc* value, which helps calculate the current *readIndex* variable used to read from the *.wav* file data. Each core obtains an *IPCMSampleSource* interface pointer that is used to query and load samples into the database in a very similar manner as the *IWavetableSource* objects.

Sections 11.6.1 through 11.6.5 summarize the five operational phases plus constructor for the wavetable cores. Make sure to examine the code while digesting their operational phase details.

11.6.1 Construction Phase

All cores:

- The module strings are the PCM sample file names, and their index values map to the GUI control selection values; the strings will be used to query the database for the selected waveform
- The mod knobs are not assigned
- The cores demonstrate multiple was to deal with samples: the legacy files use transient plus loop, the Mellotron samples are long one-shot files, and the wave slices play in their original pitches and are mapped to individual keys for sample playback

11.6.2 Reset Phase

The *reset* function queries the PCM sample database and adds the sources as needed. The *IPCMSampleSource* object handles parsing the PCM data from the wave files. For SynthLab, the samples are located within a special folder that will sit in the same folder as your plugin DLL. The DLL folder is acquired when the plugin loads and is available in the *processInfo.dllPath* variable. You only need to provide the outer containing folder name and the sub-directories with the instrument samples – these are your *coreData.moduleStrings[ ]* values that you set in the constructor. You may also set a simple hard-coded location for the samples (e.g. *C:\samples*). This code demonstrates the legacy core operation.

```
// --- initialize samples
std::string sampleFolder = concatStrings(processInfo.dllPath,
                           "\\SynthLabSamples\\Legacy\\");

for (uint32_t i = 0; i < MODULE_STRINGS; i++)
{
     std::string sampleFile =
          concatStrings(sampleFolder, coreData.moduleStrings[i]);

     checkAddSampleSet(sampleFile.c_str(),
                              coreData.moduleStrings[i], processInfo);
}
```

11.6.3 Note-On Phase

The note-on event is easily serviced; you save the incoming MIDI pitch to use for update calculations and reset the *readIndex* variable.

```
// --- save pitch
midiPitch = processInfo.noteEvent.midiPitch;

// --- reset to new start phase
readIndex = 0.0;
```

11.6.4 Update Phase

The pitched core update phases follow the same three steps that you will find on the other pitched oscillators. The *update* function's main goal here is to have the correct PCM sample selected and its interface pointer stored for the render phase that will immediately follow.

1   Calculate the pitch modulation value based on GUI controls and pitch modulation sources
2   Select the PCM source based on the user's waveform selection string
3   Select the sample based on the final modulated pitch value

To get the sample source, you use the GUI control index value:

```
// --- get the wave string
const char* wave = coreData.moduleStrings[parameters->sampleIndex];

// --- select the source
selectedSampleSource =
                   processInfo.sampleDatabase->getSampleSource(wave);
```

With the PCM source selected, you can get the *phaseInc* value by calling the *selectSample* function, which also chooses the *PCMSample* object for rendering. It returns the *phaseInc* value to use in the next phase.

```
phaseInc = selectedSampleSource->selectSample(oscillatorFrequency);
```

11.6.5 Render Phase

The PCM rendering is efficient and simple. The sample source object will handle reading and interpolating the buffer. The render function first acquires the audio buffers, then runs a loop over the block, rendering both left and right channels using the *readSample* method, which also updates the *phaseInc* value:

```
float* leftOutBuffer = processInfo.outputBuffers[LEFT_CHANNEL];
float* rightOutBuffer = processInfo.outputBuffers[RIGHT_CHANNEL];

for (uint32_t i = 0; i < processInfo.samplesToProcess; i++){

// --- read sample
PCMSampleOutput output = selectedSampleSource->readSample(readIndex,
                                                          phaseInc);
leftOutBuffer[i] = output.audioOutput[LEFT_CHANNEL];
rightOutBuffer [i] = output.audioOutput[RIGHT_CHANNEL];
```

11.7 Exercises

11.7.1 SynthLab-PCM$_{DM}$ Mellotron Core: Loop Points

Mellotron samples are taken from the beginning to the end of the note-event and do not include loop points. In this state, this creates a one-shot sample playback synth, but the samples are six to ten seconds in length. Using software such as *Wavosaur* (free), you can set the loop points for the sustain sections and embed the MIDI unity note. Create a set of transient plus loop samples from the original Mellotron files. There are 35 files per patch, so you will become very good at identifying the transient loop points, and you will find that it is quite challenging to get a click-free loop. You might also investigate software such as *SampleRobot* that can find loop points for you.

11.7.2 SynthLab-PCM$_{DM}$ Mellotron Core: Start Point Mod Knob

All mod knobs are unassigned for the PCM cores. The Mellotron samples are delivered in long one-shot un-looped form. Use two mod knobs to set the loop start and end points on-the-fly. HINT: You will need to modify the *IPCMSampleSource* object to set the loop points.

11.7.3 SynthLab-WT$_{DM}$: Hard Sync

PCM samples are usually not hard-sunk as their information is often instrument-specific. Use a mod knob and implement the same self hard-sync as the wavetable cores. Then, implement shape modulation using a mod knob as the controller and using a similar waveshaping technique.

11.7.4 Advanced Module: Create a PCM Split Core

Splitting a synth keyboard involves mapping one patch (PCM sample set) to one range of notes and another patch to the remaining notes. Middle-C is often chosen as the split note. Create a core that splits the keyboard and chooses from two different patches depending on the key being depressed.

11.7.5 Advanced Interface: On-Demand PCM Sample Access

If you are already knowledgeable about multi-threaded applications, propose and implement a system for loading PCM samples on-demand from the disc. This will require numerous heuristic options regarding how a worker thread that accesses the disc can add data to a growing audio buffer (HINT: see the lock-free ring buffers, as described in Chapter 20 of *Designing Audio Effects Plugins in C++ 2nd Ed.*).

Bibliography

Braut, Christian. 1994. *The Musician's Guide to MIDI*, Chap. 5–7. Alameda: SYBEX.

MIDI Manufacturer's Association. 1999. *Downloadable Sounds Level 1*. https://www.midi.org/specifications-old/item/dls-level-1-specification, Accessed October 14, 2020

MIDI Manufacturer's Association. 1999. *Downloadable Sounds Level 2*. https://www.midi.org/specifications-old/item/dls-level-2-specification, Accessed October 14, 2020

12 Synthesizer Filters

Filters play a critical role in most synthesizer algorithms, from simple damping in the Karplus-Strong algorithms to searing filter sweeps in analog modeling synths. Interestingly, many classical DSP textbooks explain the design theory, but they rarely reveal the implementations that we need in audio applications: independent controls for cutoff frequency (f_c) and quality factor (Q) and stability over the audio spectrum from 20 Hz to ~20,480 Hz (10 octaves). Early digital synth filters, designed directly in the z-plane, can be found in Chamberlain, F.R. Moore, and Dodge and Jerse. In the late 1980s, Motorola introduced a set of DSP application notes that demonstrated algorithms with independent controls and which were implemented as IIR filters. More recently, Zavalishin's excellent and free book *The Art of VA Filter Design* has added a new set of synth filter designs to our repertoire. In fact, this chapter is devoted entirely to these virtual analog designs because they work well for modulation and are simple to implement. In addition, you can find almost all of the other audio filter design types in my FX plugin book.

12.1 Design Summary

As with analog filters, digital filter design has multiple approaches. These include:

1   *Direct z-plane design*: early synth filters, including resonator and all-pole designs
    Pros: simple to design and implement; CPU friendly
    Cons: limited design flexibility
    Sources: Moore, Dodge and Jerse, Chamberlain
2   *Bilinear z-Transform IIR* (BZT): classical analog-to-digital filter designs via the bilinear z-transform
    Pros: maps analog s-plane to digital z-plane, preserving the frequency axis
    Cons: does not preserve impulse response, and LPF edges have errors due to incorrect mapping of zeros at infinity
    Sources: numerous, including Pirkle (2018)
3   *Impulse invariant filters*: classical filter design that preserves the impulse response of the analog filter prototype
    Pros: impulse response preserved
    Cons: can alias but only useful for lowpass types; filter f_c has errors that get worse as the frequency increases
    Sources: Ifeachor and Jarvis, Pirkle (2018)

4   *Wave Digital Filters (WDF)*: model the analog circuit components directly using scattering parameter theory
Pros: design techniques are well documented and may include passive or active components
Cons: advanced circuits with multiple loops and nodes may be difficult to implement
Sources: Fettweis, Smith: RT-WDF, Pirkle (2018)

5   *SPICE modeled filters*: uses a real-time SPICE engine and SPICE scripts for circuit simulation
Pros: exact modeling of components with a long history and thousands of existing models
Cons: CPU intensive
Sources: usually a trade secret

6   *Virtual Analog filters (VA)*: model analog filter block diagrams or analog signal flow graphs at a conceptual level, instead of circuit components
Pros: excellent sound quality and ability to tolerate intense f_c modulation; simple to implement
Cons: ultimately, these are bilinear transform variants and suffer from the same errors with LPF edges and zeros at infinity; it is still possible to produce harsh or erroneous filter output with extreme f_c modulation
Sources: Zavalishin, Pirkle (2018)

12.2   *Q* and Self-Oscillation

One aspect of synth filter design that differs from FX and other applications is that self-oscillation is generally desirable. The filter will self-oscillate when its Q (resonant peaking) value becomes infinite. For our synth filters, this will always be based on a feedback loop gain value that represents a 100% feedback. However, this value is different for every filter, and in one case, the value is 0.0. To create filters that can use the same pair of GUI controls for f_c and Q, I am using a single scale of 1 to 10 for the Q control. Each filter will take this value and map it to a range of values that works for its design. The maximum setting will produce self-oscillation. Self-oscillation becomes particularly interesting when key-track modulation is used; the filter can act as a secondary oscillator and may be tuned to musical intervals based on the MIDI note that is playing.

12.3   Analog Magnitude Matching at Nyquist

One annoyance with bilinear z-transformed filters is that lowpass and bandpass filters do not have a matched analog frequency response due to the zero at Nyquist – this is discussed in detail in my FX plugin book. Each of my synth filters includes a modification to produce a finite gain at Nyquist in order to more closely mimic the analog counterparts. As with the MMA, impulse invariant, and Vickanek analog matched filters in the FX book, there is some error from the true analog magnitude, and it varies from −12.4% to +1.1%. Even with the error, I feel that these are superior to the BZT versions because of the added top-end to the response. In this chapter, the option is named "analog FGN" (Finite Gain at Nyquist). All filters produce both standard and analog FGN outputs, so you are free to choose whichever you like.

12.4   Zavalishin's Virtual Analog Filters

Zavalishin's VA design technique (2012) simulates analog filters by implementing the analog block diagrams, consisting of summers, multipliers (amplification or attenuation), and integrators, with their digital versions. The summers and multipliers translate easily into their corresponding DSP structures, and there are more than two-dozen different digital integrators that may be considered. This idea goes back to El-Masry's *RLC* simulation technique (El-Masry and Sakla 1979) and has been re-packaged over the years in different forms, but it is based on the notion of digital integrator replacement. This method did not gain traction early on because it usually results in delay-free loops, also called "zero delay feedback loops" or "zero delay feedback" or ZDF. Zavalishin presents an algebraic solution to the delay-free loop problem. In 2015, I extended Härmä's "Implementation of Recursive Filters Having Delay Free Loops" (1998) to provide another method of solving the problem that uses simple filter stimuli and responses with a universal transfer function. For this chapter, the phrase "Virtual Analog," or VA, refers to these integrator replacement designs.

12.4.1 Digital Integrator Replacement

Figure 12.1 shows the fundamental concept behind integrator replacement as a method of digitizing an analog filter. A simple first order *RC* filter is shown in Figure 12.1(a), and it is easy to derive the cutoff frequency $\omega_c = 1/RC$. The analog block diagram is shown in Figure 12.1(b), and you can see the location of the multiplier and integrator inside of a delay-free loop. This is well documented in Zavalishin's text, using simple voltage dividers as well as Laplace transforms. You can also download an alternate derivation from www.willpirkle.com/synth-lab that uses signal flow graph theory – in any event, you need to know a bit about analog block diagrams and filtering theory to understand these derivations.

While digital summers and coefficient multipliers are simple to implement, the analog integrator does not have a directly corresponding digital version. The analog integrator's transfer function $H(s) = 1/s$ may be analyzed in the frequency domain as a kind of first order lowpass filter with a magnitude response of infinity at $\omega = 0$, or as a time domain algorithm that calculates the area under the analog signal's curve. If we think about calculating the area under the signal's curve, we know that any digital version will have errors because the signal itself is discretized where the smooth analog curve is broken into samples.

The bilinear integrator approximates the analog integrator with a trapezoidal area calculation. Figure 12.2(a) shows two samples from the audio input, the current input $x(n)$, and the previous input $x(n - 1)$. If the integrator output $y(n)$ represents the area under the input signal's curve, then the area of this trapezoid can be found using the familiar geometric equation, where the value $T/2$ represents the halfway point between the two input samples and $T = 1/f_s$.

$$y(n) = y(n-1) + \frac{T}{2}(x(n) + x(n-1))$$

(12.1)

Taking the *z*-transform of (12.1) by inspection, we get:

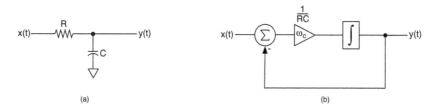

(a)   (b)

Figure 12.1 (a) A simple RC lowpass filter and (b) the analog block diagram

$$H(z) = \frac{T}{2}\frac{1+z^{-1}}{1-z^{-1}} = \frac{T}{2}\frac{z+1}{z-1} \tag{12.2}$$

Figure 12.2(b) shows the bilinear integrator in transposed canonical form and has been labeled with an intermediate node, $s(n)$, that represents the output of a storage block or z^{-1} storage register and shows that the output is a scaled version of the input, plus the output of that storage register. This separates the equation into two parts: the part dependent only on the current input signal $x(n)$ and the part dependent only on the output of the storage system $s(n)$ or the delayed part. Equation (12.3) shows how the output $y(n)$ is separated into these two components and that it is a function of the input $x(n)$, the static coefficient $T/2$, and the storage component $s(n)$.

$$y(n) = \frac{T}{2}[x(n)] + s(n) \tag{12.3}$$

Performing digital integrator substitution on the first order lowpass filter produces the diagram in Figure 12.3(a). The coefficient multiplier that was $\omega_c = 1/RC$ has been replaced with ω_a, which represents the pre-warped analog cutoff frequency that is inherent in the bilinear transform calculation. The original analog cutoff frequency is assigned directly to the desired digital frequency, ω_d, and then the "incorrect" analog version is calculated with the standard pre-warping Equation (12.4).

$$\omega_a = \frac{2}{T}\tan\left[\frac{\omega_d T}{2}\right] \quad T = \frac{1}{f_s} \tag{12.4}$$

Figure 12.3(b) combines the series multipliers into one value, $g = \omega_a T/2$, and ignores the details of the delay structure. Figure 12.3(c) takes this one step further and simplifies the whole feed-forward structure into a block with *input, output, g* and *s* values. This notation will be used throughout the chapter. At this point, everything is in place, but we still have to deal with the delay-free loop.

12.5 Resolving Delay-Free Loops in VA Structures

The underlying issue with delay-free feedback loops is that you wind up with equations that look like (12.4), where the discrete output $y(n)$ appears on both sides of the equation, implying that you

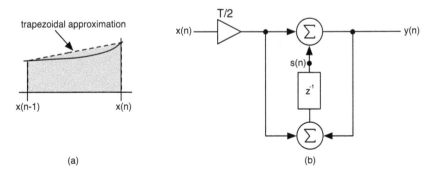

(a) (b)

Figure 12.2 (a) The bilinear (trapezoidal) approximation of the area under a curve, showing the error portion between the dotted line and the curve, and (b) transposed canonical form of the bilinear integrator

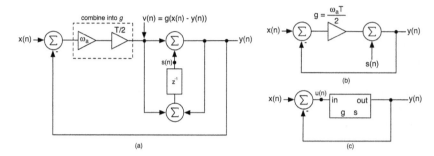

Figure 12.3 (a) The analog integrator is replaced with a digital bilinear integrator (b) a shorthand version
after combining the two input multipliers into one, and ignoring the exact details of the bilinear
structure and (c) simplified notation showing a block with input, output, *g*, and *s* ports

need the current output value in order to calculate the current output value. Prior to the late 1990s,
you had to place a z^{-1} storage register in the loop to prevent feedback loop dependence, but this
would alter the transfer function of the structure.

12.5.1 Zavalishin's Algebraic Method

Consider the structure in Figure 12.3(c), where the input to the shorthand block has been labeled
$u(n)$ (commonly used in signals and systems theory). Tracing the signal, you can write (12.5), which
places $y(n)$ on both sides of the equal sign.

$$u(n) = x(n) - y(n)$$
$$y(n) = gu(n) + s(n)$$
$$= g(x(n) - y(n)) + s(n)$$
(12.5)

Zavalishin's technique requires you to make somewhat of a leap of faith regarding the difference
equation in (12.4) – ignore the independent variable *n*, which results from the discretization of the
signal, and treat the equation as instantaneous. This results in Equation (12.6).

$$y = g(x - y) + s$$
$$y = \frac{gx + s}{1 + g} = \frac{g}{1 + g}x + \frac{s}{1 + g}$$
$$y = Gx + S$$
(12.6)
$$G = \frac{g}{1 + g} \quad S = \frac{s}{1 + g}$$

At this point, you let $G = g/(1 + g)$ and $S = s/(1 + g)$, which shoehorns the equation into the format
$y = Gx + S$, which follows the idea of separating the difference equation into input and storage
parts. Now, refer to Figure 12.3(a), and look at the node marked $v(n) = g(x(n) - y(n))$. Ignoring the
discrete time variable *n*, you get $v = g(x - y)$. Now, substituting Equation (12.5) as the *y* component,
you can write:

$$v = g(x - y) = g\left[x - \frac{g}{1+g}x - \frac{1}{1+g}s \right] = g\left[x\frac{1+g}{1+g} - \frac{g}{1+g}x - \frac{1}{1+g}s \right]$$

$$= g\left[\frac{x + gx - gx - s}{1+g} \right] = \frac{g}{1+g}(x - s)$$

$$= G(x - s)$$

(12.7)

Now, by observation, you resolve the delay-free loop. This is accomplished with two steps:

1   Change the input coefficient multiplier to $G = g/1 + g$, and note that this is the same as cascading the original g coefficient with another $1/1 + g$ coefficient
2   Relocate the original feedback loop from the output to the $s(n)$ location

Both steps are shown in Figure 12.4, where 12.4(a) shows the setup with $v(n)$, and 12.4(b) relocates the delay loop and merges the coefficients into one G value. When you use Zavalishin's method, these will always be true – the loop coefficient gain multiplier will be merged with another factor (g becomes G), and the loop source will be relocated from the output to a storage location, where $s(n)$ is the output of a pure delay network.

12.5.2 Modified Härmä Method

My loop resolution method is called the Modified Härmä (MH) method because it is based on Härmä's original design, which resolved one specific type of delay-free loop where the processing is in the feedback path, and the feed-forward path consists only of non-storage components. The MH method extends that theory to resolve any kind of delay-free loop. You can find the derivation that does not require ignoring the discrete time variable n and that uses a familiar infinite series in Pirkle (2014). The methodology is also different – instead of algebra, you stimulate the loop by injecting two values (0.0 and 1.0) into it under specific conditions and tabulating the results. Next, you use a universal difference equation template and plug in the values – the loop can then be resolved by inspection. The MH method requires five steps. The first three involve stimulating the loop to find three values:

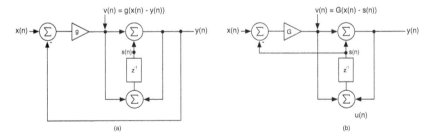

Figure 12.4 (a) The delay-free loops structure with $v(n)$ labeled and (b) the resolved loop done by examination of Equation (12.7)

1   $u_o(n)$ = the temporary loop input value
2   $y_o(n)$ = the temporary loop output value
3   X = the loop gain without any delay (storage) elements in place
4   The fourth step is to plug these values into the delay-free resolved difference equation for a single loop system; this is the result of the derivation of the method and is covered in the source.

$$y(n) = y_o(n)\frac{1}{1-X} \tag{12.8}$$

5   The last step is to find $u_o(n)$ for the filter implementation to see how the new difference equation will alter the structure – it is here that you will be able to relocate the loop and modify the loop coefficient by inspection. You can then prove to yourself that the difference equation implements the new structure.

Figure 12.5 shows the MH method's first three steps for a system consisting of a single loop, with the processing block in the feedback path. With these values and Equation (12.8), you can easily write the difference equation:

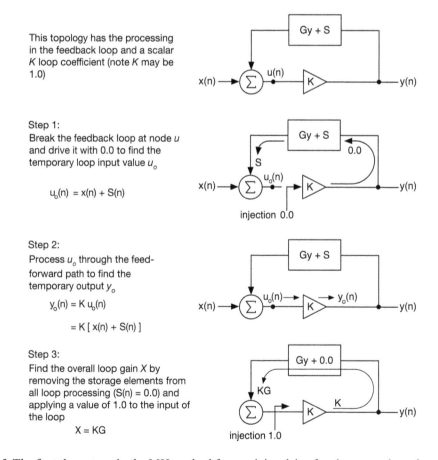

This topology has the processing in the feedback loop and a scalar K loop coefficient (note K may be 1.0)

Step 1:
Break the feedback loop at node u and drive it with 0.0 to find the temporary loop input value u_o

$u_o(n) = x(n) + S(n)$

Step 2:
Process u_o through the feedforward path to find the temporary output y_o

$y_o(n) = K u_o(n)$

$= K[x(n) + S(n)]$

Step 3:
Find the overall loop gain X by removing the storage elements from all loop processing ($S(n) = 0.0$) and applying a value of 1.0 to the input of the loop

$X = KG$

Figure 12.5 The first three steps in the MH method for resolving delay-free loops produce the values $u_o(n)$, $y_o(n)$, and loop gain X

$$y(n) = y_o(n) \frac{1}{1-X}$$
$$= \frac{K[x(n)+S(n)]}{1-KG}$$

(12.9)

For the final step, find the exact value for $u_o(n)$ – this will vary depending on the loop structure. Notice that the operations are the same as those in Zavalishin's algebraic method: the loop is re-located from the output $y(n)$ to a storage location $S(n)$, and the loop coefficient is augmented with another series multiplier.

$$u_o(n) = x(n)+Gy_o(n)+S$$
and
$$y_o(n) = Ku_o(n)$$
therefore
$$u_o(n) = x(n)+GKu_o(n)+S$$
$$u_o(n) = \frac{x(n)+S}{1-KG}$$

(12.10)

Now you can inspect (12.8) and (12.9), and set up the final structure shown in Figure 12.6. Notice that the output of the loop-processing block seems to go nowhere – this is correct as the output value is not applied anywhere else. In fact, you don't need to calculate the output value in this case as the loop is dependent on the $S(n)$ value.

For completion, in multiple loop systems, the generalized difference equation solution is shown in Equation (12.11).

$$y(n) = \frac{1}{1-X}\left[f(u(n)) + \sum_{i=1}^{M} \beta_i s_i \right]$$

$f(u(n)) =$ the processing functon in the feed-forward path
            or $x(n)$ if no function in path

(12.11)

$M =$ the number of delay elements in the structure
$X =$ the loop gain coefficient
$s_i =$ the output of delay element i
$\beta_i =$ the feedback multiplier for delay element i

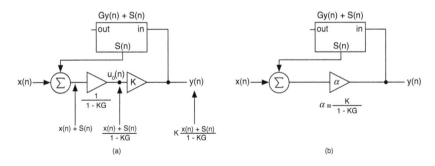

Figure 12.6 (a) The final structure after loop resolution and (b) combining the series loop coefficients into a single value α

12.6 VA Filters from Primitive Analog Block Diagrams

The simplest VA filters are derived from first and second order primitive analog filter block diagrams. Primitive means that the diagrams consist only of summers, multipliers, and integrators, with no higher-level structures embedded.

12.6.1 First Order VA Filters

Figure 12.7(a)–(c) shows the analog filter block diagrams and virtual analog realizations for the three basic first order filters: LPF, HPF, and APF. In all cases, the single coefficient α is calculated the same, using Equation (12.5). Converting this to C++ code, we can write the update calculation for α (note that the calculation for *wa* and *g* may be combined and simplified a bit).

```
double wd = 2*pi*Fc;
double T = 1/SampleRate;
double wa = (2/T)*tan(wd*T/2);
double g = wa*T/2;   // <--- i.e. g = tan(wd*T/2)

// --- final calculation
double alpha = g/(1.0 + g);
```

These three filters may be combined into a single structure that implements all of them at once as they are based on the same core structure, and we only need to resolve that delay-free loop once. We will use this kind of structure for the Korg35 filters.

12.6.1.1 First Order LPF Analog FGN

I modified this algorithm to produce better analog matching gain at Nyquist using the Korg35 sub-circuit in Figure 12.9(c). The method involves blending in some of the HPF response, whose gain at Nyquist is fixed at 1.0. It turns out that for this design, the alpha coefficient may be used directly as a scaling factor, albeit with a bit of magnitude matching error. Figure 12.7(d) shows the normal VA LPF frequency response, with the Nyquist magnitude pinned down to 0.0, while 12.7(e) shows the matched-analog response, with finite gain at Nyquist. Figure 12.7(f) and (g) shows the HPF frequency and APF phase responses.

12.6.2 Second Order State Variable Filter

For filters higher than first order, there will almost always be multiple analog circuit realizations and varying block diagram implementations. The well-documented State Variable Filter (SVF), also known as the Kerwin-Huelsman-Newcomb (KHN) filter after its inventors, is a second order structure that produces all four basic filters at once: LPF, HPF, BPF, and BSF. Figure 12.8(a) shows the analog block diagram that consists of two synchronously tuned integrators inside of two delay-free loops, an inner loop, and an outer loop. Figure 12.8(b) shows Zavalishin's VA realization. Notice that the analog block diagram references ζ, the damping factor in classical analog filter theory, but in musical applications, we prefer to replace it with the term Q, which stands for quality factor, where:

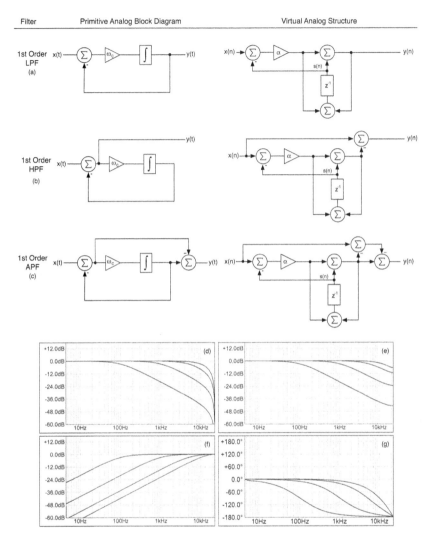

Figure 12.7 Primitive analog block diagrams and their resulting VA filter structures for (a) first order low-pass filter, (b) first order high-pass filter, and (c) first order all-pass filter (d) the normal first order BZT LPF frequency response with zero gain at Nyquist (e) analog FGN LPF frequency response (f) first order HPF frequency response and (g) first order APF phase response; all plots are shown with f_c = 100 Hz, 1 kHz, 5 kHz, and 10 kHz

$$Q = \frac{1}{2\zeta} \tag{12.12}$$

You can see that the bandpass output is fed back into the input summer via the scaling coefficient $2\zeta = 1$, so the more feedback, the lower the resonant peak. Notice the relocation of the delay-free loops to storage locations $s_1(n)$ and $s_2(n)$, and the addition of the α_o coefficient in series with the input loop gain value α. The design equations and output calculations are given in Equation block (12.13) (Zavalishin 2008). After updating the coefficients, you calculate the individual outputs in succession, starting with y_{HP}.

$$\omega_d = 2\pi f_c$$
$$T = 1/f_s$$
$$\omega_a = \frac{2}{T}\tan\left(\frac{\omega_d T}{2}\right)$$

$$\alpha = \frac{\omega_a T}{2} = \tan\left(\frac{\omega_d T}{2}\right) \qquad y_{HP}(n) = \alpha_0\left(x(n) - \beta_1 s_1(n) - \beta_2 s_2(n)\right) \qquad (12.13)$$

$$R = \frac{1}{2Q} \qquad\qquad y_{BP}(n) = \alpha_1 y_{HP}(n) + s_1(n)$$

$$\alpha_0 = \frac{1}{1 + 2R\alpha + \alpha^2} \qquad y_{LP}(n) = \alpha_1 y_{BP}(n) + s_2(n)$$

$$\rho = 2R + \alpha \qquad\qquad y_{BS}(n) = x(n) - 2R y_{BP}(n)$$

12.6.2.1 SVF Analog FGN

As with the first order filters, the SVF LPF also includes an erroneous zero at Nyquist, which is a result of the bilinear transform. In order to correct the gain at Nyquist, I observed that the value residing in the first integrator's state register, labeled $s_1(n)$ in Figure 12.8, is actually a mixture of the current bandpass output plus the high-pass output scaled by α. We can take advantage of the fact that the HPF gain at Nyquist is easily calculated (and mostly equals 1.0 except for very high combinations of f_c and Q). I used a similar method of blending in this "correction" signal knowing the values of α and the desired gain at Nyquist. This works very well up until just before Nyquist, where we observe a small high frequency magnitude offset due to the fact that the internal HP-F+BPF signal has the same value of Q applied to it. The Nyquist gain still matches the analog version, and the filter is still stable right up to f_c = Nyquist. To calculate the analog matching coefficient σ in Figure 12.8, I use Equation (12.13), evaluating the analog matching transfer functions at f = Nyquist. The equations for M_{LPF} and M_{HPF} are the standard equations to calculate the magnitude of the analog filter $H(s)$ for second order LPF and HPF, respectively. In our ratio, their denominators cancel each other out, so we are left with a relatively simple coefficient equation to calculate. Figure 12.8(c) and (d) shows the normal and analog matched LPF outputs, while Figure 12.8(e) and (f) shows the SVF HPF and BPF outputs at a variety of f_c and Q settings.

$$f_o = \frac{f}{f_c} \qquad\qquad\qquad \zeta = \frac{1}{2Q}$$

$$M_{LPF} = |H(s)_{LPF}| = \frac{1}{\sqrt{\left(1 - f_o^2\right)^2 + 4\zeta^2 f_o^2}} \qquad M_{HPF} = |H(s)_{HPF}| = \frac{f_o^2}{\sqrt{\left(1 - f_o^2\right)^2 + 4\zeta^2 f_o^2}} \qquad (12.14)$$

$$\sigma = \left.\frac{M_{LPF}}{\alpha M_{HPF}}\right|_{f = Nyquist} = \frac{1}{\alpha f_o^2}$$

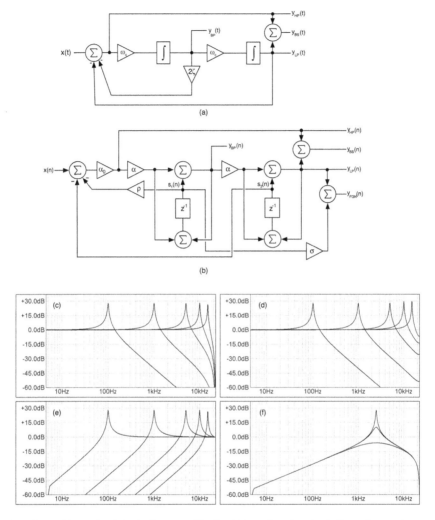

Figure 12.8 (a) The SVF analog block diagram (b) the VA realization including the analog matched LPF output $y_{LPM}(n)$ (c) normal SVF LPF frequency response and (d) LPF frequency response with analog matching at Nyquist (e) SVF HPF frequency response with f_c = 100 Hz, 1 kHz, 5 kHz, 10 kHz and 15 kHz and Q = 25 and (f) SVF BPF frequency response with f_c = 2.5 kHz and Q = 0.5, 10 and 25

12.7 VA Filters from Signal Flow Graphs

Signal flow graphs may be used as a shorthand method for notating primitive analog block diagrams. However, they excel when used to diagram more complex block algorithms consisting of series or parallel branches of sub-filters. These high-level signal flow graphs also describe summers and coefficients, but the integrators are replaced with filters: *LPF1* and *HPF1* for first order lowpass and high-pass filters, respectively. Higher order sub-filter blocks are equally possible. For these designs, each first order building block is implemented as a VA filter, then these are connected together, often involving delay-free loops around the sub-filters. The delay-free loop resolution methods still work as usual, with the sub-filters replaced with an equation that is always broken into the current input and storage components, or $y(n) = Gx(n) + S(n)$.

12.7.1 Korg35 Second Order Filters

Korg35 second order resonant filters used in the MS-10 and early MS-20 are voltage controlled versions of the Sallen-Key filter topology. Sallen-Key filters feature a positive feedback path through a narrow bandpass filter that reinforces the resonant frequency and eventually allows the filter to self-oscillate. Korg took advantage of this to produce a simple but effective highly resonant filter. Both LPF and HPF are second order types and will self-oscillate, but the Korg35 HPF has an interesting quirk; its roll-off slope is +6 dB/octave instead of the normal +12 dB/octave. This produces an HPF with more bass response. The non-standard roll-off is due to the manner in which Korg implemented the HPF, using an analog filter shortcut – take any analog filter circuit, ground the input, then lift and drive the ground connections to produce the complementary version with the same f_c and Q values.

I designed the Korg35 filters directly from their signal flow graphs, as shown in Figure 12.9(a) and (b). These filters are made of first order sub-filters that are synchronously tuned, meaning they share the same f_c value. The complete derivation is available at www.willpirkle.com/synth-book-derivations/. The Sallen-Key filter has two analog implementations that differ only in terms of the maximum loop gain K that creates the self-oscillation; these use $K = 2.0$. During the derivation, a new variable (β) was needed to act as a feedback scalar once the delay-free loops were resolved. This created the structure in Figure 12.9(c) that is used for each of the VA sub-filters; this filter can generate LPF and/or HPF outputs, and includes the new feedback coefficient. Notice that the loop resolution also generated the loop coefficient α_o as usual. The design of Equation (12.15) is straightforward; the α_N coefficients are the same for all filters, and only sub-filters 2 and 3 need a β coefficient, which is different from LPF to HPF. Figure 12.9(d) shows the normal LPF and HPF responses with their different roll-off slopes.

$$g = \tan\left(\frac{\omega_d T}{2}\right) \quad \alpha = \frac{g}{1+g} \quad \alpha_o = \frac{1}{1 - K\alpha + K\alpha^2}$$

$$\text{Korg35 LPF:} \quad \beta_2 = K\frac{(1-\alpha)}{(1+g)} \quad \beta_3 = \frac{-1}{(1+g)} \quad\quad (12.15)$$

$$\text{Korg35 HPF:} \quad \beta_2 = \frac{-\alpha}{(1+g)} \quad \beta_3 = \frac{1}{(1+g)}$$

12.7.1.1 Korg35 Analog FGN

I modified the Korg35 LPF for finite gain at Nyquist to try to match the true analog response more closely. The first order VA module shown in Figure 12.9(c) includes the analog FGN matching described in Section 12.3 and generates all three outputs at once. For the Korg35 LPF, I use the analog FGN output for the *VA1 LPF*. For the *VA2 LPF*, the normal (BZT) LPF output is used to supply the feedback loop, and the analog Nyquist matched output is routed to the filter output. Figure 12.9(e) shows the new version with finite gain at Nyquist. As with the SVF, there is a slight boost at the very highest f_c settings, and the filters are stable right up to f_c = Nyquist.

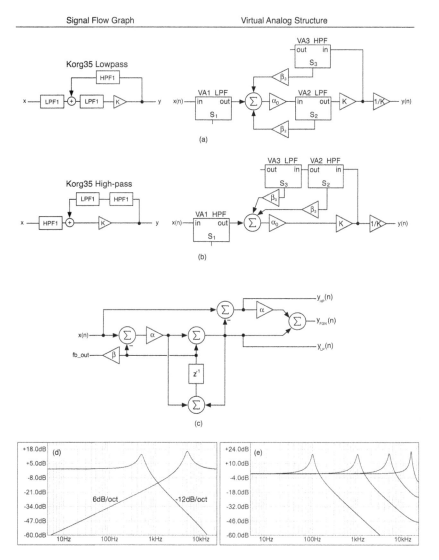

Figure 12.9 The signal flow graph and VA realizations for (a) Korg35 LPF, (b) Korg35 HPF and (c) the combined structure that is used for each of the Korg35 sub-filters (d) the LPF and HPF frequency responses show differences in the roll-off slopes with LPF f_c = 500 Hz and HPF f_c = 5 kHz and (e) the Korg35 LPF frequency response with analog Nyquist matching and f_c = 100 Hz, 1 kHz, 5 kHz and 15 kHz with K = 1.9

12.7.2 *Moog Fourth Order Ladder Filter*

Robert Moog invented a filter that became known as the Moog ladder filter; this might be the most celebrated, copied, and tweaked of any manufacturer's filters. Several integrated circuit companies made variations on this design, including the Curtis CEM3328, CEM3372, and Precision Monolithics PMI SSM2044. They optimized, modified, tweaked, and extended the design. The devices were used in countless synthesizers from nearly every company in the 1970s and 1980s. A unique feature of this filter is that changes in resonance create changes in the overall filter gain; as the Q increases, the filter gain drops, as shown in Figure 12.10(b). In addition, you can see that the resonant (peak) frequency also increases as Q increases. The roll-off slope is 24 dB/octave as a fourth order filter.

The Moog ladder filter consists of a cascade of four first order synchronously tuned LPF stages in a global negative feedback loop, as shown in Figure 12.10(a). Putting four first order LPFs in series creates a fourth order filter, but it won't be resonant. The way this filter implements resonance is based on the phase response of each first order section. The phase shift at the cutoff frequency is −45 degrees for a first order LPF stage. Each successive stage then adds another −45 degrees of phase shift. After going through four of these filters, the phase shift at f_c will be −180 degrees, exactly out of phase with the input. This output is fed back into the input through a negative scalar, $-K$, which flips the phase at the cutoff so it is back in-phase with the input. This amplifies the cutoff frequency along with the frequencies that are very close to it resulting in a resonant peak. If $K = 0$ there is no feedback and no resonance. As soon as K becomes non-zero, the Q increases, and peaking occurs. When $K = 4$, we achieve 100% feedback through the loop, and the filter will self-oscillate.

The loss of low frequency gain as the Q is increased is sometimes considered problematic, especially if the filter is being used on a bass instrument. However, the reduction in gain also prevents the filter from overloading and may be part of the device's lore as a "musical filter." Curtis Electromusic Specialists (the same company that made the CEM3328) provided a way of controlling the loss of gain all the way up to no loss at all by designing this feature into one of their ICs in 1984. The gain is compensated by feeding some of the inverted input signal into a summer prior to the gain element $-K$. The doubly inverted (in-phase) signal works against

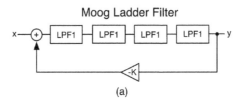

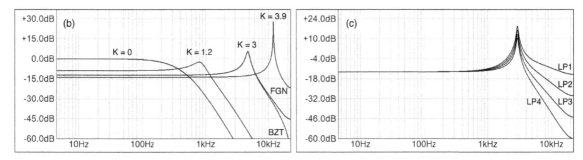

Figure 12.10 The Moog ladder filter (a) signal flow block diagram (b) notice how the bass response is reduced as the Q is increased shown with f_c = 100 Hz, 1 kHz, 5 kHz and 15 kHz each with increasing Q (K) value; the BZT and analog FGN curves are shown for $K = 3$, and for $K = 3.9$ the analog FGN response is indicated (c) the modified additional outputs generate three more filter types including a resonant first order variety

the inverted signal in the feedback path. The filter in the ARP2600 is also a Moog ladder filter derivative that incorporates gain compensation. Zavalishin proposed simply boosting the input x by a factor of $1 + K$, an elegant and simple modification. A variable version can then be implemented by making the boost factor $1 + aK$ where a is on the range of 0.0 to 1.0, as shown in Figure 12.11(a).

Figure 12.11(a) shows the final VA realization after the delay-free loop has been resolved; the complete derivation is available at www.willpirkle.com/synth-book-derivations/. Here, the single feedback loop becomes four parallel loops, each originating from one of the storage registers in the sub-filters, and the familiar loop gain coefficient appears at the input to the first filter. Note that the input scaling and extra outputs are optional. The Moog ladder filter block diagram is ripe for hacking. One easy addition is to tap off of the output of each of the series LPFs, which produces three more outputs for first order, second order, and third order versions of the filter. The first order filter also includes a resonant peak, and the frequency responses are shown in Figure 12.10(c). See the exercises for more hacks. The design equations for the Moog ladder filter are in Equation block (12.16). Note that all sub-filters share the same α coefficient value. The β coefficients are subscripted with the sub-filter number.

$$g = \tan\left(\frac{\omega_d T}{2}\right) \quad \alpha = \frac{g}{1+g} \quad \alpha_o = \frac{1}{1+K\alpha^4}$$

$$\beta_1 = \frac{\alpha^3}{1+g} \quad \beta_2 = \frac{\alpha^2}{1+g} \quad \beta_3 = \frac{\alpha}{1+g} \quad \beta_4 = \frac{1}{1+g}$$

$$(12.16)$$

12.7.2.1 *Moog Filter Analog FGN*

The Moog ladder may also be experimentally modified for finite gain at Nyquist, though it requires four more filters that run in a parallel branch with the main set, as shown in Figure 12.11(b). The reason that I cannot simply place the series filters in analog Nyquist matched mode is that this alters the phase response in a nonlinear manner across f_c values and destroys the feedback loop's behavior. A somewhat brute force method is to add the four analog Nyquist matched filters and use their outputs but keep the existing signal path that generates the proper phase response for the feedback loop. All of the filters are sync-tuned, so there is only one calculation of the α coefficient; the filters are also very CPU-friendly, so there is not much added overhead. The new version produces the finite gain at Nyquist which you can see in Figure 12.10(b) and (c). As with the others, the filter is stable right up to f_c = Nyquist. The filters in the upper row do not have the S-ports connected to anything.

12.7.3 *VCS3 Diode Ladder Filter*

The Diode Ladder Filter first appeared in the EMS VCS3 monophonic synth designed by David Cockerell in 1969. It is also incorporated into the 1982 Roland TB-303 monophonic bass synth. In 1974, Steiner presented another resonant lowpass filter using diodes, but it implemented the Sallen-Key topology. In 1977, Yamaha patented the ring-diode method of implementing a voltage controlled filter in another Sallen-Key topology, and Korg used yet another Sallen-Key ring-diode variation in numerous synths, including the S700. These ring-diode networks are unrelated to the diode ladder filter in this section.

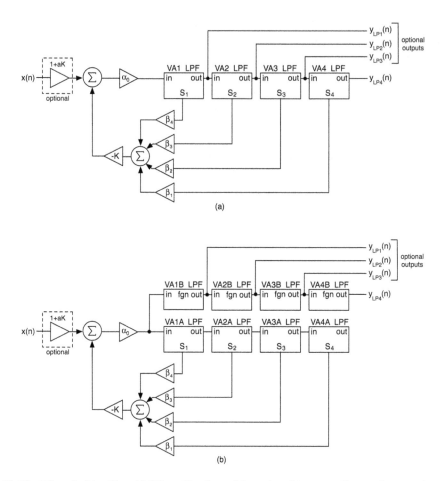

Figure 12.11 The Moog ladder filter (a) VA realization with optional input scaling and output branches, and (b) the analog FGN version; note that the β coefficients are contained in each sub-filter but shown externally here to convey their operation in the feedback loop

This diode ladder filter is based on the Moog ladder filter topology but uses diodes rather than transistors as voltage controlled elements and incorporates multiple feedback paths between sections. The effect of the feedback paths on the signal is two-fold: like the Moog filter, it reduces overall gain as the resonance increases, but the reduction is more extreme (by about 12 dB); second, as the resonance increases, the resonant frequency migrates upwards but never makes it to the cutoff point. At the point of self-oscillation, the resonant peak will have drifted up to $0.707f_c$, and the resonant frequency is never truly correct and equal to the f_c used in the calculations. Figure 12.12(a) shows the signal flow block diagram, which includes three inner delay-free feedback loops as well as the main outer loop with the $-K$ feedback value. Figure 12.12(b) shows how the gain changes more drastically than the Moog ladder filter as the loop gain K is varied. In this filter, K ranges from 0 to 17, at which self-oscillation occurs, and the filter gain is reduced by -24 dB.

There are numerous similarities to the Moog version: four synchronously tuned first order LPFs in series embedded in a global feedback loop that creates positive feedback only at the cutoff

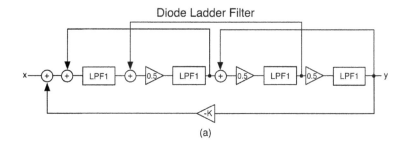

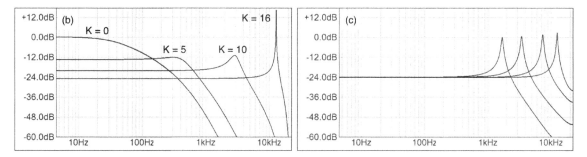

Figure 12.12 The diode ladder filter's (a) signal flow block diagram, and (b) notice how the bass response is reduced as the Q is increased shown with $f_c = 500$ Hz, 1 kHz, 5 kHz and 15 kHz each with increasing Q (K) value and (c) the experimental analog FGN output at $f_c = 2.5$ kHz, 5 kHz, 10 kHz and 15 kHz; the error in the resonant peak frequency is normal and correct for this filter

frequency. As soon as K becomes non-zero, the Q increases, and peaking occurs. However, the diode ladder incorporates multiple feedback loops around each section (LPF2 feeds back into LPF1, LPF3 feeds back into LPF2, LPF4 feeds back into LPF3), as shown in Figure 12.13(a). This is a topology known as *leap-frog-form* (LFF). In addition to the feedback paths, there are also attenuators on the inputs to the last three LPFs. Due to the complex interactions of the multiple feedback paths, the filter analysis and synthesis of the block diagram is much more difficult than any of the filters in this chapter. The full derivation is available at www.willpirkle.com/synth-book-derivations/. The crossed feedback paths necessitate adding new local feedback input and output ports to the basic VA LPF, as shown in Figure 12.13(a). Figure 12.13(b) shows the final realization after the delay-free loops have been resolved, and the inner loops have been relocated to and from storage units in each feedback pair.

The design equations for the diode loop coefficients and the coefficients for each sub-filter are given in Equations (12.17) and (12.18).

$$g = \tan\left(\frac{\omega_d T}{2}\right)$$

$$G_1 = \frac{0.5g}{1+g} \qquad G_2 = \frac{0.5g}{1+g-0.5gG_4} \qquad G_3 = \frac{0.5g}{1+g-0.5gG_3} \qquad G_4 = \frac{g}{1+g-gG_2} \qquad (12.17)$$

$$\beta_1 = G_4G_3G_2 \qquad \beta_2 = G_4G_3 \qquad \beta_3 = G_4 \qquad \beta_4 = 1$$

$$\alpha_o = \frac{1}{1+KG_4G_3G_2G_1}$$

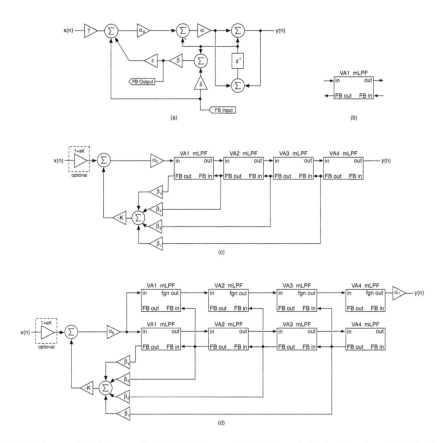

Figure 12.13 (a) The modified first order VA LPF (named mLPF) and (b) its shorthand block diagram with arrows showing the signal flow directions (c) the diode ladder filter realization and (d) the experimental analog FGN version with added α_1 coefficient at the output; note that the β coefficients are calculated within each sub-filter but are shown externally here to convey their operation in the feedback loop

	Filter 1	Filter 2	Filter 3	Filter 4
α_o	1	0.5	0.5	0.5
α	$\dfrac{g}{1+g}$	$\dfrac{g}{1+g}$	$\dfrac{g}{1+g}$	$\dfrac{g}{1+g}$
β	$\dfrac{1}{1+g-gG_2}$	$\dfrac{1}{1+g-0.5gG_3}$	$\dfrac{1}{1+g-0.5gG_4}$	$\dfrac{1}{1+g}$
γ	$1+G_1G_2$	$1+G_2G_3$	$1+G_3G_4$	1
δ	g	$0.5g$	$0.5g$	0
ε	G_2	G_3	G_4	0

$$(12.18)$$

12.7.3.1 Diode Filter Analog FGN

The diode ladder may also be experimentally modified in a similar brute-force manner as the Moog filter for finite gain at Nyquist, as shown in Figure 12.12(c). I cannot simply place the series filters in analog Nyquist matched mode because this alters the phase response in a nonlinear manner across f_c values and destroys the feedback loop's behavior. Once again, all of the filters are sync-tuned, so there is only one calculation of the α coefficient, and the filters are very CPU-friendly, so there is not much added overhead. As with the others, the filter is stable right up to f_c = Nyquist. Each filter in the upper row gets its local feedback input from the lower row of normal VA filters. As with the Moog ladder analog FGN version, the global feedback loop is taken only from the lower row of VA filters to maintain the proper phase relationship for resonance control. The analog FGN filter requires an additional gain equalizer coefficient, α_1, that is calculated to fit the measured gain as f_c varies, as given in Equation (12.19).

$$a = 1.005381 \qquad b = 0.8783896 \qquad c = 01.113067 \qquad d = -0.2110344$$

$$f = \frac{2\pi f_c}{f_s} \qquad e = \left(\frac{f}{c}\right)^b \qquad \alpha_1 = d + \frac{a-d}{1+e} \tag{12.19}$$

12.8 VA Filters from Conceptual Signal Flow Graphs

I have also created VA filters from conceptual signal flow graphs of filters that do not have an analog closed-form transfer function and even violate some classical analog filter design paradigms. This yields some bizarre results, including filters with the resonant frequency f_r and the cutoff frequency f_c, decoupled and controlled independently, allowing you to move the resonant peak anywhere you like in the response, regardless of the f_c setting, as shown for the second order LPF in Figure 12.14(a). In addition, I've developed strange filters, such as the resonant first shelving filters shown in Figure 12.14(b), and filters with multiple resonant peaks, each independently controllable, as in Figure 12.14(c) and (d). You can find the descriptions and algorithms at https://www.willpirkle.com/novel-hybrid-filters.

12.9 Nonlinear Processing and Self-Oscillation Control

All of the VA filters include the ability for nonlinear processing (NLP), and there are numerous locations within the filter structures to place nonlinear waveshapers. In some cases, the nonlinearities are placed to model nonlinearities in the circuit components: for example, the analog Moog filter is nonlinear in nature due to the way in which the transistor ladder differential pairs conduct current. The differential voltage and current are related by the hyperbolic tangent function. In other cases, the nonlinearities are due to clipping circuits placed inside the filters to try to limit the ultra-high gain that comes from high resonance settings. The nonlinear processors, all of which are based on soft-clip circuits, also aid in taming the harsh clipping that may result from self-oscillation when the filter is driven with program material that has large amounts of energy near the resonant frequency. There are a few strategies for the placement of the NLP, which is often done with *tanh()* waveshapers. Care must be taken to ensure that the waveshapers have a unity-gain or less amplification factor so they do not disrupt the gain in the sensitive feedback loops we have designed.

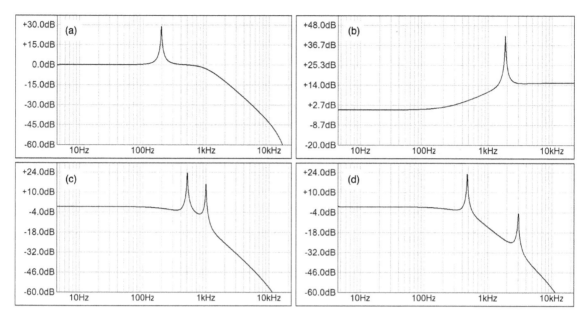

Figure 12.14 Novel VA filters contrived from conceptual signal flow graphs, including (a) second order LPF with f_r = 500 Hz and f_c = 1 kHz, (b) resonant first order high shelving filter with $f_c = f_r$ = 2 kHz and a doubly-resonant LPF with f_c = 500 Hz, (c) f_r = 1 kHz, and (d) f_r = 3 kHz

Figure 12.15(a) shows a saturating integrator (Zavalishin 2008) with a waveshaper in the feedback loop. This saturating integrator may be placed into any of the models as a non-linear filter. For the Korg35 filters, you might also experiment with placing the NLP in the feed-forward path of the overall loop, as shown in Figure 12.15(b). Both ladder filters include numerous nonlinearities within each filter and within the entire feedback loop. Zavaliahin's budget version is shown in Figure 12.15(c), with a single NLP block at the input and outside of the feedback loop.

12.9.1 NLP with Soft-Knee Peak Limiter

A fundamental issue with any kind of NLP is the addition of aliased components to the signal, which need to be mitigated with oversampling. However, for taming the self-oscillation distortion, it works quite well. After several years of experimentation, I found a solution to producing pure sinusoids during self-oscillation and avoiding distortion using a soft-knee peak limiter with the threshold set between −0.5 dBFS and −1.0 dBFS, as shown in Figure 12.15(d) on the output of the Moog ladder filter. This method is implemented for all of the SynthLab filters; you may, of course, disable the limiters if you like. In order to produce smooth distortion, you move the threshold from nearly the topmost value (0.0 dBFS) to a much lower value, then increase the limiter's makeup gain to bring the signal up to the nominal level – the soft knee and low threshold will produce rounded, soft-clipped waveforms.

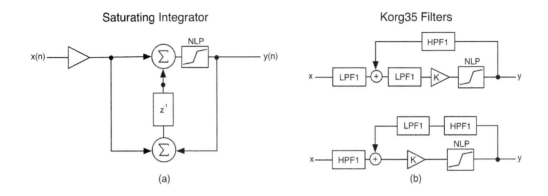

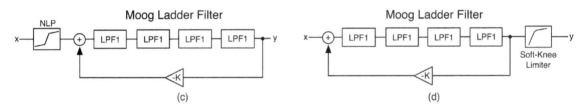

Figure 12.15 Nonlinear blocks in the VA structures shown inside (a) the saturating integrator, (b) the Korg35, and (c) Moog signal flow block diagrams, while (d) shows the location of the peak limiter on the filter output, always outside of any feedback loop

12.10 Synth Filter Objects

The SynthLab *VAFilterCore* object implements all of the filters discussed in this chapter. In order to simplify the object, I created smaller C++ objects for each filter.

1 *VA1Filter*: first order LPF, HPF, APF, and LPF with analog FGN
2 *VASVFilter*: state variable filter with second order LPF, HPF, BPF, BSF, and LPF with analog FGN
3 *VAKorg35Filter*: second order *Korg35* LPF and HPF (including HPF's 6 dB/octave roll-off)
4 *VAMoogFilter*: fourth order Moog LPF; normal and analog FGN; and the first, second, and third order LPF variations
5 *VADiodeSubFilter*: modified *VA1Filter* structure that includes the additional diode specific coefficients
6 *VADiodeFilter*: fourth order diode LPF and analog FGN

These all inherit from *IFilterBase* and do not implement shared parameter pointers as they are used as embedded sub-filter objects. *IFilterBase* requires the implementation of only four functions. The filters include outputs for all types in Table 12.1 and are written into a filter output data structure.

The *VA1Filter* and *VADiodeSubFilter* objects are used as sub-filters in the Korg, Moog, and diode filters, which are always synchronously tuned with identical α coefficients that require the *tan* function call but in general will have different β coefficients. Therefore, these filters include added functions to allow the container filter to set the coefficients directly, bypassing the costly *update* function for improved efficiency. Additionally, these filters need to provide access to their *s(n)* values for the container object to manipulate in its feedback loop. The *VA1Filter* includes these additional functions; note that *beta* is applied during the *getFBOutput* method for the Korg35 and Moog filters.

```
// --- set coeffs directly, bypassing coeff calculation
void setBeta(double _ beta);
void setAlpha(double _ alpha);
```

```
// --- added for MOOG & K35, need access to this output value
double getFBOutput();
```

The *VADiodeSubFilter* requires many more coefficients that are packaged in the *DiodeVA1Coefficients* structure. It also requires access into and out of the feedback portion, so it includes these additional methods; compare the code with Figure 12.12(a).

```
void setFilterCoeffs(const DiodeVA1Coeffs& _ coeffs);
```

```
void setFBInput(double _ feedbackIn) { feedbackIn = _ feedbackIn; }
```

```
double getFBOutput() {
     return coeffs.beta * (sn + feedbackIn*coeffs.delta); }
```

Table 12.1 shows the second order and higher VA filters, and their required *VA1Filter* sub-filters, which are stored in small arrays on the container object. The filter indexes are named according to the model, block diagram, and equations, so you can easily link the parts for study.

12.10.1 Sub-Filter Operation

The coefficient calculation starts with a function call to *setFilterParams*, which checks the incoming values and, if different, saves them and calls *update*. For filters with a Q control, you need to

Table 12.1 High order VA filters and their sub-filter types and arrays

Filter	VA1Filter Sub-filter Types	Array Name
VASVFilter	none, see model	n/a
VAKorg35 LPF	Filter1: LPF1 Filter2: LPF1 Filter3: HPF1	*lpfVAFilters[KORG_SUBFILTERS]*
VAKorg35 HPF	Filter1: HPF1 Filter2: HPF1 Filter3: LPF1	*hpfVAFilters[KORG_SUBFILTERS]*
VAMoogFilter	Filter1 = Filter2 = Filter3 = Filter4: LPF1	*subFilter[MOOG_SUBFILTERS];*
VADiodeFilter	Filter1 = Filter2 = Filter3 = Filter4: LPF1	*subFilter[DIODE_SUBFILTERS];*

map the incoming value on the range [1, 10] to the range of *K* values such that *Q* = 10 produces self-oscillation. This is accomplished with the *mapDoubleValue* function. For example, in the Korg35 filter, the *K* value goes from 0.01 to 2.0 as *Q* is increased from 1.0 to 10.0.

```
void VAKorg35Filter::setFilterParams(double _fc, double _Q)
{
    // --- use mapping function for Q -> K
    mapDoubleValue(_Q, 1.0, 10.0, 0.01, 2.0);

    if (fc != _fc || K != _Q)
    {
        fc = _fc;
        K = _Q;
        update();
    }
}
```

The *update* function performs the coefficient calculations and is based directly on the filter coefficient equations presented in the chapter, using the same variable names whenever possible. For example, the *VAKorg35Filter's update* function calculates Equation block (12.13) as follows; compare the code with the equation block for this filter, then do the same for the remaining filters so you understand how the calculation works.

```
bool VAKorg35Filter::update()
{
    double g = tan(kTwoPi*fc*halfSamplePeriod);
    alpha = g / (1.0 + g);

    // --- alpha0 same for LPF, HPF
    alpha0 = 1.0 / (1.0 - K*alpha + K*alpha*alpha);

    // --- three sync-tuned filters
    for (uint32_t i = 0; i < KORG_SUBFILTERS; i++)
    {
        lpfVAFilters[i].setAlpha(alpha);
        hpfVAFilters[i].setAlpha(alpha);
    }

    // --- set filter beta values FLT2:LPF FLT3:HPF
    lpfVAFilters[FLT2].setBeta((K * (1.0 - alpha)) / (1.0 + g));
    lpfVAFilters[FLT3].setBeta(-1.0 / (1.0 + g));

    // --- set filter beta values FLT2:HPF FLT3:LPF
    hpfVAFilters[FLT2].setBeta(-alpha / (1.0 + g));
    hpfVAFilters[FLT3].setBeta(1.0 / (1.0 + g));

    return true;
}
```

The *process* function runs the filter algorithm on a single audio input sample and varies greatly with the model. Each filter declares a *FilterOutput* structure named *output* that may hold multiple filter output values in an array of *doubles*:

```
double filter[NUM _ FILTER _ OUTPUTS];
```

Each slot in the array holds a different filter output and a helper enumeration is used for easier code readability:

```
enum { LPF1, LPF2, LPF3, LPF4, HPF1, HPF2, HPF3…, NUM _ FILTER _ OUTPUTS};
```

The *VA MoogFilter::process* method is shown here for the normal filter.

- Notice that the *getFBOutput* function is used on the sub-filters
- The bass gain compensation is hard coded with *bassComp* = 0 so that the filter operates in a normal manner
- The input value u is calculated with the α_0 loop correction factor (this is the same for all filters)
- Each filter processes into a sub-structure, whose outputs are gathered accordingly
- The *output* structure's member variables are written and will vary with the filter model; note the use of the helper enumeration
- The analog FGN code simply pumps the input u into a series of LPF1 modules, taking their analog FGN outputs while preserving the normal feedback outputs for the resonant loop and following the normal pattern; check the sample code for details.

```
FilterOutput VAMoogFilter::process(double xn)
{
        // --- 4th order MOOG:
        double sigma = 0.0;

        // --- feedback
        for (uint32 _ t i = 0; i < MOOG _ SUBFILTERS; i++)
            sigma += subFilter[i].getFBOutput();

        // --- gain comp
        xn *= 1.0 + bassComp*K; // --- bassComp is hard coded

        // --- now figure out u(n) = alpha0*[x(n) - K*sigma]
        double u = alpha0*(xn - K * sigma);

        FilterOutput subFltOut[4];
        FilterOutput subFltOutFGN[4];
```

```
// --- send u -> LPF1
subFltOut[FLT1] = subFilter[FLT1].process(u);

// --- and then cascade the outputs to form y(n)
subFltOut[FLT2] =
    subFilter[FLT2].process(subFltOut[FLT1].filter[LPF1]);
subFltOut[FLT3] =
    subFilter[FLT3].process(subFltOut[FLT2].filter[LPF1]);
subFltOut[FLT4] =
    subFilter[FLT4].process(subFltOut[FLT3].filter[LPF1]);

// --- optional outputs 1,2,3
output.filter[LPF1] = subFltOut[FLT1].filter[LPF1];
output.filter[LPF2] = subFltOut[FLT2].filter[LPF1];
output.filter[LPF3] = subFltOut[FLT3].filter[LPF1];

// --- MOOG LP4 output
output.filter[LPF4] = subFltOut[FLT4].filter[LPF1];

return output;
}
```

Now, you need to compare the rest of the object code to the block diagrams and coefficient equations to prove to yourself that the code matches the model. Each filter can produce the analog FGN output, whose implementation varies from simple to complex depending on the filter type. Table 12.2 lists the filters and their sub-filter array components.

12.11 Input Drive and Output Peak Limiter

The SVF, Korg35, Moog, and diode models include an input distortion control that sets the saturation value in a *tanh* waveshaper, as documented in my FX plugin book. When the saturation is at

Table 12.2 Synth filter models and their output types, along with notes on implementation

Synth Filter Model	Outputs	Notes
VA1Filter	LPF1, HPF1, APF1, LPF1_FGN	Uses Zavalishin's first order structure
VASVFilter	LPF2, HPF2, BPF2, BSF2, LPF2_FGN	Self-oscillation induced at max Q by letting Q = infinity so $\rho = \alpha$
VAKorg35Filter	LPF2, HPF2, LPF2_FGN	Massive gain near self-oscillation
VAMoogFilter	LPF1, LPF2, LPF3, LPF4, and analog FGN versions of each	Analog FGN version requires four more sub-filters but are sync-tuned
VA1DiodeSubFilter	LPF1, LPF1_FGN	Uses coefficient structure for extended variables
VADiodeFilter	LPF4, LPF4_FGN	Requires a gain factor for analog FGN output that is empirically derived

the minimum value, the waveshaper is disabled. Placing the nonlinear distortion at the filter input allows the filter to sculpt the added harmonics. Extreme settings will cause aliasing, which will require mitigation via oversampling, which is also covered in the FX plugin book. The output of each model passes through a peak limiter using logarithmic RMS detection with the threshold set at almost 0 dBFS, which produces pure sinusoids during self-oscillation and prevents distortion from high gain due to high *Q* settings. The limiter is a simplified version of the limiter in the second edition FX book and works extremely well. The coding details can be found in the *VAFilter* and *VAFCore* objects as they implement these blocks and not the filters themselves.

12.12 *SynthFilter* and Cores

The *SynthFilter* and filter core details are shown in block form in Figure 12.16. The custom module strings are the filter-type strings, and the mod knobs are chosen for the most common operations, including key tracking, drive, and modulation intensity controls, one each for EG and bipolar modulation inputs. Both cores are available as separate dynamic modules and work easily in stand-alone mode, so you can use them in your non-synth projects as well. Table 12.3 lists the GUI parameter structure and core descriptions.

The VA filter core produces all of the VA filters in this chapter. For easier programming, a secondary filter enumeration is used that groups the filters according to VA model:

```
enum class FilterModel { kFirstOrder, kSVF, kKorg35, kMoog, kDiode};
```

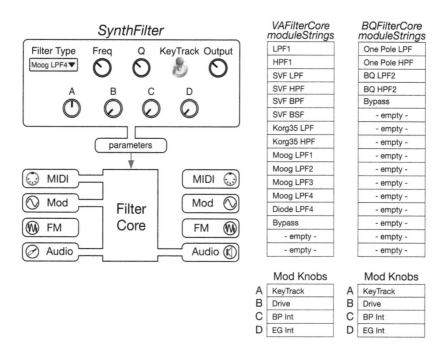

Figure 12.16 The *SynthFilter* and core block diagram, filter types, and mod knob labels

Table 12.3 *SynthFilter* custom parameter structure and cores: (*) downloadable SynthLab-DM core project

Parameter Structure	Description
FilterParameters	Used for all filters; includes additional parameters, such as bass compensation, that only apply to some filters
Example Core	Description
*VAFilterCore**	13 VA filter algorithms including the first, second, and third order Moog variants
*BQFilterCore**	A few biquad filters to get you started; use my FX plugin book for several dozen more, including impulse invariant, the MMA FGN lowpass, and multiple analog Nyquist gain matching algorithms

Table 12.4 The *SynthFilter* core GUI controls

Control	Function	Target
Filter type	Selects 1 of 13 filter types	Filter selection
Filter *f*	Sets filter center or cutoff frequency	Filter frequency
Filter *Q*	Set generic *Q* value on range [1, 10]	Filter *Q*
Key track	Enable/Disable key track modulation	Filter frequency
Output	Level in dB	Output amplitude
Mod Knob		
KT amount	Key tracking offset in semitones +/− 48 range	Filter frequency
Drive	Sets waveshaper saturation	Input amplitude
EG Int	Sets intensity of EG modulation	Filter frequency
BP Int	Sets intensity of summed bipolar modulation	Filter frequency

12.12.1 Synth Filter Controls, Modulations and Features

The synth filters share the same four controls: frequency (cut-off, center, or resonant), *Q*, a filter-keytrack enable switch, and an output control (dB). Table 12.2 lists the GUI controls and their parameter targets within the plugin. The VA filter core also includes a stereo peak limiter to produce sweet and pure sinusoidal output when driven into self-oscillation. The filter drive control adds pre-filter distortion using *tanh* waveshapers. The limiter's threshold is set to −0.5 dBFS. The filters include three modulation calculations: key-track with offset, bipolar, and unipolar (EG) modulation.

12.13 Synth Filter Core Programming Notes

With the C++ files open, compare the programming notes with the code that you see, starting with the class descriptions of each core. Sections 12.13.1 through 12.13.5 summarize the five operational phases, plus constructor for the synth filter cores. Make sure to examine the code while digesting their operational phase details.

12.13.1 Construction Phase

All cores:

- The module strings are the filter types; use whatever strings make the most sense to your users
- The mod knobs are all assigned
- The filter cores are simple in that there are no lookup tables or databases to access

12.13.2 Reset Phase

The *reset* function simply resets all of the components and sets up the limiter with a threshold of −0.5 dBFS.

```
val.reset(processInfo.sampleRate);
svf.reset(processInfo.sampleRate);
etc...

// --- output limiter
limiter.reset(processInfo.sampleRate);
limiter.setThreshold _ dB(-0.5);
```

12.13.3 Note On Phase

The note-on event is easily serviced; you save the incoming MIDI pitch to use for key tracking, and that is it.

12.13.4 Update Phase

The update operation follows the normal design pattern for pitch modulation, though here, it is for the filter f_c value that is based off of semitones and calculated the same way as f_o (pitch) modulation for oscillators. Filters are often hard-wired to a separate EG, with a dedicated EG intensity control; the same is true for the SynthLab synths that feature a dedicated filter EG object. However, a bipolar modulation input may also be applied and a bipolar intensity control used. To set or modify the range of operation, you only need to modify a bit of code in the *filtercore.h* file. Here, you use the *semitonesBetweenFrequencies* helper function to set the modulation range in semitones. The high limit is the top of the filter range, but you may decide to lower it to around 18 kHz – listen and decide.

```
freqModLow = 20.0; // <- you will want to raise this value a bit
freqModHigh = 20480.0; // <- you will want to lower this value a bit
freqModSemitoneRange = semitonesBetweenFrequencies(
                                        freqModLow, freqModHigh);
```

In the *update* function, first parse the mod knob values that set the EG and bipolar intensities, then calculate the modulation. Notice that the bipolar calculation adds a 0.5 modifier to split the modulation range around the user's f_c control setting.

```
// --- bipolar freqmod (0.5 is to split the total range)
```

```
bpInt = getModKnobValueLinear(parameters->modKnobValue[MOD _ KNOB _ C],
                              0.0, +1.0);


bpFmodSemitones = bpInt*0.5*freqModSemitoneRange*
                           processInfo.modulationInputs[kBipolarMod];


// --- EG freqmod
egInt = getModKnobValueLinear(parameters->modKnobValue[MOD _ KNOB _ D],
                              0.0, +1.0);
egFmodSemitones = egInt*freqModSemitoneRange*
                           processInfo.modulationInputs[kEGMod];
```

The key-tracking code checks to see if the function is enabled, then overrides the user's f_c control setting and calculates the key track frequency shift on a range of [−48, +48] semitones (+/− four octaves).

```
// --- setup fc mod
double fc = parameters->fc;
double ktFmodSemotones = 0.0;


// --- key tracking
if (parameters->enableKeyTrack)
{
    ktFmodSemotones = getModKnobValueLinear(
        parameters->modKnobValue[FLT _ KEYTRACK], -48.0, +48.0);
    fc = midiPitch;
}
```

The modulation calculation sums the semitone values as usual and bounds the value:

```
// --- sum modulations
fcModSSemis = bpFmodSemitones + egFmodSemitones + ktFmodSemotones;


// --- multiply by pitch shift factor
fc *= pow(2.0, fcModSSemis / 12.0);
boundValue(fc, freqModLow, freqModHigh);
```

The last chunk of code is a decision tree that sets the selection members, then calls the update function on the sub-object. The VA filters are selected by family:

```
else if (parameters->filterAlgorithm == VAFilterAlgorithm::kDiode _ LP4)
{
    // --- output array slot
    if (parameters->analogFGN)
        outputIndex = ANM _ LPF4;
    else
        outputIndex = LPF4;

    // --- model
```

```
    selectedModel = FilterModel::kDiode;

    // --- sub-filter update
    diode.setFilterParams(fc, parameters->Q);
}
```

The biquad filters calculate the filter coefficients and store them:

```
if (parameters->filterIndex == enumToInt(BQFilterAlgorithm::kLPF2))
{
    // --- see 2nd Ed FX for formulae
    double theta_c = kTwoPi*fc / sampleRate;
    double d = 1.0 / mappedQ;
    double betaNumerator = 1.0 - ((d / 2.0)*(sin(theta_c)));
    double betaDenominator = 1.0 + ((d / 2.0)*(sin(theta_c)));
    double beta = 0.5*(betaNumerator / betaDenominator);
    double gamma = (0.5 + beta)*(cos(theta_c));
    double alpha = (0.5 + beta - gamma) / 2.0;

    // --- update coeffs
    bq.coeff[a0] = alpha;
    bq.coeff[a1] = 2.0*alpha;
    bq.coeff[a2] = alpha;
    bq.coeff[b1] = -2.0*gamma;
    bq.coeff[b2] = 2.0*beta;
}
```

12.13.5 Render Phase

The VA core render phase is simple since the sub-filters do all of the heavy lifting. Therefore, the render function simply uses the filter type and output index to perform the processing. The drive control is used to apply a nonlinear waveshaper only if the control value is greater than zero. Then, the selected filter's process function runs the filter, and the output is applied to the peak limiter and scaled with the user's output control value that was calculated in the *update* function. Notice that the VA core's sub-filters calculate all outputs (LPF, HPF, BPF, etc.), which are then selected, and all filters and sub-filters are stereo, requiring double the objects. Examine the code in *vafilters.h* and *.cpp* to see how I minimize the filter calculations using the *IFilterBase* interface and functions that set the filtering coefficients directly, bypassing the update calculation. For the Korg35, Moog, and diode filters, the sub-filters are synchronously tuned so a single update function's results can be shared across multiple sub-filter components. The synth filter processes audio input buffers into output buffers.

```
// --- stereo I/O
float* leftInBuffer = processInfo.inputBuffers[LEFT_CHANNEL];
float* leftOutBuffer = processInfo.outputBuffers[LEFT_CHANNEL];

float* rightInBuffer = processInfo.inputBuffers[RIGHT_CHANNEL];
float* rightOutBuffer = processInfo.outputBuffers[RIGHT_CHANNEL];
```

At the top of the block-processing loop, notice the filter bypass code:

```
for (uint32_t i = 0; i < processInfo.samplesToProcess; i++)
{
    double xnL = leftInBuffer[i];
    double xnR = rightInBuffer[i];

    if (parameters->filterIndex ==
                    enumToInt(VAFilterAlgorithm::kBypassFilter))
    {
        leftOutBuffer[i] = xnL;
        rightOutBuffer[i] = xnR;
        continue;
    }
```

Filter drive/distortion uses a built-in waveshaper function (note that there are several to choose from):

```
// --- waveshaper drive
if (parameters->filterDrive > 1.05)
{
    xnL = tanhWaveShaper(xnL, parameters->filterDrive);
    xnR = tanhWaveShaper(xnR, parameters->filterDrive);
}
```

The VA filters are processed according to filter family; notice the array of two filters for each family:

```
FilterOutput output[STEREO];


if (selectedModel == FilterModel::kFirstOrder)
{
    output[LEFT] = va1[LEFT].process(xnL);
    output[RIGHT] = va1[RIGHT].process(xnR);
}
else if (selectedModel == FilterModel::kSVF)
{
    output[LEFT] = svf[LEFT].process(xnL);
    output[RIGHT] = svf[RIGHT].process(xnR);
}
else if (selectedModel == FilterModel::kKorg35)
{
    output[LEFT] = korg35[LEFT].process(xnL);
    output[RIGHT] = korg35[RIGHT].process(xnR);
}

etc. . .
```

The biquad core uses a single biquad filtering object, *BQAudioFilter*, that implements the direct form biquad filter, described in detail in my FX plugin book. That object performs the filtering in a simple function call:

```
// --- select output
leftOutBuffer[i] = outputAmp *
                        filter[LEFT _ CHANNEL].processAudioSample(xnL);
rightOutBuffer[i] = outputAmp *
                        filter[RIGHT _ CHANNEL].processAudioSample(xnR);
```

12.14 Exercises

12.14.1 SynthLab-DM Core: SVF Self Modulation

The state variable filter will only self-oscillate when the Q value becomes infinite and is the only model that does not have an upper feedback value limit that creates self-oscillation. The SVF has the Q control from [1, 10] mapped to a range of [0.707, 25.0], and at the top value, the filter is highly resonant, producing copious gain at the peak frequency, though it is not oscillating. Examine the equations in block (12.12) and figure out what happens to the ρ value if Q becomes infinite. Then, modify the *VASVFilter::update* function with an if/else statement, and add your own code. Now, when the user maxes the Q control, the filter will go into self-oscillation. The switching point will be inaudible as the filter will already have massive gain, and the output limiter will be maintaining distortion-free operation.

```
if (Q > 24.95)
     // --- your code here
else
     rho = 2.0*R + alpha; // normal calculation
```

The bipolar modulation intensity control (Mod Knob #4) can be removed because bipolar modulators like LFOs already have output amplitude controls that will set the modulation intensity. It can also be set with the Modulation Matrix, so this Mod Knob can be changed to give you more practice. Here are two possibilities for altering this control.

12.14.2 SynthLab-DM Core: SVF Bass Compensation

The code and parameter structure already include a *bassComp* variable that represents the *a* variable in Figures 12.11 and 12.12 for the Moog and diode filters. This value varies on the range [0.0, +1.0]. Modify the Mod Knob #4 string for "Bass Comp," then modify the *update* calculation to remove the bipolar mod intensity calculation (or set it to 1.0), and modify the *render* function to apply the bass compensation. As the user increases the bass compensation control, the filter gain reduction will be abated, and more bass will result. The output limiter will keep the distortion at bay.

12.14.3 SynthLab-DM Core: Key Tracking Slope

The key-tracking amount is a constant shift in semitones above or below the MIDI pitch of the note being played. Check out the manual for the Korg Wavestate™ from www.willpirkle.com/

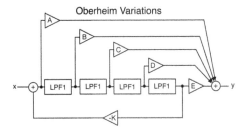

Oberheim Variations

Filter	A	B	C	D	E
2nd order BPF	0	2	-2	0	0
4th order BPF	0	0	4	-8	4
2nd order HPF	1	-2	1	0	0
4th order HPF	1	-4	6	-4	1

Figure 12.17 The Oberheim variations on the Moog ladder signal flow block diagram and table of coefficient values

Downloads/wavestate.pdf, and look at the filter key-tracking section. Notice how the added *slope* control is used to create a rate of change in the key-tracking offset as the user moves above or below the middle-note (usually middle-C or MIDI note 60). Next, change Mod Knob #4 to a key-tracking *slope* control, and use the Wavestate manual and information to create your new feature.

12.14.4 Advanced Module: Oberheim/Moog FilterCore

Finally, make your own filter core object which implements the Oberheim variations on the Moog ladder filter. Create your own Moog filter C++ object, and add it to the objects in *vafilters.h* and *vafilters.cpp*, which implements the added filters from Oberheim's Xpander® synth. Tom Oberheim realized that, if outputs were taken from each of the Moog's four LPFs and combined in various ratios, many other filters could be obtained. You can download the original XPander service manual from www.willpirkle.com/Downloads/Oberheim_Xpander_Service_Manual.pdf. The following are some of the variations available (other than the normal LPFs), and the service manual contains more options.

- second order BPF
- fourth order BPF
- second order HPF
- fourth order HPF

Figure 12.17 shows the newly added feed-forward coefficients that inject zeros into the transfer function and a table that lists the coefficient values for the four new filters. Create your own new synth filter core object that implements these four new filters, and add it to the SynthLab projects that you like, thereby increasing the number of filters to 18 in total.

Bibliography

cedos.com. 1980. "CEM3328 Four Pole Low-Pass VCF Datasheet." http://www.cedos.com/datasheets/cem3328pdf.pdf, Accessed October 14, 2020

El-Masry, E.I. and Sakla, A.A. 1979. "Low-sensitivity Digital Ladder Networks." *13th Asilo-mar Conference*, pp. 273–278.

Fettweis, Alfred. 1986. "Wave Digital Filters: Theory and Practice." *Proceedings of the IEEE*, vol. 74, no. 2. pp. 270–327.

Fontana, Fredrico. 2010. "Modeling of the EMS VCS3 Voltage-Controlled Filter as a Nonlinear Filter Network." *IEEE Transactions on Audio, Speech and Language Processing*, vol. 18, no. 4. pp. 760–772.

Huovilainen, Antti. 2006. "Nonlinear Digital Implementation of the Moog Ladder Filter." Proceedings of the International Conference on Digital Audio Effects, Naples.

Lindquist, Claude. 1977. *Active Network Design with Signal Filtering Applications*. Long Beach: Steward and Sons.

Nagahama, Yasuo. 1977. "Voltage Controlled Filter." United States Patent 4,039,980.

Oberheim, Tom. 1984. *Oberheim XPander Service Manual*. Los Angeles: ECC Development Corp.

Pirkle, Will. 2013. "Modeling the Korg35 Highpass and Lowpass Filters." Presented at the 135th Audio Engineering Society Convention, New York.

Pirkle, Will. 2014. "Novel Hybrid Virtual Analog Filters Based on the Sallen-Key Architecture." Presented at the 137th Audio Engineering Society Convention, New York.

Pirkle, Will. 2014. "Resolving Delay-Free Loops in Recursive Filters using the Modified Härmä Method." Presented at the 137th Audio Engineering Society Convention, New York.

Pirkle, Will. 2018. *Designing Audio Effects Plugins in C++*, 2nd Ed. Chap. 12. New York: Routledge.

Stilson, Tim & Smith, Julius O. 1996. "Analyzing the Moog VCF with Considerations for Digital Implementation." Proceedings of the 1996 International Computer Music Conference, San Francisco.

Stinchcombe, Tim. 2006. "A Study of the Korg MS10 and MS20 Filters." http://www.timstinchcombe.co.uk/synth/MS20_study.pdf, Accessed October 14, 2020

synthfool.com. 1974. "Oberheim SEM Schematics." http://www.synthfool.com/docs/Oberheim/Oberheim_SEM1A/Oberheim_SEM_1A_Schematics.pdf, Accessed October 14, 2020

Välimäki, Vesa & Huovilainen, Antti. 2006. "Oscillator and Filter Algorithms for Virtual Analog Synthesis." *Computer Music Journal*, vol. 30, no. 2, pp. 19–31, Cambridge: MIT Press.

Zavalishin, Vadim. 2012. *The Art of VA Filter Design*. https://www.native-instruments.com/fileadmin/ni_media/downloads/pdf/VAFilterDesign_2.1.0.pdf, Accessed October 14, 2020

13 Karplus-Strong Plucked String Model

In its simplest form, physical modeling involves creating DSP components that combine to behave like their physical counterparts, such as a pendulum or a resonating mass-spring system. The theory may be used for modeling strings, tubes, or struck-metal plates, or practically any other acoustic/mechanical system or effect, such as a piano or the reverb effect. The Yamaha VL-1®, Korg Prophecy®, and OASYS® are examples of early, commercially available physical modeling synthesizers. Today, the GeoShred® mobile app uses physical string modeling as its synthesis core. This area has matured over several decades, including texts dedicated specifically to the science. In this chapter, we will study one of the most famous and useful physical modeling algorithms: the Karplus-Strong plucked string model. This algorithm works well as an introduction to physical modeling because it includes the same set of components as other more complex algorithms. such as a saxophone. Physical modeling does away with PCM samples and wavetables, so there is little data to store or load. However, the processing may become very complicated as the output is mathematically generated.

13.1 The Exciter-Resonator

Physical modeling algorithms for acoustic instruments usually contain two components: the exciter and the resonator, which are fundamentally connected, as shown in Figure 13.1(a). The exciter stimulates the resonator that rings at the desired musical pitch. Figure 13.1(b) includes an output filter that couples the output waveform to the air load. Figure 13.1(b) also shows that the

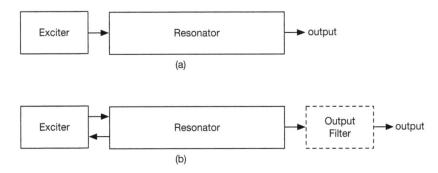

Figure 13.1 (a) The most basic exciter-resonator system, and (b) a more complex model that includes coupling from the resonator back to the exciter and an output impedance coupler

Table 13.1 Some common instruments and their physical modeling components

Instrument	Exciter	Resonator	Output Filter
Guitar	Plucked-string deformation	Transverse wave on string	Guitar bridge to body (integrator)
Saxophone	Reed flapping against mouthpiece and breath pressure	Standing wave in tube	Bell and open holes in bore (HPF)
Trumpet	Lips vibrating in mouthpiece and breath pressure	Standing wave in tube	Bell (HPF)

resonator can couple back to the exciter with the reverse arrow. Table 13.1 lists a few common acoustic instruments and their exciter, resonator, and output filter. The saxophone and trumpet both feature coupled resonators because the standing wave setup in the instrument's tube reflects off of the musician's lips/mouth. Instruments that include open holes, such as most woodwinds, have an additional complexity since there are multiple locations where the sound couples with the air load.

13.2 The Plucked String

Plucked string instruments include guitars and basses as well as harps and other similar devices. Struck string instruments include piano, clavichord, and dulcimer. In both cases, the string is deformed and released either with the finger or a hammer, as depicted in Figure 13.2(a) (the guitar) and (b) (the deformation), and acts as the excitation signal. In its simplest version, the deformation sets up a transverse wave that bounces back and forth between the bridge and the fretting finger, or nut if the string is open, as shown in Figure 13.2(c) and (d). The transverse wave bounces off of each terminal end point at the nut (or fretting finger) and the bridge. The rate of the bounces per second is the frequency in Hertz of the note. The transverse wave on the string itself is the resonator, and the bridge couples the resonator with the body that vibrates and couples the output to the air load. As the system loses energy, the transverse wave loses amplitude and eventually becomes inaudible. In addition, we observe the fact that high frequencies, which inherently do not have as much power as low frequencies, decay faster and earlier. The body behaves as a complex, multi-peaked filter that resonates well at some frequencies and not so well at others.

13.3 The Karplus-Strong Model

The Karplus-Strong (KS) model for the plucked string is simple, elegant, and effective. Its most basic form is immediately simpler than other algorithms because there is no interaction between the resonator and the exciter – once the string is plucked, the exciter is removed from the model, and the resonator takes over. Note that there are more complex models that do include coupling to the exciter. DSP building blocks are designed to implement each section of the model. Figure 13.3(a) shows the basic idea for modeling the string.

13.3.1 KS Resonator

The resonator consists of two delay lines, each of which implements half of the total delay, *D*, that is the period of the musical pitch. An LPF and attenuator at each delay output remove high

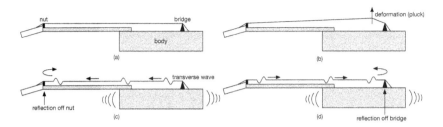

Figure 13.2 (a) An acoustic guitar with nut, bridge, and body; (b) plucking the string deforms it and (c) sets up a transverse wave that moves down the string, and (d) bounces off the nut and moves back toward the bridge

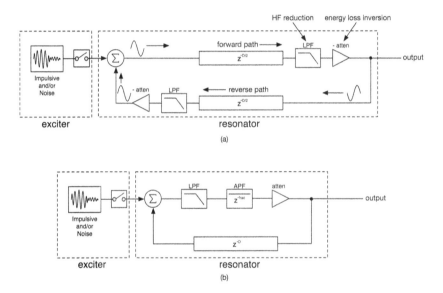

Figure 13.3 (a) Basic model of a plucked string with dual delay lines for transverse wave oscillation and (b) a simplified version that combines like components and adds the fractional delay APF

frequencies and energy on each reflection. Figure 13.3(b) shows how this loop may be simplified and improved. The two delay lines may be combined, along with the attenuators and filters to reduce complexity.

Musical pitches will rarely be exact multiples of the sample period. This means that the period of the waveform, and the calculated delay, D, will include a fractional component, as shown in Figure 13.3(b). The fractional delay is implemented with a first order all pass filter (APF) in Figure 13.4(a) that creates a linear fractional group delay, δ over the range of 0 Hz to about $0.1f_s$, as shown in Figure 13.4(b). With $f_s = 44.1$ kHz, this would be around 4,410 Hz, which is close to the top note on a piano, so it is easily usable across the range of a guitar or bass. The resonator's delay line length and APF fractional delay calculations must be exact to produce the correct pitch. The user may have control over the attenuation that corresponds to the string's decay time.

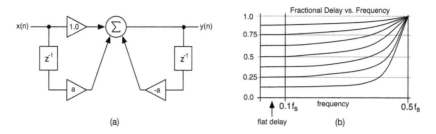

Figure 13.4 (a) A first order structure for an APF with only one coefficient *a* to calculate and (b) the group delay versus frequency for the APF; each curve represents a different APF f_c

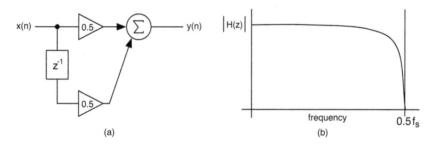

Figure 13.5 (a) The simple first order feed-forward LPF and (b) its frequency response showing a zero at Nyquist

13.3.2 KS Loop Filter

The lowpass filter in the loop is going to reduce high frequency components, but it can also introduce its own group delay, depending on the filter, f_c. This means that we cannot let the user adjust the filter, or the note will be slightly out of tune. However, if we use the simple first order feed-forward LPF, shown in Figure 13.5(a), with the coefficients $a_0 = a_1 = 0.5$, then we get the most selectivity with a zero at Nyquist, as shown in Figure 13.5(b), and we can calculate that we will get exactly ½ of a sample of delay through the filter.

13.3.3 KS Exciter

The exciter signal has numerous options: a simple unit impulse, an impulse generated from a resonant filter, and impulses that are combinations of several impulsive or noisy components. A simple and effective excitation signal consists of a short noise blast with an envelope and a spectral

The Karplus-Strong algorithm is a specific kind of plucked string model and has undergone improvements and modifications over time. The algorithms here are a combination of some of these modifications. For simplicity's sake, I am keeping the Karplus-Strong moniker for the model developed here.

content. In the traditional KS algorithm, the exciter signal is placed inside of the delay line and sets the initial state for the system.

For the *KSOscillator* core, the exciter is placed at the entrance to the loop summer, producing the first output samples immediately and without delay. Setting the spectrum of the noise exciter establishes the initial frequency response of the system. The LPF loop filter will take that spectrum and filter it repeatedly on each pass through the loop, emulating the natural harmonic decay in an acoustic stringed instrument. Unlike the resonator, which has some fixed properties and calculations, the exciter is wide open for experimentation. The harmonic content of the output depends upon the exciter's initial harmonic spectrum. If noisy signals are used, then randomness in the spectra will create slight timbral differences for each note-event, which will add a human element.

13.3.3.1 Windowed Noise Burst Exciter

You can create interesting sounds with very simple exciter signals, including the rectangular-pulsed random noise that you generate by simply counting off a few random values, as shown in Figure 13.6(a). You can also use common window functions to create a time domain signal without the discontinuities at the edges that will reduce the high harmonics, as in the Hann windowed excitation in Figure 13.6(b). The windowed exciter lends itself easily to re-triggering, which produces a stream of impulsive blasts called "sonic grains," as shown in Figure 13.6(c). Each of these may also operate on pseudo-random noise or filter noise signals.

13.3.3.2 EG Shaped Noise Burst Exciter

You can also shape the noise burst with an envelope generator (EG) using the attack-release (AR) and attack-hold-release (AHR) contours, as shown in Figure 13.6(d) and (e). As with the windowed exciter, the EG may also be retriggered. The physical model of a bowed instrument like the cello is quite complex, but the AHR shaped noise produces a surprisingly similar sound when the attack time is long. When the attack and release are set to 0.0, and the hold time is finite, we get the rectangular noise blast.

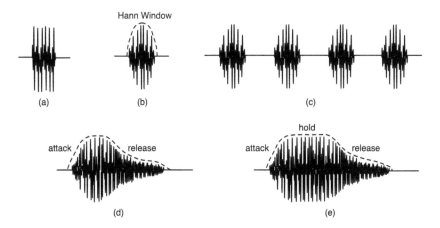

Figure 13.6 (a) Rectangular windowed noise burst; (b) Hann windowed noise burst; (c) sonic grains from re-triggered windowed exciter; (d) attack-release; and (e) attack-hold-release envelope noise bursts

13.3.3.3 Exciter by Reverse Filtering with PCM Samples

In yet another approach to generate an impulse, you start with a single PCM sample of an actual plucked string note-event. Next, you synthesize a perfectly complementary KS model that reverses (complements) all of the DSP algorithm blocks and run the model in reverse-time. This model accepts an input at the output port that flows in the reverse direction, then you recover the impulse response as the "output" of the exciter. Now you have the exact impulse response needed for the model to produce an output identical to your PCM sample. If you are interested, see the Leary reference for more information.

13.4 Pluck Position

Figure 13.2 is oversimplified but effective in explaining the transverse wave's relationship to the string's frequency. The pluck actually creates string motion, which may be thought of as two pulses that travel in opposite directions (Fletcher/Rossing) and bounce back and forth, producing a set of vibrating modes that combine to produce phase cancellations at frequencies based on the pluck position. When plucked in the exact center (twelfth fret on a guitar), the two standing waves cancel at each even harmonic, starting with the second harmonic (the octave), then the fourth, sixth, and eighth, producing a distinctly hollow timbre. As the pluck position moves towards one end, the canceled harmonics appear at exact multiples of the pluck position, as a fraction of the string length. This is modeled with an inverse comb filter whose delay length $z^{-D/M}$ is set to the pluck position fraction D/M of the string loop delay, as shown in Figure 13.7(a). If the string is plucked at ½ the string length, then the comb delay is ½ the loop delay ($D/2$), while it is 1/4 the total delay for a pluck at 1/4 the string length ($D/4$). The $z^{-D/M}$ comb filter response is shown in Figure 13.7(b), with notches which are multiples of $M = 4$. The number of notches and whether or not a zero is present at DC and Nyquist depends on the even/odd nature of the comb filter delay length. The comb filter length will rarely be an exact integer, and we use a delay line that interpolates to create the fractional delay in that filter.

13.4.1 Bridge Filter

The bridge acts as an integrator as it couples the signal pulses to the soundboard top and is implemented with a lowpass filter whose f_c is lower than the lowest pitch to synthesize (Välimäki), as shown in Figure 13.7(c). The bridge filter and pluck position filter may be combined (Välimäki) into one unit, as shown in Figure 13.7(a), whose combined frequency response is shown in Figure 13.7(d).

Figure 13.8(a) shows the output of the KS model for the *KSOscillator* taken at the bridge with the bridge filter engaged and a fundamental frequency of 110 Hz. Figure 13.8(b) includes the pluck position filter with the pluck point at half the string length, showing that every other harmonic is missing. The harmonic amplitudes have variation in them because the source is a short noise burst that does not have a perfectly flat spectrum.

13.4.2 Pickup Filter

Implementing an electric or bass guitar pickup requires us to revert to the two-delay-line KS model in Figure 13.2(a); the pickup point is tapped from locations within the integer delay line, corresponding to different locations under the strings. The pickup itself behaves like a second

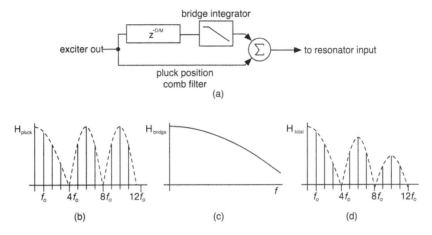

Figure 13.7 (a) The pluck position filter is a simple feed forward comb filter that is combined with the bridge integrator in the delay branch, (b) shows the comb filter response for a pluck position of ¼ the total length (M = 4), (c) the bridge filter's lowpass-integrator response and (d) the combined integrator and comb filter responses

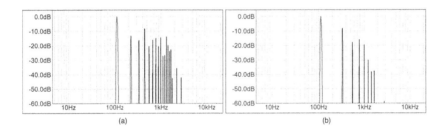

Figure 13.8 Spectra of the KS model of the note A-2 (110 Hz), showing output of (a) bridge filter only and (b) bridge filter and pluck position with pluck at ½ the length of the string

order resonant lowpass filter, with a resonant frequency between 2 kHz and 5 kHz, and a peak gain of a few *dB* for guitar. Bass pickups may exhibit much higher resonant peak frequencies. To keep the model simple, the single delay version is still implemented, with the pickup filter placed just before the bridge filter, as shown in Figure 13.8.

13.5 Karplus-Strong Algorithm Equations

For a given note-event, we will need to calculate several parameters for the resonator component that will set the delay length and calculate the APF coefficients for the fractional delay filter. We know that the delay loop will provide $L + \frac{1}{2}$ samples when we include the loop filter. The loop filter has coefficients a_0 and a_1 fixed at 0.5, so there is nothing to calculate for it.

To calculate the fixed delay length L and APF coefficient a, we only need a few equations, and we can show these by example: suppose the user plays MIDI note 60 or middle-C with $f_o = 261.6256$ Hz.

Calculate the exact delay length L_E:

$$L_E = \frac{f_s}{f_o} = \frac{44,100}{261.6256...} = 168.5614 \tag{13.1}$$

We will get ½ sample of delay from the simple LPF, so subtract back, and find the nearest integer length that will result in a fractional delay of less than one sample:

$$L_D = \text{int}(L_E - 0.5) = \text{int}(168.0614) = 168 \tag{13.2}$$

L_D is the length of the delay in samples. Now, find the fractional amount that the APF must make up:

$$\delta = L_E - (L_D + 0.5) = 0.0614 \tag{13.3}$$

Another way to think about L_D and δ is that they are the integer and fractional components of L_E. With this fractional delay time, you can calculate the single APF coefficient a as:

$$\begin{aligned} \omega_0 &= \frac{2\pi f_o}{f_s} \\ a &= \frac{\sin((1-\delta)(\omega_0 / 2))}{\sin((1+\delta)(\omega_0 / 2))} \\ &= 0.8842 \end{aligned} \tag{13.4}$$

For the pluck position filter, the comb delay is set to L_E/M, as described in Section 13.4, where M is the denominator of the pluck position fraction. This requires a comb filter that interpolates to create fractional delay times. The bridge integrator is a first order, all pole lowpass filter with the f_c set to 20 Hz, which is about half of the bass guitar's low E-string frequency of about 44 Hz.

13.6 Karplus-Strong C++ Objects

Technically, the KS algorithm constitutes a complete patch and renders a plucked/struck event complete with decay time setting. However, the KS algorithm also works well as an oscillator used within the SynthLab architecture that includes LFOs, EGs, etc. In order to facilitate the operation, I've created a set of very small, very specific C++ objects that perform dedicated processing, which are listed in Table 13.2. These objects are lightweight and dedicated to KS algorithms, with simple *set*, *process*, and *render* functions.

13.6.1 Exciter, Resonator, and PluckPosFilter C++ Objects

The *Exciter* and *Resonator* objects complete the *KSCore* for the *KSOScillator* and implement three KS models: nylon string guitar, distorted electric guitar, and electric bass guitar. The exciter object implements the block diagram in the dotted box in Figure 13.9 and uses an EG-shaped noise burst as the excitation. The simple Attack-Hold-Release (AHR) EG is implemented and can produce both short noise bursts and longer, quasi-bowed-string excitation signals. When dealing with short noise bursts or impulsive signals, a DC offset may be present that will build up in the resonator. A simple first order HPF is used to block the DC. The *Resonator* object implements the single delay architecture in Figure 13.2(b) and is unchanged.

Table 13.2 List of lightweight objects specifically for KS algorithms

Object Name	Functionality	Important Methods	Notes
ResDelayLine	Resonator integer length delay line	*readDelay* *writeDelay* *setDelayTime*	Length set to correspond to MIDI note 0 at ~8 Hz
FracDelayAPF	Resonator fractional delay element	*setAlpha* *processAudioSample*	Single coefficient α sets fractional delay
ResLoopFilter	Simple feed-forward LPF with ½ sample delay	*processAudioSample*	$a_0 = a_1 = 0.5$
ExciterEG	Dedicated AHR EG with analog EG curvature	*setParameters(AHR)* *startEG* *render*	Lean version of *AnalogEG* with only A, H, and R
DCRemovalFilter	First order HPF with f_c = 2 Hz to remove DC offsets	*reset* *processAudioSample*	Coefficients are hard-coded
PluckPosFilter	Inverse comb filter with selectable bridge integrator and pickup filter	*reset* *processAudioSample*	Options for output at pluck position, pickup, and bridge, and combinations of them
HighShelvingFilter	High shelving filter with f_c (Hz) and boost/cut (dB)	*setParameters* *processAudioSample*	Adds HF energy to exciter signal with shelf f_c = 2 kHz
ParametricFilter	Non-constant-Q parametric filter for body resonance	*setParameters* *processAudioSample*	Used for body filter, post processing; varies with model
LP2Filter	Second order biquad LPF	*setParameters* *processAudioSample*	Used for the amp simulator and pickup filters
LP1PFilter	First order one-pole LPF	*setParameters* *processAudioSample*	Used for the bridge pickup

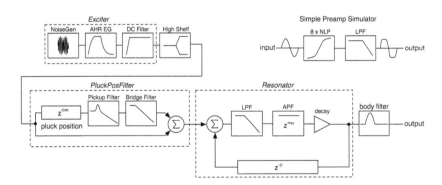

Figure 13.9 The block diagram of the KS algorithm packaged as the *KSOCore* includes the exciter, pluck, pickup, and bridge filters, and the resonator and body filter; the inset shows the very simple guitar preamp simulator, consisting of eight stages of waveshaping followed by a second order LPF

Table 13.3 shows the *Exciter* object's member objects and methods. The sub-objects do the work, and the *render* method simply generates the noise and shapes it with the EG. Notice that the function takes an argument *coupledInput* that allows you to couple the resonator back into the exciter for experimentation. Finally, the DC is removed and the excitation value returned.

```
double render(double coupledInput = 0.0)
{
    double noise = noiseGen.doWhiteNoise();
    double eg = noiseEG.render();
    double ahr = (noise * eg) + coupledInput;
    return dcFilter.processAudioSample(ahr);
}
```

Table 13.4 shows the *Resonator* object's member objects and methods. Once again, the sub-objects do the work, and the *process* method follows Figure 13.6, starting with reading the output of the delay line to sum with the incoming exciter signal:

```
double Resonator::process(double xn)
{
    // --- read delay
    double delayOut = delayLine.readDelay();

    // --- filter input + delay output
    double filterOut = loopFilter.processAudioSample(xn + delayOut);

    // --- create fractional delay with APF
    double yn = fracDelayAPF.processAudioSample(filterOut);

    // --- write the value into the delay and scale
    delayLine.writeDelay(yn*decay);

    // --- done
    return yn;
}
```

Table 13.3 The *Exciter* members and brief description

Exciter Member	Argument/Variable	Description
NoiseGenerator	*noiseGenerator*	Creates white noise; see Section 8.1
ExciterEG	*noiseEG*	AHR EG for shaping the noise burst
DCRemovalFilter	*dcFilter*	HPF to remove DC offset, f_c fixed at 2 Hz
setParameters( )	*attackTime_mSec* *holdTime_mSec* *releaseTime_mSec*	Sets EG parameters
startExciter( )	None	Places the EG into attack state, ready to render
render( )	None	Renders the exciter output samples, one at a time

Table 13.4 The *Resonator* members and brief description

Resonator Member	Argument/Variable	Description
ResDelayLine	*delayLine*	Circular buffer for integer resonator delay
FracDelayAPF	*fracDelayAPF*	Generates fractional delay for loop tuning
ResLoopFilter	*loopFilter*	Simple feed forward LPF with ½ sample group delay
setParameters( )	*frequency* *decay*	Sets the resonator's frequency and attenuation parameters
process( )	*xn*	Process a sample through the resonator loop, taking output, as shown in Figure 13.6

Table 13.5 shows the *PluckPosFilter* object's member objects and methods. This object is set up to allow you to choose from any output point using multiple combinations of filters according to the *PluckFilterType*; each model will use a different output point.

```
enum class PluckFilterType {kPluck, kPluckAndBridge, kPickup,
                            kPluckAndPickup, kBridge,
                            kPluckPickupBridge};
```

The *PluckPosFilter* requires a delay line for the comb filter, a one-pole LPF for the bridge integrator, and a second order resonant LPF for the pickup filter, which are set up in the reset function as follows:

1 *combDelay*: length is set for the lowest possible pitch, MIDI note 0 at the current f_s
2 *bridgeIntegrator*: f_c = 20 Hz (you may lower this, but you will need to boost the output to accommodate the loss of energy)
3 *pickupFilter*: f_c = 2.5 kHz, Q = 1.5 (Q plays an important role in the pickup's tonal coloration; experiment with this filter)

The *processAudioSample* function decodes the input parameter and returns the desired output value. Notice the scalar multipliers that make up for lost energy in the bridge and pickup filters; feel free to experiment with these as needed.

```
if (type == PluckFilterType::kBridge)
    return 12.0*bridgeIntegrator.processAudioSample(xn);


if (type == PluckFilterType::kPickup)
    return pickupFilter.processAudioSample(xn);


// --- pluck position
double yn = combDelay.readDelay();
combDelay.writeDelay(xn);

// --- output pluck
double pluck = 0.5*(xn - yn);
```

```
if (type == PluckFilterType::kPluck)
    return pluck;

// --- pluck and pickup
if (type == PluckFilterType::kPluckAndPickup)
    return pickupFilter.processAudioSample(pluck);

// --- pluck and bridge
if (type == PluckFilterType::kPluckAndBridge)
    return 12.0*bridgeIntegrator.processAudioSample(pluck);

if (type == PluckFilterType::kPluckPickupBridge)
{
    double pu = 2.0*pickupFilter.processAudioSample(pluck);
    return 12.0*bridgeIntegrator.processAudioSample(pu);
}
```

13.7 KSOscillator and KSOCore

The *KSOscillator* and *KSOCore* objects are shown in block form in Figure 13.10. The model implements a nylon string guitar, and distorted electric and bass guitar KS algorithms. The differences between the three variations lies mainly in filter settings and the addition of a simple preamp simulator for the distorted guitar. This is the only SynthLab oscillator that has just one core as it is a very specific kind of algorithm.

13.7.1 *KSOCore Mod Knobs*

The *KSOscParameters* structure contains the GUI parameters, which are very application-specific and consist of the AHR EG controls and the decay control. You will notice that there are no tuning controls; however, in unison mode, the four voices will be detuned as with the other oscillators. You may decide to remove this functionality. The mod knobs are set up for the rest of the functionality shown in Figure 13.9 and consist of:

1 *AmpTweak*: +/−12 dB of final amplitude adjustment, corresponding to the output control on the other oscillators
2 *Body*: a medium-Q parametric filter is placed at the output of the system to mimic the fundamental body resonances of the models
3 *Bite*: a high-shelving filter after the *Exciter* to add high harmonics and brightness to the excitation signal

Table 13.5 The *PluckPosFilter* members and brief description

Exciter Member	Argument/Variable	Notes
DelayLine	combDelay	Length defaults to lowest MIDI note
LP1PFilter	bridgeIntegrator	Lossy integrator with f_c = 20 Hz
LP2Filter	pickupFilter	Resonant LPF; avoid high Q, or feedback may result

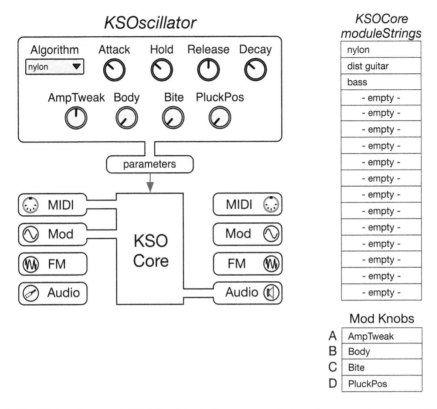

Figure 13.10 The *KSOscillator* and *KSOCore* block diagrams, module strings, mod inputs, and GUI controls

4   *PluckPos*: controls the pluck position and works backwards on a range of [10, 2], establishing the denominator of the pluck position fraction

13.8 *KSOCore* Member Objects

Table 13.6 lists the core member objects and their KS functionality.

13.9 Core Programming Notes

With the C++ files open, compare the programming notes with the code that you see, starting with the class descriptions of each core. Sections 13.9.1 through 13.9.5 summarize the five operational phases, plus constructor for the wavetable cores. Make sure to examine the code while digesting their operational phase details.

13.9.1 Construction Phase

As with all of the *ModuleCore* objects, you first assign the module name and module type, then set the module strings. For the KS oscillator, these are the names of the plucked string instruments.

Table 13.6 KSOCore member objects/variables

KS Functionality	C++ Object/Variables	Notes
Exciter	*Exciter*	AHR noise exciter
Resonator	*Resonator*	One-delay-line resonator
Pluck position, pickup, & bridge	*PluckPosFilter*	Includes scalar values to make up for energy losses; feel free to adjust as needed
Brightness	*HighShelfFilter*	Adds high harmonics to the exciter
Body resonance	*ParametricFilter*	Different center frequencies for the three models
Distortion	*LP2Filter*	The simple preamp simulator uses a second order filter to smooth harsh harmonics

13.9.2 Reset Phase

The *reset* method simply calls the *reset* method on each of the member objects. In addition, the distortion filter is hardcoded for f_c = 2 kz and Q = 1.0 (feel free to experiment)

```
distortionFilter.reset(sampleRate);
distortionFilter.setParameters(2000.0, 1.0); // fc and Q
```

13.9.3 Note-On Phase

The note-on event is easily serviced; we first save the incoming MIDI pitch to use for update calculations. Then, the sub-objects have their delay lines flushed with the *flushDelays* or *clear* functions, depending on the object. This is crucial to avoid corrupted information in the delays. Most importantly, the exciter's *startExciter* method is called, placing the exciter EG into the attack state and making it ready for render.

```
// --- parameters
midiPitch = processInfo.noteEvent.midiPitch;

// --- reset
resonator.flushDelays();
pluckPosFilter.clear();

// --- start excitation
exciter.startExciter();
```

13.9.4 Update Phase

The core's *update* method follows the normal pitch modulation calculation detailed in Section 6.8.1. After the modulated oscillator frequency is calculated, the resonator and pluck position objects are updated using the oscillator frequency to calculate the delay lengths. Notice that the resonator's *setParameter* function returns the newly calculated delay line length, including the fraction. The pluck position mod knob is quantized to an integer value and used to calculate the pluck position filter's new delay length.

```
// --- BOUND the value to our range
boundValue(oscillatorFrequency, OSC _ FMIN, OSC _ FMAX);
```

```
// --- Resonator:
double delayLen = resonator.setParameters(
                        oscillatorFrequency, parameters->decay);
```

```
// --- Pluck Position:
pluckPosition = (uint32 _ t)getModKnobValueLinear(
                    parameters->modKnobValue[MOD _ KNOB _ D], 10.0, 2.0);
```

```
pluckPosFilter.setDelayInSamples(delayLen / pluckPosition);
```

The exciter attack, hold, and release times are updated, followed by the bite and body filters. Notice how the mod knobs map to boost-only values for both filters and that the center frequencies are different for each model. The high shelf "bite" filter has f_c = 2 kHz with boost from 0.0 to 20.0 dB.

```
// --- filters
bite _ dB = getModKnobValueLinear(parameters->modKnobValue[MOD _ KNOB _ C],
                            0.0, 20.0);
```

```
highShelfFilter.setParameters(2000.0, bite _ dB);
```

The "body" filter is a parametric boost-only filter with 0.0 to +6 dB of gain, and various f_c and Q values depending on the model – these too are highly experimental.

```
body _ dB = getModKnobValueLinear(parameters->modKnobValue[MOD _ KNOB _ B],
                        0.0, 6.0);
```

```
// --- fc, Q vary with model
if (parameters->algorithmIndex == kNylonGtr)
    bodyFilter.setParameters(400.0, 1.0, body _ dB);
else if (parameters->algorithmIndex == kDistGtr)
    bodyFilter.setParameters(300.0, 2.0, body _ dB);
else if (parameters->algorithmIndex == kBass)
    bodyFilter.setParameters(250.0, 1.0, body _ dB);
```

13.9.5 Render Phase

The *render* function is fairly simple because the member objects do most of the work; it follows the flow of Figure 13.8, from exciter to pluck position filter to resonator to body filter in that order. The fundamental differences are in the pluck position filter, whose output is tapped from different locations for each model, and the added preamp simulator for the distorted guitar model. The process starts with the exciter and high-shelf filter:

```
double input = exciter.render();
input = highShelfFilter.processAudioSample(input);
```

The pluck position is altered by model:

```
if (parameters->algorithmIndex == kNylonGtr)
    input = pluckPosFilter.processAudioSample(input,
                              PluckFilterType::kPluckAndBridge);


else if (parameters->algorithmIndex == kDistGtr)
    input = pluckPosFilter.processAudioSample(input,
                              PluckFilterType::kPluckAndPickup);
else if (parameters->algorithmIndex == kBass)
    input = pluckPosFilter.processAudioSample(input,
                            PluckFilterType::kPluckPickupBridge);
```

The bass is lowpass filtered twice through the pickup and bridge filters, and has the least high harmonics. The input is applied to the resonator object, then the preamp simulator is applied to the distorted guitar output only.

```
// --- resonate the excitation
double oscOutput = resonator.process(input);

// --- VERY simple guitar preamp sim
if (parameters->algorithmIndex == kDistGtr)
{
    int stages = 8;
    for (int i = 0; i < stages; i++)
        oscOutput = tanhWaveShaper(oscOutput, 1.0);

    // --- drop -6dB; make up for energy boost
    oscOutput = 0.5 * distortionFilter.processAudioSample(oscOutput);
}
```

Finally, the body filter and output amplitude values are applied, and the output is written:

```
// --- add resonance if desired
oscOutput = bodyFilter.processAudioSample(oscOutput);
oscOutput *= outputAmplitude;

// --- write to output buffers
leftOutBuffer[i] = oscOutput;
rightOutBuffer[i] = oscOutput;
```

13.10 Extensions to the KS Algorithm

The plucked string algorithm has been augmented over the years, with numerous extensions and improvements. An excellent source you may use as a starting point is Valamaki, which documents the additions and contains a plethora of references and sources for more information and study. These additions include:

- Electric guitar and bass pickup output (requires dual delay lines)
- Pluck shaping to model variations in pluck and pick stroke angles
- Sympathetic vibration of open strings; applications to the old-fashioned harp-guitar

The chapter references here also contain information about hammered and bowed-string models, which include coupling between resonator and exciter, and involve scattering junctions.

13.11 Exercises

13.11.1 SynthLab-DM: High Register Accommodations

The high-shelving filter allows the boosting of high frequencies in the exciter; however if you play very high notes, you will notice that the attack loses its sharpness (Jaffe and Smith 1983). Implement a system that adjusts the high-shelving filter's gain value and/or shelving frequency to accommodate notes in the upper register. Next, note that, for the nylon string model, the notes lose energy very quickly in the upper register, and though that is similar to the real instrument, you may want to try to extend the note duration by manipulating the loop's *decay* parameter, which is set in the resonator model (see the code in Section 13.6.1).

13.11.2 SynthLab-DM: 12-String Guitar

A 12-string guitar uses pairs of strings, called courses, that are tuned one octave apart for the lower four strings and in unison for the upper pair of B and E strings. You can implement these extra strings as additional resonators and feed the excitation signal to each in parallel. For the unison-tuned string pairs, you can apply a bit of detuning for a thicker sound. Implement your own 12-string guitar model as a new *KSOCore*, or modify the existing core to add the 12-string option. If you want to go further with realism, research the sympathetic vibration modeling for open-string chords, and add that to your implementation.

13.11.3 SynthLab-DM: Body Resonance and Electric Guitar Feedback

The exciter's *render* method includes an input so that the exciter may be re-stimulated from the resonator. This has two immediate applications: first, the body of the guitar usually has multiple resonant peaks (see Fletcher and Rossing), and this may be simulated with resonant filters that feed back from the resonator into the exciter. Many electric guitarists feature feedback in their styles; one method to create this is to rest the headstock of the guitar on the vibrating amp to couple the energy back into the instrument. This is equivalent to coupling part of the resonator's output back into the exciter directly or through a filter; in both cases, care is needed to avoid runaway feedback. Postulate a model for body resonances and/or guitar feedback that re-energize the exciter with part of the resonator's signal and implement it. Guitar feedback is often on octave boundaries, so that would be a place to start your experiments. Use the *coupledInput* variable for the exciter object's render function to channel audio back to the exciter.

Bibliography

Karjalainen, Matti, Välimäki, Vesa & Tolonen, Tero. 1998. "Plucked String Models: From the Karplus-Strong Algorithm to Digital Waveguides and Beyond." *Computer Music Journal*, vol. 22, no. 3, pp. 17–32, Cambridge: MIT Press.

Jaffe, David & Smith, Julius. 1983. "Extensions of the Karplus-Strong Plucked-String Algorithm." *Computer Music Journal*, vol. 7, no. 2, pp. 56–69, Cambridge: MIT Press.

Kahrs, Mark & Karlheinz, Brandenburg. 1998. *Applications of Digital Signal Processing to Audio and Acoustics*, Chap. 10. Boston: Klewer Academic Publishers.

Karjalainan, Matti, Välimäki, Vesa & Jánosy, Zoltan. 1993. "Towards High-Quality Sound Synthesis of the Guitar and String Instruments." Proceedings of the 1993 International Computer Music Conference, San Francisco, California: International Computer Music Association, pp. 56–63.

Karplus, Kevin & Strong, Alex 1983. "Digital Synthesis of Plucked-String and Drum Timbres." *Computer Music Journal*, vol. 7, no. 2, pp. 43–55. Reprinted in C. Roads, ed. 1989. *The Music Machine*. Cambridge: MIT Press.

Smith, Julius Orion. 1993. "Efficient Synthesis of Stringed Musical Instruments." Proceedings of the 1993 International Computer Music Conference, San Francisco, California: International Computer Music Association, pp. 64–71.

Smith, Julius. 2010. *Physical Audio Signal Processing*, Chap. 9. Stanford: Center for Computer Research in Music and Acoustics.

14 The Modulation Matrix

Chapter 6 detailed the various types of modulations and calculations, then each of the synth modules implemented an *update* function that used one or more of the modulations and corresponding calculations. These synth modules are modulation destinations because they change their internal parameters when modulation values are applied. The LFO and EG modules are modulation sources because their outputs are applied to the modulation destinations. For FM synthesis, pitched oscillators are used as both modulation sources and modulation destinations; this is possible for other modules as well, as it is with the LFOs that can modulate each other's oscillator frequency. The modulation matrix is used to connect sources and destinations during the voice object's update phase. The matrix must therefore know the locations of all of the source values (the outputs of the LFOs and EGs) as well as the locations of the destinations (the modulation inputs). We will use the *ModMatrix* object to connect our modules together.

14.1 Modulation Inputs and Outputs

Each *SynthModule* object includes two *Modulators* member objects: one for incoming modulation values and another for modulation outputs named *modulationInput* and *modulationOutput*. The *Modulators* object is a thin wrapper for a statically declared array of 32 *double* values, with get/set function access to the array elements and a special array pointer access for the modulation matrix. The elements are indexed with a simple *enum*, and all *SynthModules* share the same modulation input array index names, as shown in Figure 14.1(a). There are currently 22 modulation inputs when you include the additional wave-sequencing object in SynthLab-WS, and you may add as many more as you like as the array will be self-sizing. Each module that generates a modulation output writes into its *modulationOutput* using its own module-specific index names, as shown for the LFO core in Figure 14.1(b) and (c). The EG has another set of index names, as shown in Figure 14.1(d).

14.2 Modulation Routings

A modulation routing (or mod routing) is a specific connection between the modulation output array of one object and the modulation input array of another, such as the connection shown in Figure 14.2, where the mod source is LFO1's normal output (array slot 0), and the mod destination is OSC2's bipolar input (array slot 3). Each routing is a unique (source, destination) pair. In the SynthLab *ModMatrix* object, any number of sources may modulate the same destination. The modulation matrix's parameter object stores a set of modulation routings, and you may add, remove, or re-configure the routings at any time. You may also define pre-wired routings for a

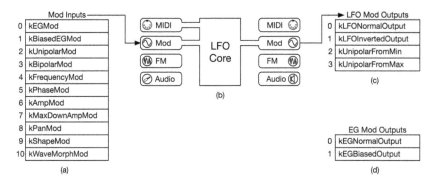

Figure 14.1 (a) The modulation input array is indexed the same way for all *SynthModules* using constant declarations for kEGMod, kBiasedEGMod, etc… (b) the LFO Core exposes a modulation input and a modulation output (c) the modulation output array is indexed specifically for the LFO using constant declarations while (d) shows the indexing for the EG's modulation output array for comparison

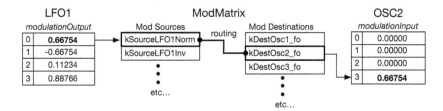

Figure 14.2 A modulation routing that connects LFO1's normal output to OSC2's bipolar modulation input, which modulates the oscillator's frequency

semi-modular design: for example, the amp EG's output is always hardwired to the DCA's EG input, while a filter EG's output is always connected to a filter's f_c modulation input.

The *ModMatrix* source and destination arrays are indexed with their own simple *enums* that need to be separate from the module *enums*, and you can easily add more, as needed. Mod sources are prefixed with "source" and likewise with destinations, so the constants are easy to decode.

```
enum modSource
{
    // --- LFOs here
    kSourceLFO1 _ Norm,
    kSourceLFO1 _ Inv,

    kSourceLFO2 _ Norm,
    kSourceLFO2 _ Inv,

    // --- EGs here
    kSourceAmpEG _ Norm,
    kSourceAmpEG _ Bias,
    // etc . . .
```

```
    // --- remain last, will always be the size of modulator array
    kNumberModSources
};

enum modDestination
{
    kDestOsc1 _ fo,
    kDestOsc2 _ fo,
    // etc . . .

    kDestOsc1 _ Amp,
    kDestOsc2 _ Amp,
    // etc . . .

    // --- remain last, will always be the size of modulator array
    kNumberModDestinations
};
```

14.2.1 Mod Routing Selection and Intensity Controls

Modulation matrices take on varying forms in different synth designs. Figure 14.3 shows two out of the many possible GUI design choices for a modulation matrix. The modulation matrix in Figure 14.3(a) looks like an actual matrix, with rows (sources) and columns (destinations). On the EMS VCS3, pins are inserted into holes, which make the electrical connection between the analog source and the destination (the pins contain resistors for summing and attenuating). On the Arturia Prophet VS plugin, GUI buttons are used to create the mod routings, and this synth includes intensity controls for the sources and destinations. You can think of them as global send and receive controls per source and destination. In this mod matrix, the user can map any or all sources to any or all destinations, as desired. You can see that both the LFO2 and EG2 modulate the same destination – in this case, the mod values are summed together without scaling.

Figure 14.3(b) shows a different type of mod matrix; here, the user is restricted to only four modulation routings and presented with a selection list for each routing pair. This matrix features individual intensity controls for each routing, allowing for finer control per mod routing connection. In this version, the selection lists must also include a "no connection" choice.

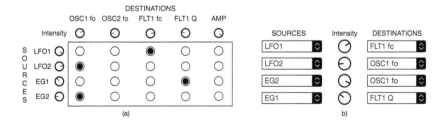

Figure 14.3 Modulation matrix designs include (a) pin/button programmable with global source and destination intensity controls, and (b) a limited choice matrix with individual channel routing intensity controls

14.3 Mod Matrix Channel Routing

The modulation matrix is packaged as a C++ object named *ModMatrix*. Figures 14.1–14.3 make apparent that the *ModMatrix* object will need to know the source and destination locations in order to pull and push the mod values into place. On the destination end, it will need to accumulate the mod values since multiple sources can modulate a single destination. There are numerous ways in which to handle this, including individual arrays for sources and destinations. The method in *ModMatrix* is to store pointers to the statically declared modulation input and output array locations on each synth module; it reads from the source array slot and accumulates into the destination array location. This must be done at the voice level, and the *SynthVoice* constructor sets up the sources, destinations, and hardwired routings.

In order to accommodate many mod matrix schemes, the *ModMatrix* object includes multiple intensity controls, a hardwired bypass path that overrides the channel path, and channel enable and disable controls, as shown in Figure 14.4(a). The intensity controls are source, channel, and destination; these may look like overkill, but they are there for maximum flexibility in your designs. And you will rarely use all three intensity controls. Figure 14.4(b) shows how the object is configured to match the mod matrix in Figure 14.3(a). In this case, there is a single GUI intensity control for each source and destination, but they connect to the same parameter within each modulation routing. Figure 14.4(c) shows the configuration for Figure 14.3(b), which only requires an enable switch and channel intensity control.

14.4 *ModSource* and *ModDestination* for GUI Controls

Ultimately, the user programs the *ModMatrix* via the GUI, or you can set up the object programmatically from within the *SynthVoice* object. There is only one set of *ModMatrix* controls on the synth, but these routings apply to all of the voices. However, each voice contains its own set of modules (LFOs, EGs, etc.), which are locally owned, and they have their own local modulation

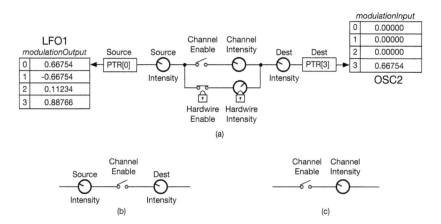

Figure 14.4 (a) The *ModMatrix* configuration for a single routing shows the multiple intensity controls and enable-switches; in this example, the hardwire enable switch is overriding the channel branch while (b) and (c) demonstrate the routing configurations that match Figures 14.3 (a) and (b), respectively

input and output arrays, and therefore need their own set of array pointers – these are not shared resources. To manage this issue, I use one *ModMatrix* object per voice, which stores pointers to the voice's member object modulation array slots. In order to share the GUI parameters for routing and intensity functions, I use *std::shared_ptrs* to *std::arrays* in the *ModMatrixParameters* structure, which handles user input from the GUI. These arrays are named "rows" for sources and "columns" for destinations. There are two *std::arrays*, one each for the sources and destinations, holding tiny C++ structures called *ModSource* and *ModDestination*; these store the GUI routing and intensity settings.

The *ModSource* structure contains a single intensity parameter, while the *ModDestination* contains its own intensity variable plus the channel and hardwire-enable and intensity parameters. The *ModDestination* is special because there may be many routing channels merging into a single destination. Thus, the *ModDestination* parameters are stored in arrays of 48 channels, providing the capacity for up to 48 rows of modulation sources in the matrix; if you require more, simply change the constant definition for the array size. Notice that the array objects are sized to *modSourceRows* and *modDestinationColumns* from the *enums* in Section 14.2, so, as you add or remove your own, these sizes will automatically reset.

14.5 *ModMatrixParameters*

The *ModMatrixParameters* structure contains only two member variables: the shared pointers to the source and destination parameter arrays. The GUI controls are parsed into these arrays.

```
// --- modulation matrix rows and columns
std::shared _ ptr<std::array<ModSource, kNumberModSources>>
                                    modSourceRows;

std::shared _ ptr<std::array<ModDestination, kNumberModDestinations>>
                                    modDestinationColumns;
```

To facilitate transferring the GUI control information into the structures, several helper functions are provided that accept the source and destination index values and intensity controls.

```
void setMM _ SourceIntensity
void setMM _ DestIntensity

void setMM _ ChannelEnable
void setMM _ ChannelIntensity

void setMM _ HardwireEnable
void setMM _ DestHardwireIntensity
void setMM _ DestDefaultValue
```

A final function allows a single call to set a complete hardwired routing, including source and destination index values and the hardwired channel intensity.

```
void setMM _ HardwiredRouting(uint32 _ t source, uint32 _ t destination,
                            double intensity = 1.0)
```

14.6 The *ModMatrix* Object

There will be one *ModMatrix* object for each voice, and it is simple, containing only three member variables: a shared pointer to the parameters and source and destination arrays, sized exactly as needed for holding pointers to the source and destination value locations.

```
// --- parameters
std::shared_ptr<ModMatrixParameters> parameters = nullptr;

// --- arrays to hold source/destination pointers
double* modSourceData[kNumberModSources];
double* modDestinationData[kNumberModDestinations];
```

The *ModMatrix* object also includes a set of functions for adding and removing sources or destinations, along with functions for populating the arrays with local pointers. The only other method is for running the modulation matrix that will happen once per render block – after the modulator components have rendered their values and before the destinations have updated their parameters. The simple *for* loop is organized with columns (destinations) as the outer loop since the destinations may have multiple sources. If the *channelEnable* is not set, the loop continues. This short and simple function provides all of the modulation routing and calculations.

```
// --- loop over destinations columns & calculate the accumulated
//     modulation value
double modDestinationValue = 0.0;

for (int col = 0; col < kNumberModDestinations; col++)
{
    ModDestination destination = parameters->
                                   modDestinationColumns->at(col);

    modDestinationValue = destination.defautValue;

    for (int row = 0; row < kNumberModSources; row++)
    {
        if (!modSourceData[row] ||
            destination.channelEnable[row] == 0)
            continue;

        // --- get local modulation value
        double modSourceValue = *modSourceData[row];

        ModSource source = parameters->modSourceRows->at(row);

        // --- scale it
        modSourceValue *= source.intensity;

        // --- choose intensity
```

```
        if (destination.channelHardwire[row])
            modDestinationValue += modSourceValue *
                                    destination.hardwireIntensity[row];
        else
            modDestinationValue += destination.intensity *
                                                    modSourceValue;
    }
    // --- write to the output array
    if (modDestinationData[col])
        *modDestinationData[col] = modDestinationValue;
}
```

14.7 Initializing the *ModMatrix*

The *SynthVoiceParameters* structure declares the shared pointer to the *ModMatrixParameters* and uses the *make_shared* function such that the first *SynthVoice* that is created will create the shared structure for the rest of the voices so the GUI controls are handled without a problem.

The *SynthVoice* uses *std::unique_ptrs* for its modules as they are never shared across voices. The *ModMatrix* is declared in the class definition, then created in the constructor, passing the shared parameters during *ModMatrix* construction.

```
// --- each voice has a modulation matrix
//    but rows/columns are shared via matrix parameters
std::unique _ ptr<ModMatrix> modMatrix;


// --- creation
modMatrix.reset(new ModMatrix(parameters->modMatrixParameters));
```

In order to use the *ModMatrix*, the *SynthVoice* object needs to program its member object with several pieces of information. First, it needs to set up the pointers to each module's source or destination array location. To add sources or destinations, you use the helper functions. Setting up the LFO1 as a source and OSC2's f_o as a destination is simple – the oscillators all use the *kBipolarMod* array slot for modulating the f_o, so you request pointers via *getModArrayPtr* and provide the index:

```
// --- add LFO1 Output Source index and pointer
modMatrix->addModSource(kSourceLFO1 _ Norm,
    lfo1->getModulationOutput()->getModArrayPtr(kLFONormalOutput));


// --- add wavetable oscillator fo as destination
modMatrix->addModDestination(kDestOsc1 _ fo,
    wtOsc->getModulationInput()->getModArrayPtr(kBipolarMod));
```

To remove a mod source or destination during runtime, you use the *clear* methods:

```
modMatrix->clearModSource(kSourceLFO1 _ Norm);
modMatrix->clearModDestination(kDestOsc1 _ fo);
```

14.8 Programming the *ModMatrix*

Each *SynthVoice's* mod matrix object is specific to it and only contains the arrays of local pointers. To program the *ModMatrix*, you use the *ModMatrixParameters*, either via GUI control information or programmatically from within the voice object.

To set up a hardwired routing from the *AmpEG* to the DCA's EG mod input, you write:

```
parameters->modMatrixParameters->setMM _ HardwiredRouting(
                        kSourceAmpEG _ Norm, kDestDCA _ EGMod);
```

All destinations have a default value that is set to 0.0 on creation, but there are some routings that require a default setting of 1.0 to prevent accidental silence. This is necessary for the *AmpEG* to DCA EG mod and is handled with another helper function:

```
parameters->modMatrixParameters->setMM _ DestDefaultValue(
                                    kDestDCA _ AmpMod, 1.0);
```

To enable the routing from LFO1 to OSC2's f_o, you write the following; notice that the enable argument *true* may come from a GUI control switch.

```
parameters->modMatrixParameters->setMM _ ChannelEnable(
                        kSourceLFO1 _ Norm, kDestOsc2 _ fo, true);
```

To set the channel intensity to 0.707 for this routing, you write the following; as with the channel enable, the 0.707 value may come from a GUI knob or slider.

```
parameters->modMatrixParameters->setMM _ ChannelIntensity(
                        kSourceLFO1 _ Norm, kDestOsc2 _ fo, 0.707);
```

The source and destination global intensity values are set with the same types of functions:

```
setMM _ SourceIntensity(kSourceLFO1 _ Norm, 0.456);
setMM _ DestIntensity(kDestOsc2 _ fo, 0.789);
```

14.9 Mod Matrix Transforms

The SynthLab modulation matrix consists of sources that are both bipolar (LFO and wave sequencer) and unipolar (EG). For most modulations, you may freely mix these together. On occasion, you may need to declare a destination as requiring a unipolar-to-bipolar or bipolar-to-unipolar transform, as happens with the EG re-triggering modulation in Section 7.7. The MMA DLS specs also list inversion (multiply by −1), along with the curved transforms as transform possibilities. When you declare a modulation destination, you may also add an optional transform into the function arguments.

```
modMatrix->addModDestination(kDestAmpEGRetrigger,
            ampEG->getModulationInput()->getModArrayPtr
            (kTriggerMod), kMMTransformUnipolar);
```

14.10 Running the *ModMatrix*

The *ModMatrix* is executed after the modulators have generated their outputs and before the destinations are updated during the *SynthVoice::renderVoice* operation. For example, in a wavetable synth voice, you would write this:

```
// --- render modulators
lfo1->render(samplesToProcess);
lfo2->render(samplesToProcess);

// --- update/render (add more here)
ampEG->render(samplesToProcess);
filterEG->render(samplesToProcess);
auxEG->render(samplesToProcess);

// --- run the mod matrix
modMatrix->runModMatrix();

// --- update and render everything else
wtOsc1->render(samplesToProcess);
wtOsc2->render(samplesToProcess);

// --- etc...
```

Bibliography

MIDI Manufacturer's Association. 1999. *Downloadable Sounds Level 1*. https://www.midi.org/specifications-old/item/dls-level-1-specification, Accessed October 14, 2020

MIDI Manufacturer's Association. 1999. *Downloadable Sounds Level 2*. https://www.midi.org/specifications-old/item/dls-level-2-specification, Accessed October 14, 2020

SynthLab Documentation. 2020. www.willpirkle.com/synthlab-docs, Accessed October 14, 2020

15 Wave Morphing and Wave Sequencing

In recent years, there has been a resurgence in dynamic timbral synthesis with waveform cross-fading. Wolfgang Palm, Sequential Circuits, and Korg have released synths that generate long evolving sounds, percussive loops, and searing lead patches using fairly simple waveform crossfade techniques. These include:

1   **Wave morphing**: crossfading a series of waveforms, one after the other, using an LFO, EG, or other modulation source that smoothly morphs between them; there are only ever two waveforms that are being crossfaded or mixed at a given time
2   **Wave sequencing**: crossfading a series of waveforms, one after another, based on a sequencer designed in order to perform a combination of crossfading and holding such that the waveform morphing follows a rhythmic sequence or pattern; unlike wave morphing, sequencing often involves holding the waveforms using rhythmic note durations between crossfades or allowing for silent gaps that break up the sequence, producing rhythmic patterns without necessarily needing drum sounds
3   **Vector synthesis**: implements waveform crossfading using a joystick or pre-programmed mix envelopes; one, two, three, or four waveforms may be mixed at any given time corresponding to the joystick's four extremes when an x, y grid is superimposed on the joystick's motion

Vector mixing is covered in Section 6.4 and requires an X-Y track-pad on the GUI; the original Sequential Circuits equations are given so you can translate the joystick's x, y location into a set of four mix values for performing the four-way crossfading that is central to this synthesis method. This chapter is about wave morphing and wave sequencing.

15.1 Wave Banks

Before getting into the details, we need to consider the fact that wave morphing will require multiple data sources, and for simplicity, only wavetables are used for morphing and sequencing. The *SynthEngine* already maintains a wavetable database, as discussed in Section 9.2, so we already have a system for storing and sharing the tables. Wave morphing synths usually employ sets of waveforms that are designed to work together as a group. In SynthLab, a group of wavetables that is imported all at once is called a wave *bank*. The tables are stored in the normal manner and may be used like any other wavetable, but the importing mechanism only involves one step, and the morphing wavetable core has access to all of the waveform names in each bank; thus, it has the unique strings necessary to select the waveforms in succession from the database as it morphs during the render phase. The *SynthLabBankSet* structure stores pointers to the tables as well as a list of waveform names for the database. All of this is documented online.

15.2 Wave Morphing

Wave morphing involves crossfading over a series of oscillator waveforms in succession using a modulation signal that may come from GUI controls or from a modulator component. Wavetable and PCM samples lend themselves easily to this kind of crossfading, especially when the tables or files are all the same length; here, I use the term *table* to represent any tabular data source, including PCM samples. Wolfgang Palm's Infinite® and Korg's Electribe Wave® are excellent examples, among many others. Infinite is special because it displays morphing in the frequency domain, showing the spectra of the waveform slices rather than the time domain representation that is more common. In addition, Infinite allows you to precisely control the spectral components – for example, you may manually cut out every other harmonic or alter the harmonic envelope of each slice.

Wave morphing requires a set of source tables (slices) that are distributed along a morphing dimension; you need at least two waveforms to morph over, but commercial morphing table collections usually range from four to hundreds of different tables for generating only one note-event. Figure 15.1 shows several variations, and the double-arrows show the morphing dimension. The morphing table sets (or banks) may be made of dissimilar waveforms, as in Figure 15.1(a), which includes a sinusoid, triangle, square, and sawtooth waveform (from back to front), and is named *PrimalWaves* in the SynthLab-WT project. Another bank preparation involves starting with a common waveform and varying one or two parameters of it, taking sample slices at regular intervals, as shown in Figure 15.1(b)'s square wave, whose duty cycle is changed over the course of the bank's waveforms. Figure 15.1(c) shows a bank that starts with a complex waveform processed through filters, waveshapers, and other effects to produce a related set of waveforms.

15.2.1 Wave Morph Modulation

The crossfade modulation that occurs between the fixed waveforms includes a starting point, intensity, and a modulation control signal. The modulation signal that controls the location of the current morphing point is typically a low frequency modulator, such as an LFO, EG, or MIDI CC. Figure 15.2(a) shows an LFO morphing back and forth across a range of four waveforms. The dotted waveforms are the interpolated or in-between combinations of the two fixed waveforms on either side. With slow modulators, there will be thousands of interpolated waveforms between the fixed sources. Figure 15.2(b) shows morphing with an EG that is significantly different. The EG

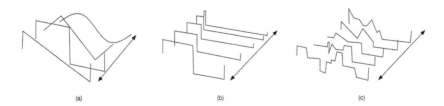

(a)   (b)   (c)

Figure 15.1 Three sets of tables for morphing, including (a) dissimilar waveforms, (b) one waveform whose parameters are adjusted for each slice, and (c) a complex waveform that has undergone multiple passes of filtering or other processing

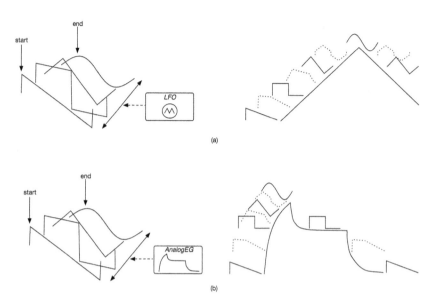

Figure 15.2 (a) An LFO modulates the wave-morphing index, producing a smoothly interpolated succession of waveforms back and forth along the range, while (b) the EG also morphs the waveforms but stops during the sustain portion, holding the current waveform constant prior to release

curve morphs over the waveforms but stops at the sustain morph point and holds that waveform until the key is released, when the morphing moves backward toward the starting waveform. The user can typically control the starting morph waveform with a floating-point control value that allows the starting point to be in between waveforms.

15.3 The *MorphWTCore*

The wavetable oscillator from Section 9.3 loads wavetable module cores that use the wavetable database it provides via the engine. The *ClassicWTCore* is designed to load statically declared wavetables, which are provided in a set of *.h* files and use the *SynthLabTableSet* structure to store the data. Since SynthLab uses interfaces for the wavetable databank, you are free to use whatever mechanism you wish for storing and importing by modifying the existing structure or sub-classing *IWavetableDatabase*. The *MorphWTCore* is also a wavetable core and snaps into the SynthLab-WT project alongside the other cores, though with two differences: it uses the *SynthLabBankSet* to import the tables to the database, and it stores interface pointers for two table sources instead of one, interpolating between them as required. As the morphing index moves along, the two table sources always point to the waveform pair needed for interpolation. The mechanisms for reading and interpolating the individual tables do not change, and the *auxEG* is used as the hardwired morphing modulator, so everything is already present in the SynthLab architecture to support the *MorphWTCore*.

Figure 15.3 shows how the *MorphWTCore* works as a wavetable oscillator core object, and the modules' strings point to wavetable banks, which are really just a pre-set list of wavetables in the database. The *auxEG* is hardwired to the *kWaveMorphMod* array slot, which acts as a unipolar

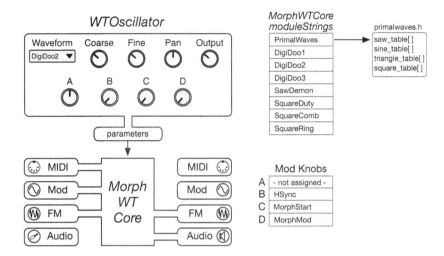

Figure 15.3 The *MorphWTCore* snaps into the *WTOscillator* object and exposes its mod knobs, which are slightly different and include morph start index and morph mod intensity; notice that the module strings point to a bank of wavetables

morph position modulator. The unique modulation input may be connected to an LFO and accepts bipolar modulation based around the center point, which is set with the morph start control.

15.4 *MorphWTCore* Programming Notes

The *MorphWTCore* is fundamentally the same as the other wavetable cores except for the fact that it uses two wavetable sources whose tables are blended through constant power morph modulation (Section 6.2.2). It also initializes the wavetable database using a *SynthLabBankSet*, which is simply an array of *SynthLabTableSet* pointers and a corresponding array of unique wavetable names. The code for setting up the banks is straightforward and involves two parts: first, the core stores a set of *MorphBankData* structures for each set of wavetables that includes the bank name and the table names. There is one structure for each module string, so for the *PrimalWaves* bank, the information would include that bank name plus an array of table names, *DigiSaw, DigiSine*, etc. This is the mechanism that connects the bank name the user selects to the set of tables and allows the core to find and load those tables to morph between. The second part simply iterates over the wavetables, querying the database during the reset phase and adding tables as needed, which is just a big loop over the same code that you saw for the normal wavetable oscillator.

15.4.1 **MorphWTCore** *Construction Phase*

The constructor is identical to the other wavetable core constructors except for the fact that it uses banks of wavetables. The object uses the function *addMorphBankData* to store the set of unique wavetable name strings for each bank. The user only sees the bank names, but the oscillator needs the waveform names to morph across. The *BankDescriptors* are part of my implementation of the

SynthLabBankSet, which contains an array of *SynthLabTableSets*. Remember that you are free to set up your wavetables as you wish as long as you use the *IWavetableDatabase* interface on your wavetable object.

```
moduleType = WTO _ MODULE;
moduleName = "Morph WT";

// --- this must be done before setting module strings
uint32 _ t count = 0;
addMorphBankData("PrimalWaves", PrimalWaves _ BankDescriptor, count++);
addMorphBankData("DigiDool", DigDool _ BankDescriptor, count++);
```

etc…

The module strings are then set, using the morph bank names that are stored in the previous operation.

```
for(uint32 _ t i=0; i<MODULE _ STRINGS; i++)
    coreData.moduleStrings[i] = morphBankData[i].bankName.c _ str();
```

Finally, the mod knobs labels are assigned according to Figure 15.3.

15.4.2 MorphWTCore *Reset Phase*

The *reset* function is fundamentally the same as it is for the other wavetable cores, but it queries the database for banks of wavetables rather than individual tables, using a helper function that loops through the bank's waveforms, ensuring each is registered with the database.

```
// --- query and add all waveforms in each bank
checkAddWaveBank(PrimalWaves _ BankDescriptor, processInfo);
checkAddWaveBank(DigDool _ BankDescriptor, processInfo);
etc…
```

15.4.3 MorphWTCore *Update Phase*

After performing the usual pitch modulation calculations from Section 6.8.1, the core needs to use the morph modulation input value to select a pair of tables to morph between. The morph start and end index values are used to set up a range that is normalized to the range [0, +1]. Then the wave morph modulation value (from the *auxEG*) is applied to select the pair of tables. The fractional distance between the tables is used as the interpolation point.

```
// --- get the floating point morph position
morphMod = processInfo.modulationInputs->getModValue(kWaveMorphMod);

// --- NOTE -1
morphTables = morphBankData[parameters->wavetableIndex].numTables - 1;

// --- mod knob C is the intensity control
```

```
morphStart = morphTables * parameters->modKnobValue[MOD_KNOB_C];

// --- calculate morph location and save for render
morphLocation = morphMod * (morphTables - morphStart);

boundValue(morphLocation, 0.0, (double)morphTables);

uint32_t table0 = (uint32_t)morphLocation;
uint32_t table1 = (uint32_t)morphLocation + 1;
if (table1 > morphTables)
    table1 = table0;
```

The two table index values are used to identify the tables via their unique waveform names, which were stored in the *MorphBankData* structure during the first step in Section 14.4. The waveform names for *table0* and *table1* are found in the structure, then used to select the wavetables:

```
bankIndex = parameters->wavetableIndex;
table0str = morphBankData[bankIndex].tableNames[table0].c_str()
table1str = morphBankData[bankIndex].tableNames[table1].c_str()

selectedTableSource[0] =
    processInfo.wavetableDatabase->getTableSource(table0str);

selectedTableSource[1] =
    processInfo.wavetableDatabase->getTableSource(table1str);
```

   With the two tables selected and the fractional morph location stored, all that remains is blending the two tables during the render phase.

15.4.4 MorphWTCore *Render Phase*

The *render* function is identical to the same function in the other wavetable cores, even in its ability to self hard sync the morphing oscillator. The only difference is in the *renderSample* helper function that performs the morph. If the morph location happens to be a pure integer value, then only one table is used.

```
double MorphWTCore::renderSample(SynthClock& clock){

double mCounter = clock.mcounter;

// --- integer morph location
if (selectedTableSource[0] == selectedTableSource[1])
    return selectedTableSource[0]->readWaveTable(mCounter);
```

   After the table read operations, the morph location is split into integer and fractional parts, and the fraction is used to interpolate points between the tables. After the output is formed, the clock is advanced as usual.

```
// --- two table reads
double oscOutput0 = selectedTableSource[0]->readWaveTable(mCounter);
double oscOutput1 = selectedTableSource[1]->readWaveTable(mCounter);

// --- split the fractional index into int.frac parts
double intPart = 0.0;
double morphFraction = modf(morphLocation, &intPart);

// --- const power summing:
double mixValueA = 0.0;
double mixValueB = 0.0;

// --- calculate mix values
calculateConstPwrMixValues(morphFraction, mixValueA, mixValueB);

// --- morph
double oscOutput = oscOutput0*mixValueA + oscOutput1*mixValueB;
```

The self hard sync code is identical to the other wavetable cores since the *renderSample* function does all of the work.

15.5 Wave Sequencing 1.0

Korg introduced another type of crossfade modulation called wave sequencing in the Wavestation® line, which also included vector synthesis. The idea is to set up a sequence of waveforms in steps that are both crossfaded over some duration and held for another duration according to a pattern, often rhythmic in nature. Each track in the sequencer is made up of a sequence of steps. A wave sequence track stores the crossfade and step durations that are applied to morph each successive pair of waveforms into and out of one other, as shown in the "Waves" track of Figure 15.4. The step durations are carried over into other tracks, which adjust pitch and amplitude so these

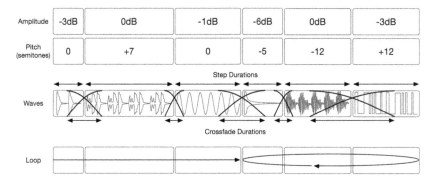

Figure 15.4 Korg's wave sequencer from the Wavestation featured the ability to hold and crossfading waveforms while also modulating each segment's pitch and amplitude; the waveforms actually blend together during the crossfades and are shown separated for easier viewing; the amplitudes were not displayed in dB in the Wavestation

parameters are modulated along with the crossfaded waveforms. A loop system, shown as a loop track in Figure 15.4, sets the looping points with numerous looping options available, including a no-loop (one-shot) setting. Finally, it is also possible to create silent (rest) segments, and this is key to creating complex drum tracks with interesting rhythmic variations using just one wave sequence.

In the original Korg wave sequencing (now called Wave Sequencing 1.0), all of the tracks were locked together in time and controlled with the loop track so that each step applied the same pitch and amplitude to the crossfaded waveforms in the same manner: for example, the waveform in Step Two in Figure 15.4 would always be shifted +7 semitones and always play at unity gain. The Wavestation took this concept to the extreme: a wave sequence was rendered from one oscillator, and the Wavestation had four of these oscillators running in parallel, each with its own wave sequence and timing patterns, that could be mixed with the four-way vector synthesis modulation in Section 6.3, creating bass lines, drum tracks, slowly modulating pads, and a searing lead sound all in one patch.

15.5.1 Wave Sequencing 2.0

Nearly 30 years after the Wavestation's release, in January 2020, Korg released the Wavestate®, which was designed and voiced with some of the original Wavestation engineers and sound designers, and uses both wavetables and PCM samples, referring to all of them, simply, as samples. The Wavestate features what Korg calls "Wave Sequencing 2.0," which re-thinks the wave sequencer and its possibilities for generating dense, unique, and even un-repeatable patterns. The synth itself has deep modulation capabilities, some of which affect the wave sequencing, but its design and operation are outside the book's scope. In the Wavestate, the wave sequencer is divided into lanes made up of steps. There is one timing lane, which sets up the crossfade and segment duration times; a sample lane that stores the waveform for each step; lanes for modulating parameters that apply to the waveforms (pitch, amplitude, note/rest); and a step sequencer lane, also for modulating other parameters in the synth (e.g. filter f_c). In addition to the use of the name lanes, some of the fundamental additions to the 2.0 version also include:

1   The ability for each lane to operate independently with its own looping setup; all segments in the lanes are still locked to the timing lane's segment *durations*, but they may move freely on their own, loop back and forth, or jump around randomly
2   The steps in each lane, including the timing lane, have their own probability setting which randomly enables or disables them; for a non-timing step, disabling it shuts off the output value so it is not applied (note that this is different from transmitting a zero value)
3   A disabled timing step is absorbed into the previous step, elongating the segment duration and crossfade times
4   Each timing step has three operational modes: *note* (play normally), *rest* (silence), or *gate* (hold this step during the sustain portion of the amp envelope)

Figure 15.5(a) shows how the Wavestate wave sequencer is set up so that each lane has its own start, end, loop start, and loop ending points, removing the original Wavestation's step locking. The non-timing steps are shown in dotted lines because they will inherit the duration from the timing lane. In addition to amplitude and pitch, there are lanes that include shape (a contour applied as an amplitude scalar) and segment gating, where you set the amount of time the waveform plays as a percentage of the timing step's duration, which itself is powerful: since the lanes are not

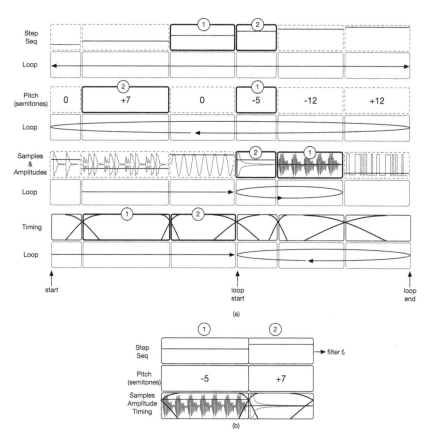

Figure 15.5 (a) The Wavestate's wave sequencer splits out each lane with its own start, stop, loop start, and loop end points (b) a possible combination of lanes showing the lane steps marked (1) and (2); the timing lane is used to synchronize the other lane step durations and crossfade timing

locked together, this step's on and off times will be applied to whatever waveform happens to be in the sample lane at the time. This also means that each segments pitch, amplitude, and contour may vary over time, and with the use of probability settings, the sequencer can generate a non-repeating stream of melodies, rhythmic patterns, and modulations during a single note-event. Due to a combination of independent lane looping and probability values, Figure 15.5(b) shows how steps labeled (1) and (2) might be combined from the various other lanes' pieces using the timing step durations and the other lane step values or waveforms. You can also see how a small number of waveforms and parameters can generate a massive number of combinations when probability is applied. Now consider this: practically every parameter for each kind of step and lane is modulate-able, and the step sequencer can even modulate its wave sequencer's own parameters. There are 16 steps in a wave sequence, and the Wavestate implements four separate wave sequencers (A, B, C, and D) per note-event.

15.6 SynthLab *WaveSequencer*

The SynthLab-WS project uses a single wave sequencer that is based on the Wavestate's multi-lane system and includes eight steps per lane. You may easily expand this to use more steps or even add another wave sequencer. For simplicity, there are a few features not included, such as the wave contour lane and lack of probability on the timing lane, but it is nonetheless a very powerful sequencer. It includes one step-sequencer lane as with the Wavestate, and you may expand that to include more lanes and hereby emulate a traditional step sequencer gone wild. Figure 15.6 shows the wave sequencer's GUI controls and interface. There are four lanes, with controls corresponding to Figure 15.5's parameters and the specifications in Section 15.5.1. There are also status lights (LEDs) to allow the user to see which steps are active in each lane at a given instant. There is a bank of global controls for each lane that has its own loop start and end points, and a loop mode control: forward, backwards, or forwards-backwards. All lanes also include a shuffle switch that randomizes the step sequence on each trip around that lane's loop points. These combine with the probability controls to create some very interesting sequences – as with the Wavestate, make sure that the DAW is in record mode all the time to catch your inventions as they happen.

15.6.1 C++ *Implementation:* WaveSequencer *Overview*

The *WaveSequencer* object acts as a pure modulation source and is run at the same time as the EGs and LFOs. The *SynthVoice* implements one *WaveSequencer* that is created, reset, and updated along with the other modules. The *WaveSequencer* writes numerous values into its modulation output array, which you may access via the modulation matrix. A special wave-sequencing oscillator (*WSOscillator*) maintains internal oscillators that are the targets for the wave sequencer modulation values: oscillator amplitude, waveform index, and pitch, along with the crossfading values to blend the two output waveforms during the morph. Figure 15.7(a) shows the *WaveSequencer* block diagram and member objects: *Lanes*, *LaneSteps*, and the *XHoldFader*. The *XHoldFader* contains the timers that set the hold and crossfade times, and generates the crossfade gain values. In one

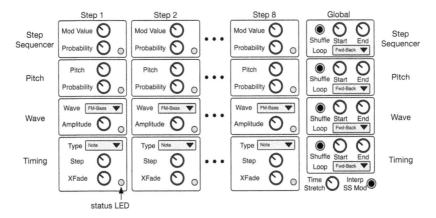

Figure 15.6 SynthLab's wave sequencer interface includes individual settings for all steps and a global control over the lanes

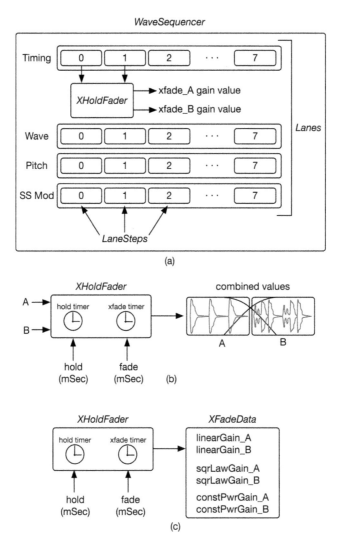

Figure 15.7 (a) The *WaveSequencer* and its member objects; (b) the *XHoldFader* can hold and crossfade signals or values, and (c) it can output the crossfade gain values in the *XFadeData* structure and operate in both modes at once, if needed

operational mode, shown in Figure 15.7(b), the *XHoldFader* performs the holding and crossfading of two input values, *A* and *B*, that may be audio signals or control values. In the second mode, in Figure 15.7(c), the object outputs the *A* and *B* gain values that an external object applies to its own signals, and it generates both linear and the two crossfade modulation gain values from Section 6.2.2 (linear, square law, and constant power). The *WaveSequencer* acts as the external object that applies the hold and crossfade gain values.

The *WaveSequencer* also provides a visual output of the current steps operating in each lane that have the ability to connect to your GUI to turn on and off as each step is activated or deactivated, which happens when the crossfade is halfway completed. You access these metering values through the engine, which provides a set of arrays corresponding to the four lanes of eight steps. You can use that to illuminate your GUI. The stock version provides status indicators for the first voice that is running. In poly mode, each note will generate its own new sequence as each new note is triggered.

15.6.2 C++ Implementation: Setting Step and Crossfade Durations

The step and crossfade durations may be set in milliseconds or with note durations. Using note durations allows you to easily set up musically interesting patterns. In addition, there is a time stretch/shrink control that will allow you to speed up or slow down the sequence while maintaining the note duration ratios between steps and crossfades. We already saw one implementation in the LFO's *BPM Sync* mod knob control. To facilitate both the GUI controls and timing calculations, I've included a strongly typed enum and helper functions that will convert note durations to time in seconds. The *NoteDuration* enum corresponds to the GUI control you set up for your user, and you display either duration strings or GUI note graphics that are indexed according to this enum. The *kOff* enum corresponds to a step or crossfade duration of zero seconds.

```
enum class NoteDuration {
k32ndTriplet, k32nd, k16thTriplet, kDot32nd, k16th, k8thTriplet, kDot16th,
k8th, kQuarterTriplet, kDot8th, kQuarter, kHalfTriplet, kDotQuarter,
kHalf, kWholeTriplet, kDotHalf, kWhole, kDotWhole, kOff,
kNumNoteDurations
};
```

Then, the function *getTimeFromTempo* will convert the duration into a time value using the BPM value from your DAW.

```
getTimeFromTempo(double BPM, NoteDuration duration,
                 bool returnMilliseconds = false)
```

15.6.3 C++ Implementation: Holding and Crossfading

To understand the modulation values that the sequencer outputs, first consider how the timing lane operates from the very start of the note-event. Consider the wave steps and timing sequence in Figure 15.8(a). At any given time, the sequencer will either be holding the current waveform (A) or crossfading waveform A into waveform B, as shown in Figure 15.8(b). Once the crossfade is done, the first timing step is discarded, the next is loaded, wave B moves to the wave A location, and the series repeats, as shown in Figure 15.8(c) and (d). Each pair of steps goes through the same process: hold for some duration, then crossfade into the next, or hold-crossfade-hold-crossfade, etc. This produces two gain values: one for the first (A) step and one for the second (B) step. When holding, wave A's gain will always be 1.0, and after the crossfade, it will be 0.0. Then, wave B becomes the "holding" step. The wave sequencer writes the current wave A, and wave B gain values into its modulation output array.

The waves themselves are indexed to correspond to the wave sequencing oscillator's unique waveform names, and these values are also written to the modulation output array, along with the amplitude values you set on the GUI. Each oscillator may have a different pitch, and the pitch

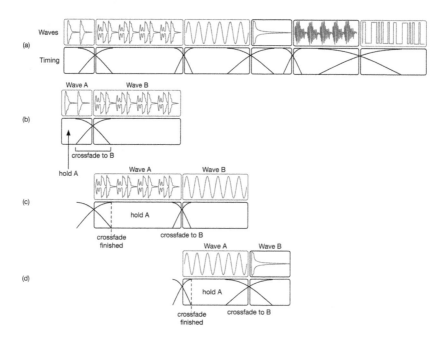

Figure 15.8 (a) A set of timing and waves to be sequenced shows the hold-then-crossfade pattern where you
(b) hold wave A and crossfade to B on first step then (c) wave B is labeled as the new wave A and
the next segment is loaded as wave B (d) the hold-then-crossfade process repeats with each new
segment

values are also written. Finally, the step sequencer modulation value, which may be stepped or
interpolated, is written to its location. If you want to add more step sequencer modulation lanes,
you will need to add more slots into the modulation output array to handle their values. The enumeration for the wave sequencer's modulation output array is:

```
enum {
    kWSWaveMix _ A,
    kWSWaveMix _ B,
    kWSWaveIndex _ A,
    kWSWaveIndex _ B,
    kWSWaveAmpMod _ A,
    kWSWaveAmpMod _ B,
    kWSPitchMod _ A,
    kWSPitchMod _ B,
    kWSStepSeqMod,
    kWSXFadeDone,
    kNumWSOutputs
};
```

You can see one additional output, *kWSFadeDone*, that is toggled when a new crossfade has finished. The target wave sequencing oscillator uses this indicator to swap oscillators so that oscillator B becomes oscillator A, then the next step is loaded as the new oscillator B.

15.6.4 C++ Implementation: Lanes and LaneSteps

The wave sequencer is actually relatively simple because it is really a big loop management system. The best way to understand it is to use the homework problems that will force you to examine the code and go deeper into the loop timing operations. The timing lane generates the step-timing information that is used to switch the other lane steps on and off, and they all switch steps at the same time – but each lane calculates its next step based on its own loop settings and each next step's probability value. To create a C++ solution, I made two C++ structures to encapsulate each component, as shown in Figure 15.9(a), with a *Lane* structure that maintains an array of *LaneStep* structures. The jump table is a circular buffer that contains the indexes of the lane steps for a given loop. After the first timing loop's crossfade, the steps are incremented so that the next step becomes the new current step, and a new next step is selected, as shown in Figure 14.9(b). Without randomization, the loop start and end points will cycle through the same series of steps, as shown in Figure 15.9(c), after the loop end point is hit. With randomization, once the loop end point is crossed, the *Lane* reshuffles the contents of the jump table, and that changes the sequence of the steps, as shown in Figure 15.9(d). So, the jump table sequences the lane steps, and the *Lane* delivers the current and next lane values to the sequencer.

Table 15.1 lists the C++ structures and objects used to create the *WaveSequencer*. The *LaneStep* holds information about both timing steps (step and crossfade durations) and modulation steps (pitch, wave, or step sequencer values).

The *Lane's* C++ code for setting the loops and maintaining the jump table, current step, and next step is reasonably simple, and involves creating the equivalent of a shuffle-able linked list. I also added the ability to create outside loops: if the user sets the loop start point to be <u>lower</u> than the loop end point, the loop will still operate but on the "outside" of the loop. If the start index is 6, and the end index is 2, then the outside loop sequence will be: 6, 7, 0, 1, 2, 6, 7, 0, 1, 2, … Each *LaneStep* keeps track of a previous step and next step index value; if these values are −1, then the *Lane* will use the jump table's value to set the next step. If the value is non-zero, then that indicates a loop start or end point. The function *updateLoopPoints* is called each time the jump table is shuffled

Table 15.1 WaveSequencer C++ objects and structures

Structure/Object	Description
LaneStep	Stores information about the step: step and crossfade durations (timing steps) and control values (non-timing steps), and previous and next step indexes; also includes a random number generator for probability
Lane	Stores an array of *LaneSteps* and a jump table for ordering the steps; also provides shuffling when randomness is applied
WaveSequencer	Stores a set of *Lanes*, one each for timing, wave, pitch, and step sequencer, and uses the *XHoldFader* object to set the step timing and generate the waveform gain values

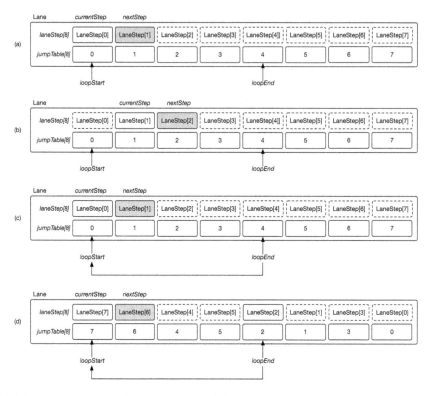

Figure 15.9 (a) A *Lane* structure maintains an array of *LaneStep* structures that are sequenced according to a jump table; the current step/next step pairs are shown in white and grey boxes (b) after the timing lane's first crossfade, the current step/next step pair advances according to the loop direction (to the right in this example) (c) without randomization, the segments will loop in the same order after the loop end point is hit (d) with randomization, the jump table is shuffled after each loop restarts which then shuffles the lane steps accordingly

and sets these next-step values to −1 or the next/previous index value; it is used in conjunction with *getNextStepIndex* to make the looping work properly. The user also sets a probability variable that is used each time the *Lane* advances to the next step. A random percentage value is generated and compared to the probability percentage value; the step is active if the random percentage value is less than or equal to the user's setting. Timing steps do not include probability. When a step is not used, its value is simply held over from the previous step's value to keep continuity in the modulation signals (Table 15.2).

15.7 The *WSOscillator* Object

The wave-sequencing oscillator is called *WSOscillator* and is a nice example that shows how to combine multiple modules. Unlike all the other SynthLab projects, SynthLab-WS does not feature a set of four oscillators that expose their waveforms, pitch controls, and mod knobs. In fact, the oscillator is somewhat hidden from the GUI, and there is no standard block diagram or module core

Table 15.2 The *WaveSequencer's SynthModule* overrides and descriptions

SynthModule Function	Operational Description
Reset	Sets current and next step indexes to 0; initializes a sample counter for generating status (for blinking lights)
Update	Updates each *Lane* with start/end times, step values, and probabilities; for the timing lane, it calculates the step and crossfade durations in *mSec* from the user's entry in *NoteDuration*; instructs *Lanes* to randomize sequences if user selects that option
doNoteOn	Initializes each lane with the first pair of steps, resets the status variables (for blinking lights), and resets the jump tables on each *Lane* to start from the original positions
Render	Gets next *crossfade* values from *XHoldFader* object and monitors the crossfade done flag; when finished, it advances each lane's next step. Writes the modulation values to its output array and turns the status lights on and off as each step moves to the next location
doNoteOff	Not used

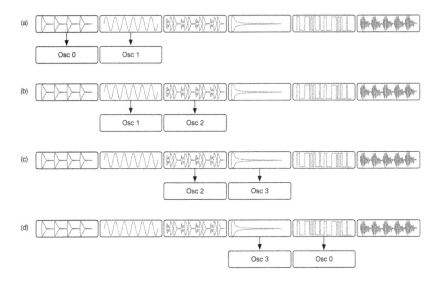

Figure 15.10 The four *WSOscillators* are used in a round-robin manner starting with (a) the oscillator pair (0, 1); after the first crossfade is completed, (b) the sequence shifts to oscillator pair (1, 2) then (c) to pair (2, 3) then (d) wrapping around to pair (3, 0), and so on

strings to reveal as in the other oscillators. The *WSOscillator* contains several underlying *WTOscillator* objects, each of which exposes up to four module cores that may render 16 waveforms each. This provides up to 64 waveforms for the user to select, including the morphing wavetable bank names, in the wave sequencer's GUI, so there is plenty of variation available.

As you can tell from Figures 15.7 to 15.9, there are two oscillators running at any given time, one for the A waveform and the other for the B waveform – unlike wave morphing that occurs on the input to a single oscillator, this morphing occurs on the outputs of two oscillators that may have different pitches as well as waveforms. However, all of the other SynthLab projects feature four oscillators, and the modulation matrix is set up with that paradigm. In order to allow you to modulate the underlying oscillators, the *WSOscillator* implements four member oscillators as well but only uses two of them at a time in a round-robin fashion, as shown in the sequence of Figure 15.10(a) through (d). Notice that this is identical to the way in which the waveforms are held and crossfaded in Figure 15.8; the oscillators switch when the waveforms switch, and this is why the *WaveSequencer* outputs an indicator that the crossfade has occurred.

15.7.1 WSOscillator Members

The *WSOscillator* maintains four *WTOscillators* as well as four *WTOscParameter* structures, one for each oscillator. These parameter structures are used to set the oscillator amplitudes in dB and the pitch offsets in semitones as the sequencer updates these values on each block processing cycle. To facilitate the round-robin behavior, an active oscillator array holds the two currently running oscillator index values. The *WSOscillator* member variables and descriptions are listed in Table 15.3.

Table 15.4 lists the *WSOscillator's SynthModule* member function overrides and describes how they operate.

Table 15.3 The *WSOscillator* members and descriptions

WSOscillator Member	Operational Description
waveSeqOsc[4]	The four oscillator members
waveSeqParams[4]	Parameter structures for each oscillator
activeOsc[2]	Array containing the indexes of the two currently active oscillators
oscMixCoeffs[4]	Hold or crossfade gain values for the oscillators; only two are used at a time
vector<WaveStringData> waveStringFinder	Set of structures used to connect the 64 possible waveforms to their module cores

Table 15.4 The *WSOscillator's SynthModule* overrides and descriptions

SynthModule Function	Operational Description
Reset	Sets current and next step indexes to 0; initializes a sample counter for generating status (for blinking lights)
Update	Updates each *Lane* with start/end times, step values, and probabilities; for the timing lane, it calculates the step and crossfade durations in *mSec* from the user's entry in *NoteDuration*; instructs *Lanes* to randomize sequences if user selects that option
doNoteOn	Initializes each lane with the first pair of steps, resets the status variables (for blinking lights), and resets the jump tables on each *Lane* to start from the original positions
Render	Gets next *crossfade* values from *XHoldFader* object and monitors the crossfade done flag; when finished, it advances each lane's next step. Writes the modulation values to its output array and turns the status lights on and off as each step moves to the next location
doNoteOff	Not used

15.8 *WSOscillator* Programming Notes

Like the *FMOperator*, the *WSOscillator* maintains a set of modules and orchestrates their use. This is a great object to study as it shows how one module can create and control numerous member modules. The only sticky detail here is how the waveform list is populated. All *SynthModules* include two built-in functions for populating the dynamic lists. The *getModuleStrings* function returns the module strings for a given core, and the function *getAllModuleStrings* loops through all four cores and compiles a std::vector of all the strings. Your plugin framework calls the function *getAllModuleStrings* in order to populate the wave sequencer's waveform lists. The *WSOscillator* includes a function that performs the same looping as *getAllModuleStrings* in order to populate its own vector of *WaveStringData* structures, which include the module core index and corresponding waveform index that maps to each of the 64 waveform strings that the user chooses. The *WSOscillator* can then easily find the core and waveform index for each wave step. You can find the code for this in *WSOscillator::makeWaveStringMap*.

15.8.1 *WSOscillator* Construction Phase

The wave-sequencing oscillator creates its member oscillators, along with corresponding parameter structures, in the constructor to control each object. The morphing wavetable cores use mod knob D to control the morph intensity, and we want to hard code that to 1.0 or full intensity as the default value. The code for setting up the parameter structures and instantiating the oscillators is below – notice how each oscillator has its own parameter structure.

```
for (uint32_t i = 0; i < NUM_WS_OSCILLATORS; i++)
{
    waveSeqParams[i].reset(new(WTOscParameters));
    waveSeqParams[i]->modKnobValue[0] = 0.5;
    waveSeqParams[i]->modKnobValue[1] = 0.0;
    waveSeqParams[i]->modKnobValue[2] = 0.0;
    waveSeqParams[i]->modKnobValue[3] = 1.0; // morph intensity
}

// --- four wavetable oscillators
waveSeqOsc[0].reset(new WTOscillator(_midiInputData, waveSeqParams[0],
                 _waveTableDatabase, blockSize));
waveSeqOsc[1].reset(new WTOscillator(_midiInputData, waveSeqParams[1],
                 _waveTableDatabase, blockSize));
waveSeqOsc[2].reset(new WTOscillator(_midiInputData, waveSeqParams[2],
                 _waveTableDatabase, blockSize));
waveSeqOsc[3].reset(new WTOscillator(_midiInputData, waveSeqParams[3],
                 _waveTableDatabase, blockSize));
```

15.8.2 *WSOscillator* Reset Phase

The reset phase involves creating the waveform map; initializing the member variables; and, most importantly, forwarding the *reset* function call to the member oscillators. Notice how the *activeOsc* array is initialized with (0, 1) – these are the first two oscillators that will be used in the round-robin loop.

```
// --- create string map
makeWaveStringMap();
for (uint32_t i = 0; i < NUM_WS_OSCILLATORS; i++)
{
      oscMixCoeff[i] = 0.0;
      waveSeqOsc[i]->reset(_sampleRate);
}

// --- initial pair of oscillators
activeOsc[0] = 0;
activeOsc[1] = 1;
```

15.8.3 *WSOscillator Note-On & Note-Off Phases*

The *doNoteOn* function cycles through each core of the four member oscillators and simply forwards the *doNoteOn* function call to each, synchronizing all cores at once. Note the Boolean flag that is set at the end of the function, which will initialize the round-robin sequence. There is nothing to do for the note-off phase, so that function is empty.

```
for (uint32_t core = 0; core < NUM_MODULE_CORES; core++)
{
      for (uint32_t i = 0; i < NUM_WS_OSCILLATORS; i++)
      {
          waveSeqOsc[i]->selectModuleCore(core);
          waveSeqOsc[i]->doNoteOn(noteEvent);
      }
}

initRoundRobin = true;
```

15.8.4 *WSOscillator Update Phase*

The oscillator includes two helper functions, called *setNewOscWaveA* and *setNewOscWaveB*, that greatly simplify the *update* function. The *setNewOscWaveA* function demonstrates how the *waveStringFinder* is used to load the correct oscillator core and set the waveform index it will use during its own update handler. The wave sequencer's modulation outputs have been hard-wired to the *WSOscillator's* modulation inputs during the voice construction. The code for connecting the wave mix A value is shown below.

```
modMatrix->addModSource(kSourceWSWaveMix_A,
waveSequencer->getModulationOutput()->getModArrayPtr(kWSWaveMix_A));

modMatrix->addModDestination(kDestOsc1_WSWaveMix_A,
wsOsc1->getModulationInput()->getModArrayPtr(kWaveSeqWave_AGainMod));

parameters->modMatrixParameters->setMM_HardwiredRouting(
                        kSourceWSWaveMix_A, kDestOsc1_WSWaveMix_A);
```

The *setNewOscWaveA* function fetches the sequencer's pitch and amplitude values for waveform A and uses the parameter structure to set the information in the oscillator. The *setNewOscWaveB* function uses the wave B index, pitch, and amplitudes, and calls the *doNoteOn* handler on the new oscillator in case the user selected a one-shot drum or sound effect for that step.

```
void setNewOscWaveA(uint32_t oscIndex, uint32_t waveAIndex,
                    double oscAMixCoeff)
{
    // --- choose oscillator core
    waveSeqOsc[oscIndex]->selectModuleCore
        (waveStringFinder[waveAIndex].coreIndex);

    // --- then set the oscillator waveform index
    waveSeqParams[oscIndex]->wavetableIndex =
        waveStringFinder[waveAIndex].coreWaveIndex;

    // --- next set the pitch and amplitude from the sequencer
    waveSeqParams[oscIndex]->oscSpecificDetune =
        getModulationInput()->getModValue(kWaveSeqPitch_AMod);

    waveSeqParams[oscIndex]->outputAmplitude_dB =
        getModulationInput()->getModValue(kWaveSeqAmp_AMod);

    //--- store the mix coefficient for render
    oscMixCoeff[oscIndex] = oscAMixCoeff;
}
```

The *update* function starts by fetching the waveform index and hold/crossfade mix values from its modulation input:

```
wave_AIndex = getModulationInput()->getModValue
                                        (kWaveSeqWaveIndex_AMod);

wave_BIndex = getModulationInput()->getModValue
                                        (kWaveSeqWaveIndex_BMod);

oscAMixCoeff = getModulationInput()->getModValue
                                        (kWaveSeqWave_AGainMod);

oscBMixCoeff = getModulationInput()->getModValue
                                        (kWaveSeqWave_BGainMod);
```

If this is the very first update, the two oscillators are set up with the helper function, and then the update function is done.

```
if (initRoundRobin)
{
    setNewOscWaveA(activeOsc[0], wave_AIndex, oscAMixCoeff);
    setNewOscWaveB(activeOsc[1], wave_BIndex, oscBMixCoeff);
```

```
            initRoundRobin = false;
            return true;
}
```

All subsequent *update* function calls will then perform two steps. First, wait for the crossfade-done signal from the sequencer; if the crossfade is done, the *activeOsc* array is incremented and wrapped to implement the round-robin behavior. Then, the helper functions are used to set the new oscillator data.

```
xfadeDone = getModulationInput()->getModValue(kWaveSeqXFadeDoneMod) ==
                                                0 ? false : true;

if (xfadeDone)
{
      // --- rotate to next pair of oscillators
      if (++activeOsc[0] >= NUM_WS_OSCILLATORS) activeOsc[0] = 0;
      if (++activeOsc[1] >= NUM_WS_OSCILLATORS) activeOsc[1] = 0;

      // --- set wave index and mix coeff
      setNewOscWaveA(activeOsc[0], wave_AIndex, oscAMixCoeff);
      setNewOscWaveB(activeOsc[1], wave_BIndex, oscBMixCoeff);
      return true;
}
```

Finally, if we are in the middle of a hold or crossfade operation, just set the updated pitch and amplitude information using the oscillator parameter structures.

```
// --- just forward the settings: OSC 0
waveSeqParams[activeOsc[0]]->oscSpecificDetune =
            getModulationInput()->getModValue(kWaveSeqPitch_AMod);

waveSeqParams[activeOsc[0]]->outputAmplitude_dB =
            getModulationInput()->getModValue(kWaveSeqAmp_AMod);

oscMixCoeff[activeOsc[0]] = oscAMixCoeff;

// --- just forward the settings: OSC 1
waveSeqParams[activeOsc[1]]->oscSpecificDetune =
            getModulationInput()->getModValue(kWaveSeqPitch_BMod);

waveSeqParams[activeOsc[1]]->outputAmplitude_dB =
            getModulationInput()->getModValue(kWaveSeqAmp_BMod);

oscMixCoeff[activeOsc[1]] = oscBMixCoeff;
```

15.8.5 *WSOscillator Render Phase*

The rendering operation is very simple – after updating, call the render method on the two active oscillators, then mix their audio output arrays into the *WSOscillator's* output array.

```
// --- update parameters for this block
update();

// --- render each osc
waveSeqOsc[activeOsc[0]]->render(samplesToProcess);
waveSeqOsc[activeOsc[1]]->render(samplesToProcess);

// --- mix output buffers into our buffer
getAudioBuffers()->flushBuffers();

// --- add osc 0
mixOscBuffers(waveSeqOsc[activeOsc[0]]->getAudioBuffers(),
                    samplesToProcess, oscMixCoeff[activeOsc[0]]);

// --- mix osc 1
mixOscBuffers(waveSeqOsc[activeOsc[1]]->getAudioBuffers(),
                    samplesToProcess, oscMixCoeff[activeOsc[1]]);
```

15.9 Exercises

15.9.1 Wave Sequencing

First, download the Korg Wavestate user manual from www.willpirkle.com\Downloads\wavestate. pdf. There are several features missing from my *WaveSequencer* object, and you should try implementing them yourself. This will force you to go deeper into the *WaveSequencer* code and understand its looping operations as well as manipulate the four round-robin oscillators in the *WSOscillator* object.

15.9.2 Crossfade Selection

The crossfades in my sequencer object are always set to constant power for crossfading waveforms and linear for crossfading the step sequencer's values. Allow the user to choose the type of crossfade they want for the waveform and the step sequencer, and alter the code to apply it. HINT: the *XHoldFader* object outputs the gain values for all three options at once (Figure 15.7(c)).

15.9.3 Fade-In and Fade-Out control

The Wavestate allows the user to manipulate both the fade-in and fade-out curvature independently for the waveform crossfade. Modify the sequencer and *XHoldFader* to allow for the manipulation of both fade-in and fade-out curvature using the two GUI control knobs that set the curvature values. Use the Wavestate manual as your guide. HINT: One easy way to provide a curvature control is to simply combine the *XHoldFader's* linear gain coefficients with the square law coefficients in a ratio that corresponds to the user's curvature control setting.

15.9.4 Timing Probability

My *WaveSequencer* does not include a probability control for the timing steps. Use the Wavestate manual to understand how this probability value works – when probability causes a timing step to be skipped, its step duration is combined into the previous step, and the crossfade point is moved out accordingly. Implementing this probability will then generate numerous different sequences that are locked to the DAW BPM but will vary in step durations.

15.9.5 Timing Swing

Use the Wavestate manual to see how Korg implements timing swing by delaying the onset of every other step in the sequence, and add a swing control to the other sequencer global GUI components.

Bibliography

Korg.com. 2014 "Electribe Wave Owner's Manual." https://www.korg.com/us/support/download/product/0/797/#manual, Accessed October 14, 2020

Korg.com. 2016. "iWavestation Wave Owner's Manual." https://www.korg.com/us/support/download/manual/0/739/3510/, Accessed October 14, 2020

Korg.com. 2019. "Wavestate Owner's Manual." https://www.korg.com/us/support/download/product/0/840/, Accessed October 14, 2020

16　The SynthLab Synth Projects

The SynthLab engine and voice architectures are fundamentally identical across all of the projects, as shown in Figure 16.1. The projects' quad oscillator banks are different, but everything else remains the same. The wave sequencing SynthLab-WS includes the additional *WaveSequencer* object, but it also uses four oscillators in its implementation.

Table 16.1 lists the projects and the type of oscillators that are used for the quad oscillator core.

16.1　SynthLab Modulation Matrix

All SynthLab projects use the same modulation matrix, except the wave sequencing synth, which adds an additional modulation source row, as shown in Figure 16.2. The sources on the left column are the main synth modulators, and you can add many more rows if you like since the LFOs and EGs have multiple outputs. The destinations across the top are common to many synth designs. Notice how I save space by having two destinations that apply to OSC1, OSC2, and OSC3 simultaneously. If you make oscillator #4 a sub-oscillator, playing an octave down, you may not want to apply the same modulation or intensity so that oscillator has its own destination columns.

Notice the two destination columns for "OSC mod" – this is a catchall for each oscillator's ability to provide a special modulation that works with its algorithm. Table 16.2 lists the oscillators and their special modulation destinations.

16.1.1　*Modulation Matrix Programming*

Mod matrix programming is covered in Chapter 14. Make sure you examine the *SynthVoice* constructors for each project to see the mod matrix programming operations. If you are using multiple cores, notice how the voice object enables and disables the mod matrix routings as different cores are loaded. Here is the code for selecting a new wavetable oscillator #1 core; notice how the old modulation destinations are removed, and the new destinations are added. This does not require any dynamic memory allocations.

```
wtOsc1->selectModuleCore(index);
```

```
// --- reset mod matrix pointers to new core modulation arrays
modMatrix->clearModDestination(kDestOsc1 _ fo);
```

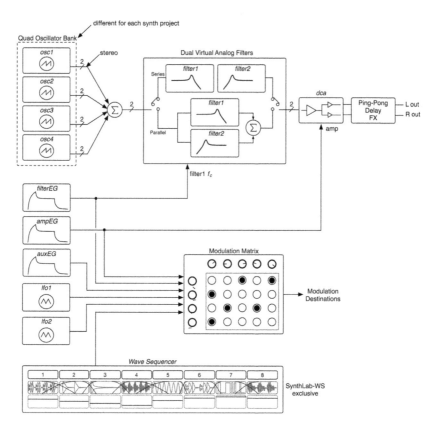

Figure 16.1 SynthLab voice architecture; the quad oscillator bank is different for each project, and the *WaveSequencer* is only in SynthLab-WS

Table 16.1 SynthLab projects and oscillators

SynthLab Project	Oscillators	Notes
Wavetable (WT)	WTOscillator	May freely mix normal, one-shot, sound effect, and morphing wavetables
Virtual analog (VA)	VAOscillator	Oscillators based on the Oberheim SEM® that output both square and saw in a user-controlled ratio
Sample based (PCM)	PCMOscillator	PCM samples stored in *.wav* files
Physical model (KS)	KSOscillator	Oscillators can be augmented with additional resonators (e.g. 12-string emulation)
Chowning FM (DX)	FMOperator	The four FM operators require significantly more GUI controls due to their built-in DX EGs
Wave-sequencing (WS)	WSOscillator that aggregates four WTOscillators and is modulated with a WaveSequencer	May freely mix normal, one-shot, sound effect, and morphing wavetables while wave sequencing at the same time

Table 16.2 SynthLab oscillators and their special modulation destinations

Oscillator	C++ Object	Special Modulation
Wavetable	*ClassicWTCore*	Oscillator shape
Morphing wavetable	*MorphWTCore*	Morphing index (added to other modulation sources)
Virtual analog	*VAOCore*	Square wave duty cycle
Sample based	All *PCMCores*	Pan modulation (per oscillator)
Plucked string model	*KSOCore*	Pluck position

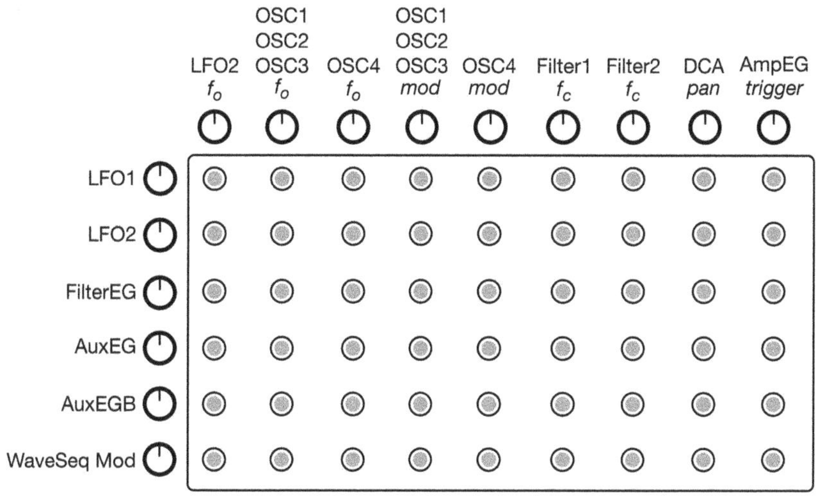

Figure 16.2 The SynthLab modulation matrix uses a pin-programmer style interface and source and destination intensity controls

```
modMatrix->clearModDestination(kDestOsc1_Mod);
modMatrix->clearModDestination(kDestOsc1_Morph);

modMatrix->addModDestination(kDestOsc1_fo,
    wtOsc1->getModulationInput()->getModArrayPtr(kBipolarMod));

modMatrix->addModDestination(kDestOsc1_Mod,
    wtOsc1->getModulationInput()->getModArrayPtr(kUniqueMod));

modMatrix->addModDestination(kDestOsc1_Morph,
    wtOsc1->getModulationInput()->getModArrayPtr(kWaveMorphMod));
```

16.2 SynthLab Render Phase: Modulators

All SynthLab projects have the same initial code for the voice *render* method, which first renders the modulator outputs, then runs the modulation matrix. SynthLab-WS runs its wave sequencer object along with the other modulators and prior to the modulation matrix. To facilitate oscillator mixing, the voice has its own sub-mix buffers that it uses to accumulate each oscillator's output buffer. This buffer must be cleared so that the first accumulation mixes with the cleared (0.0) values.

```
bool SynthVoice::render(SynthProcessInfo& synthProcessInfo)
```

```
uint32 _ t samplesToProcess = synthProcessInfo.getSamplesInBlock();

// --- clear for accumulation
mixBuffers->flushBuffers();

// --- update/render (add more here)
lfo1->render(samplesToProcess);
lfo2->render(samplesToProcess);

ampEG->render(samplesToProcess);
filterEG->render(samplesToProcess);
auxEG->render(samplesToProcess);

// --- sequencer generates modulation values
waveSequencer->render(samplesToProcess); // <- SynthLab-WS only!!

// --- do all mods
modMatrix->runModMatrix();
```

16.3 SynthLab Render Phase: Quad Oscillator Mixing

All synths except SynthLab-WS blend four oscillators together to render the synthesized audio signal. SynthLab-WS only uses a single *WSOscillator*, but that oscillator blends the outputs of two of its four internal oscillators in round-robin format, as detailed in Section 15.7. After the modulation matrix renders its values, the four oscillators are rendered and accumulated in series; the accumulation function accepts a scalar mixing-coefficient that prevents overflow and is set to 0.25 here since we have four oscillators.

```
wtOsc1->render(samplesToProcess);
accumulateToMixBuffer(wtOsc1->getAudioBuffers(), samplesToProcess,
                      0.25);

wtOsc2->render(samplesToProcess);
accumulateToMixBuffer(wtOsc2->getAudioBuffers(), samplesToProcess,
                      0.25);

wtOsc3->render(samplesToProcess);
accumulateToMixBuffer(wtOsc3->getAudioBuffers(), samplesToProcess,
                      0.25);
```

```
wtOsc4->render(samplesToProcess);
accumulateToMixBuffer(wtOsc4->getAudioBuffers(), samplesToProcess,
                      0.25);
```

SynthLab-WS uses only a single oscillator, and to simplify the filtering code that follows, it accumulates into the same mix buffer but with a mixing coefficient of 1.0.

```
// --- wave sequencer
wsOsc1->render(samplesToProcess);
accumulateToMixBuffer(wsOsc1->getAudioBuffers(), samplesToProcess,
                      1.0);
```

16.4 SynthLab Render Phase: Filtering

All synths include a pair of *SynthFilter* objects that may be run in series or parallel. A GUI controlled parameter switches between modes. This code takes advantage of the audio buffer mixing functions in *synthfunctions.h* to perform the series/parallel operation. The first step is to copy the oscillator mix buffers into either *filter1* (series) or both filters (parallel):

```
// --- setup filtering
if (parameters->filterModeIndex == enumToInt(FilterMode::kSeries))
{
    // --- to Filter1
    copyBufferToInput(mixBuffers, filter1->getAudioBuffers(),
                      STEREO _ TO _ STEREO, samplesToProcess);
}
else
{
    // --- to Filter1
    copyBufferToInput(mixBuffers, filter1->getAudioBuffers(),
                      STEREO _ TO _ STEREO, samplesToProcess);

    // --- to Filter2
    copyBufferToInput(mixBuffers, filter2->getAudioBuffers(),
                      STEREO _ TO _ STEREO, samplesToProcess);
}
```

Next, the filters are rendered in series, where *filter1's* rendered output buffer is copied to *filter2's* input and then rendered, or parallel, where both filters are rendered and outputs are accumulated in the mix buffer. In both cases, the last step is to copy the buffers to the output DCA.

```
if (parameters->filterModeIndex == enumToInt(FilterMode::kSeries))
{
    // --- update and render
    filter1->render(samplesToProcess);

    // --- to Filter2
    copyOutputToInput(filter1->getAudioBuffers(),
```

```
                            filter2->getAudioBuffers(),
                    STEREO _ TO _ STEREO, samplesToProcess);

      // --- update and render
      filter2->render(samplesToProcess);

      // --- to DCA
      copyOutputToInput(filter2->getAudioBuffers(),
                        dca->getAudioBuffers(),
                    STEREO _ TO _ STEREO, samplesToProcess);
}
else
{
      // --- flush
      mixBuffers->flushBuffers();

      // --- render and accumulate
      filter1->render(samplesToProcess);
      accumulateToMixBuffer(filter1->getAudioBuffers(),
                            samplesToProcess, 0.5);

      // --- update and render
      filter2->render(samplesToProcess);
      accumulateToMixBuffer(filter2->getAudioBuffers(),
                            samplesToProcess, 0.5);

      // --- to DCA
      copyBufferToInput(mixBuffers, dca->getAudioBuffers(),
                        STEREO _ TO _ STEREO, samplesToProcess);
}
```

The DCA processes the audio and provides gain and panning, and the final mix is copied into the *SynthProcessInfo* structure that the engine provided during the *render* function call. After that, the small piece of logic is run to see if the *ampEG* has expired and the note-event has ended. This is part of the note-lifecycle and voice-stealing operation.

```
// --- update and render
dca->render(samplesToProcess);

// --- to mains
copyOutputToOutput(dca->getAudioBuffers(), synthProcessInfo,
                   STEREO _ TO _ STEREO, samplesToProcess);
```

16.5 SynthLab Render Phase: Global Volume and Delay FX

The engine code is identical across all SynthLab projects and discussed in detail in Chapter 2. After rendering the active voices, the engine's last step is to mix them and apply the delay FX and final global volume control. This code also shows how the wave sequencer status meter values are parsed for the first voice only (otherwise, metering would be very confusing for the user).

```
// --- blend active voices
if (synthVoices[i]->isVoiceActive())
{
    // --- render and accumulate
    synthVoices[i]->render(voiceProcessInfo);
    accumulateVoice(synthProcessInfo, gainFactor);

    // --- only show first voice , WS only
    if (i == 0)
        parameters->wsStatusMeters =
        parameters->voiceParameters->
        waveSequencerParameters->statusMeters;
}
```

The ping-pong delay FX is also derived from *SynthModule*, so it behaves the same as the other processor objects that process an input to an output (DCA and filters). The algorithm is straight out of my FX plugin book. The engine owns the *std::unique_ptr* to the ping-pong delay and treats it the same way the voice treats the filters using the input and output audio buffers that all *Synth-Modules* expose. The global volume control is the last part of the engine processing and is done with another helper function that simply iterates through the output buffer and applies the scaling (volume control) factor.

```
if (parameters->enableDelayFX)
{
    // --- copy synth output to delay input
    copySynthOutputToAudioBufferInput(synthProcessInfo,
                            pingPongDelay->getAudioBuffers(),
                            STEREO _ TO _ STEREO, samplesToProcess);

    // --- run the delay
    pingPongDelay->render(samplesToProcess);

    // --- copy to output
    copyAudioBufferOutputToSynthOutput(
                            pingPongDelay->getAudioBuffers(),
                            synthProcessInfo, STEREO _ TO _ STEREO,
                            samplesToProcess);
}

// --- add master volume
applyGlobalVolume(synthProcessInfo);
```

16.6 SynthLab-DX: the FM Synthesizer

Yamaha produced and marketed the first commercially available FM synthesizer, the DX-7, in 1983, based off of John Chowning's seminal paper *The Synthesis of Complex Audio Spectra by*

Means of Frequency Modulation, published a decade prior. The DX-7 became the second-best-selling synthesizer of all time at about 160,000 units sold (not far behind the Korg M1 at about 250,000 units). Yamaha spun off the product into multiple DX synths, all marketed as FM synths. The manuals refer to this method as "digital FM tone generation." However, neither the DX-7 nor any of the DX variants were FM synths; instead, they were all Phase Modulation (PM) synthesizers. PM is virtually identical to frequency modulation so that much of the theory is interchangeable. FM and PM synthesis require accurate sinusoidal oscillators that can run forwards or backwards; all SynthLab oscillators except the Karplus-Strong variant have this capability. FM (and PM) synthesis are capable of producing a vast range of timbres, from searing, paint-peeling lead sounds to muted piano sounds to the most convincing bell and gong sounds you will probably ever synthesize without using samples.

16.6.1 FM and PM Basics

Both frequency and phase modulation theory are very well documented, and the mathematical concepts were around long before Chowning's 1973 paper. FM and PM synthesis generate dynamic and interesting waveforms using just two sinusoidal oscillators: the modulator and the carrier. In FM, the modulator waveform varies the carrier oscillator's instantaneous frequency by adding and subtracting its own frequency, as shown in Figure 16.3(a). In PM, the modulator waveform varies the carrier oscillator's instantaneous phase by adding and subtracting a phase offset (φ) in Figure 16.3(b), which, in turn, varies the frequency. You can see that the resulting time domain audio signals look very similar but phase-shifted from one another. Taking the magnitude FFT produces the frequency spectrum, and in both cases, that spectrum consists of the carrier frequency plus and minus multiples of the modulator frequency: $f_c + f_m, f_c - f_m, f_c + 2f_m, f_c - 2f_m$, and so on. These additional spectral components are called the sideband frequencies or sidebands. From Figure 16.3, you can see three important features about the sidebands:

1   The sidebands may be negative frequencies
2   The amplitudes of the sidebands don't appear to follow a pattern other than being symmetrical across the carrier frequency
3   A sideband component may occur at 0 Hz or DC

When the sidebands are negative frequencies, they reflect across the 0 Hz axis, flip in phase, and add back into the positive frequency domain's components. The reflected frequencies may line up with existing spectral components, in which case they may add or subtract from them, or they may land in-between existing frequencies. The amplitudes of the sideband harmonics, which may first appear to modulate randomly, actually follow a set of mathematical equations called Bessel functions; they produce a specific kind of undulation (up-down motion), but predicting how they will move and sound is difficult without copious experience in playing and listening to the results.

For synth implementation, the most important of the three features is that PM does not produce sidebands at DC or 0 Hz. Another issue is that for FM, the carrier oscillator needs to know the frequency of the modulator so that it may add and subtract this value to modulate the oscillation frequency; this is not required for PM, which simply offsets the current *phaseInc* value of the synth clock by adding or subtracting some amount. The DC offset problem is a deal-breaker for FM as a synthesis technique. For a single modulator-carrier pair, the DC offset may cause the output signal to move outside the bounds of [−1, +1], which creates distortion and will add a DC offset to the audio signal. More importantly, when cascading multiple modulator-carrier pairs, a DC offset

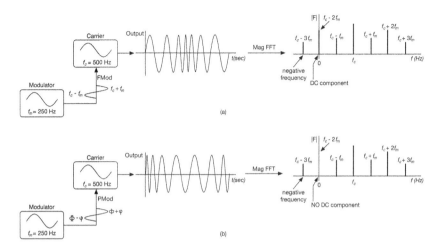

Figure 16.3 (a) FM and (b) PM time and frequency domain output signals; the spectral amplitudes shown are for visual reference; the actual amplitudes follow Bessel functions and are more complex

at the output of the first pair will produce a constant detuning offset on the second pair that will cause the note to play sharp or flat – and that is unacceptable.

16.6.2 *Index of Modulation*

When we use pitch modulation with an LFO modulating the oscillator frequency in semitones, we usually include a modulation depth control – either the LFO output control, the modulation matrix intensity control, or a combination of both. You can do the same thing with FM or PM and increase or decrease this modulation "strength" to likewise affect the amount of the resulting FM or PM. Here, the depth of modulation is called the "index of modulation" (*I*), and this control has a profound effect on the amount of sideband harmonics that are generated. Figure 16.4(a) shows how a modulator-carrier pair is connected for FM or PM synthesis. The carrier oscillator's frequency is the MIDI note pitch. The modulator's frequency is some ratio of that and set with a GUI "ratio" control. The modulator output is adjusted with a modulation index control, and as the index increases, so do the harmonics. In Figure 16.4(b), the modulation index control is replaced with an envelope generator that dynamically changes the index value as the note-event progresses, which, in turn, alters the harmonics in a dynamic manner that resembles a strange filter that adds or removes sideband harmonics as the index changes, producing interesting timbral shifts in the output. Notice how the amplitudes of the individual sideband components undulate up and down as the index changes. In this case, the maximum index value is 4.0; this is called the I_{MAX} value.

16.6.3 *FM Operators*

"FM operator" is the name Chowning gives to the combination of a sinusoidal oscillator and an output amplitude EG, and he has a specific way of diagramming various operator combinations called algorithms. Figure 16.5(a) shows the FM operator and the square symbol, while Figure 16.5(b) shows how two operators are connected as modulator (operator 2) and carrier (operator 1). Chowning's algorithms allow the last modulator in a series connection to modulate itself.

SynthLab's *FMOperator* object consists of a sinusoidal wavetable oscillator paired with a DX-EG. To create the patches, you connect the audio outputs and phase modulation inputs according to the algorithm diagram.

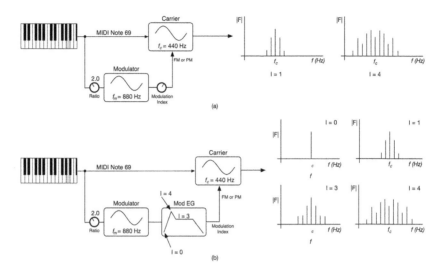

Figure 16.4 (a) A modulation index control modifies the output spectrum; (b) replacing the control with an EG allows the spectrum to morph as the note-event progresses

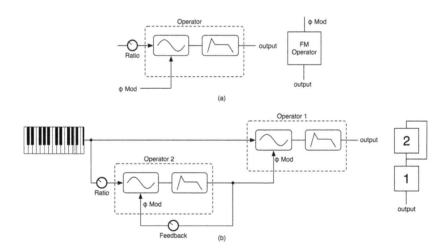

Figure 16.5 (a) An FM operator consists of a sinusoidal oscillator and EG that adjusts its output amplitude along with Chowning's FM operator notation (b) a two-operator patch that includes self-modulation; notice that Operator 1's output EG acts as the amp EG since it is the very last in the chain and Chowning's notation that indicates self-modulation

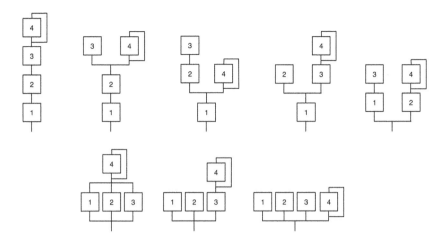

Figure 16.6 The eight DX-100 FM algorithms

16.6.4 DX Algorithms

Yamaha produced several DX variants with different numbers of operators. The DX-7 implemented six FM operators arranged in 32 different combinations, while the smaller DX-100 featured four operators in eight combinations. Since all SynthLab synths use quad-oscillator blocks, the DX style synth will likewise use four FM operators that implement the DX-100 algorithms, shown in Figure 16.6, that are simple series and parallel connections of various combinations. The three algorithms on the bottom row use parallel summing and can sound mellow and soft. The series algorithms on the first row tend to produce harsher sounds (be careful – you can peel the paint off your walls with some of them). The eight algorithms do not have specific names, so the user must select them from a text or graphic GUI control.

16.7 FM/PM Rules

So far, we've only discussed the effect of the index of modulation on the FM and PM spectra. As the index increases, so does the sideband spectral density. The ratio of the carrier and that of the modulator play an equally important role in the timbre of the sound. Programming a DX-style synth is challenging because the spectral components follow the complicated Bessel functions as they undulate with changes in the modulation index. There are a few rules that will help you understand how the algorithms affect what you hear. These are the FM/PM rules of thumb and are based on the ratio of the carrier to modulator. You first need to fashion the f_c/f_m ratio, as shown in Equation (16.1), where N_1 and N_2 are <u>integers</u> with no common divisors.

$$\frac{f_c}{f_m} = \frac{N_1}{N_2}$$

(16.1)

16.7.1 Fundamental Frequency

The fundamental frequency of the resulting patch is:

$$f_o = \frac{f_c}{N_1} = \frac{f_m}{N_2} \tag{16.2}$$

Depending on the N_1/N_2 ratio, the pitch of the resulting note may be f_c or f_m, or neither.

16.7.2 Spectral Purity

The value of N_2 affects the purity of the spectrum – whether it has gaps.

$N_2 = 1$ spectrum contains all harmonic multiples

$N_2 \geq 2$ spectrum is missing every N_2th harmonic   (16.3)

16.7.3 Reflected Frequencies

The value of N_2 also governs the way in which negative frequency components are reflected across the 0 Hz axis.

$N_2 = 1$ or $N_2 = 2$ all reflected harmonics line up perfectly with (+) harmonics

$N_2 > 2$ none of the reflected harmonics line up with any of the (+) harmonics   (16.4)

16.7.4 Inharmonicity

As inharmonicity increases, it becomes more difficult to locate the fundamental frequency or pitch as the sidebands deviate from whole number integer relationships. High inharmonicity is used to produce bell, gong and struck-metal or wood sounds. The N_1/N_2 ratio predicts the inharmonicity.

$\dfrac{N_1}{N_2} \geq 5$ f_o is low in amplitude, difficult to locate pitch

$N_1, N_2 \neq$ integers f_o does not exist, pure inharmonicity   (16.5)

16.8 FM Operator

The *FMOperator* object is a specialized combination of a sinusoidal wavetable oscillator and an envelope generator that applies its envelope as an output scaling factor, as shown in Figure 16.7(a). The wavetable oscillator uses a single sinusoidal table for all operations. The update phase only applies pitch modulation and nothing else – no self hard sync or shape modulation. There are no waveforms to select because we only use the sinusoid for traditional FM synthesis, but the module-core paradigm is still used so that you can design and test your own variations, which might use different waveforms or EGs. The object is designed and used like an augmented sinusoidal wavetable oscillator and follows the same table initialization and read/interpolate as the others in Chapter 9. However, its wavetable code demonstrates how to implement phase modulation, and this code can be lifted and applied to the rest of the wavetable oscillator cores.

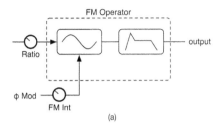

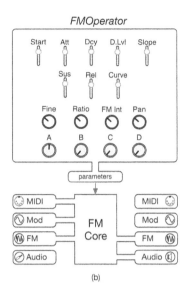

Figure 16.7 (a) The block diagram for the *FMOperator* object includes a self-modulation routing path and FM intensity control, and (b) the SynthLab implementation block diagram

16.8.1 *Implementing Phase Modulation with* SynthClock *Oscillators*

All of the SynthLab oscillators except the Karplus-Strong algorithm use a *SynthClock* for the timing base. The *SynthClock* object is a simple modulo counter, and it exposes methods to adjust the instantaneous phase to a new phase point or restore it back to the original counter location. These methods make phase modulation easy to implement, and you can experiment with any of the oscillators, but note that non-sinusoidal waveforms will likely alias and/or produce bloodcurdling noises, so be careful! The *FMOperator* object is really a specialized sinusoidal wavetable oscillator with an additional DX EG member object that controls the oscillator output amplitude and is scaled with a user-specified I_{MAX} GUI control value. To phase modulate the oscillator, you first set its PM buffer input with a simple function call. In the render loop, you apply the values from the PM buffer as phase offsets to the *SynthClock*. In order to adjust the instantaneous phase, the offset is removed at the end of each sample render loop. Examine the *FMOCore* object's render method to see the phase modulation and application of the EG value to the operator.

```
bool FMOCore::render(CoreProcData& processInfo)


// --- audio outputs
float* leftOutBuffer = processInfo.outputBuffers[LEFT_CHANNEL];
float* rightOutBuffer = processInfo.outputBuffers[RIGHT_CHANNEL];

// --- PM inputs (which are always audio outputs of another oscillator)
float* pmBufferL = processInfo.fmBuffers[LEFT_CHANNEL];
float* pmBufferR = processInfo.fmBuffers[RIGHT_CHANNEL];
```

Before entering the loop, you generate the EG scaling value and pick up the self-modulation feedback value if non-zero.

```
// --- get the EG output
dxEG->render(processInfo.samplesToProcess);
egOutput = dxEG->getModulationOutput()->getModValue(kEGNormalOutput);

// --- self modulation
bool selfModulate = parameters->modKnobValue[FMO_FEEDBACK] > 0.0;
```

Upon entering the loop, the PM buffers are summed to mono, and the resulting value is used as the phase offset and scaled with the user's I_{MAX} GUI control value.

```
for (uint32_t i = 0; i < processInfo.samplesToProcess; i++)
{
    // --- PHASE MODULATION
    if (pmBufferL && pmBufferR)
    {
        // --- convert PM buffer to mono
        double modValue = parameters->phaseModIndex *
                        (0.5*pmBufferL[i] + 0.5*pmBufferR[i]);

        // --- perform PM operation
        oscClock.addPhaseOffset(modValue);
    }
```

Self-modulation works nearly the same way, but we cannot allow a zero-delay feedback loop, so the *outputValue* variable below is the previous output from the loop, and it is stored as a member variable on the object.

```
    else if(selfModulate)
    {
        double modValue = parameters->phaseModIndex *
                parameters->modKnobValue[FMO_FEEDBACK] * outputValue;

        // --- perform PM operation
        oscClock.addPhaseOffset(modValue);
    }
```

The wavetable is then read as normal, and the procedure reversed to set up for the next iteration by removing the original phase offset and performing a modulo wrap that may be needed as a result of removing (subtracting) the phase offset.

```
// --- read table and scale with EG value
outputValue = egOutput *
                sineTableSource.readWaveTable(oscClock.mcounter);

// --- scale by gain control
outputValue *= outputAmplitude;
```

```
// --- write to output buffers
leftOutBuffer[i] = outputValue * panLeftGain;
rightOutBuffer[i] = outputValue * panRightGain;

if ((pmBufferL && pmBufferR) || selfModulate)
{
    oscClock.removePhaseOffset();
    oscClock.wrapClock();
}

// --- set up for next cycle
oscClock.advanceWrapClock();
```

16.9 SynthLab-DX Voice Render Phase

The SynthLab-DX creates four *FMOperators*, resets and initializes them, and forwards note-on and note-off messages as with all of the other SynthLab oscillator objects. The voice is responsible for performing the PM modulation operation and summing modulators and carriers, as per the algorithms in Figure 16.6. Let's take a look at a couple of examples. First, the FM1 algorithm consists of four operators in series. The code below uses the same numbering scheme as Figure 16.6.

```
if (parameters->fmAlgorithmIndex == enumToInt(DX100Algo::kFM1))
{
    // --- start with op4
    fmOp4->render(samplesToProcess);

    // --- 4 modulates 3
    fmOp3->setFMBuffer(fmOp4->getAudioBuffers());
    fmOp3->render(samplesToProcess);

    // --- 3 modulates 2
    fmOp2->setFMBuffer(fmOp3->getAudioBuffers());
    fmOp2->render(samplesToProcess);

    // --- 2 modulates 1
    fmOp1->setFMBuffer(fmOp2->getAudioBuffers());
    fmOp1->render(samplesToProcess);

    // --- write to mix buffers
    writeToMixBuffer(fmOp1->getAudioBuffers(), samplesToProcess);
}
```

Now look at algorithm #4, which has two parallel branches. Notice how the modulator outputs are summed into the standby mix buffers, then applied as the PM buffer for operator #1.

```
// --- render 4
fmOp4->render(samplesToProcess);
```

```
// --- 4 modulates 3
fmOp3->setFMBuffer(fmOp4->getAudioBuffers());
fmOp3->render(samplesToProcess);

// --- render 2
fmOp2->render(samplesToProcess);

// --- sum the two modulator outputs
accumulateToMixBuffer(fmOp3->getAudioBuffers(), samplesToProcess, 0.5);
accumulateToMixBuffer(fmOp2->getAudioBuffers(), samplesToProcess, 0.5);

// --- apply to final operator
fmOp1->setFMBuffer(mixBuffers);
fmOp1->render(samplesToProcess);

// --- write output
writeToMixBuffer(fmOp1->getAudioBuffers(), samplesToProcess);
```

Lastly, check out algorithm #8, which is comprised of four parallel operators summed together:

```
// --- all
fmOp4->render(samplesToProcess);
fmOp3->render(samplesToProcess);
fmOp2->render(samplesToProcess);
fmOp1->render(samplesToProcess);

// --- sum
accumulateToMixBuffer(fmOp4->getAudioBuffers(),
                      samplesToProcess, 0.25);

accumulateToMixBuffer(fmOp3->getAudioBuffers(),
                      samplesToProcess, 0.25);

accumulateToMixBuffer(fmOp2->getAudioBuffers(),
                      samplesToProcess, 0.25);

accumulateToMixBuffer(fmOp1->getAudioBuffers(),
                      samplesToProcess, 0.25);
```

From this point on, the mix buffers contain the oscillator render and are pushed downstream into the filters and the rest of the voice architecture, identical to the rest of the synths.

Bibliography

Chowning, John. 1973. The Synthesis of Complex Audio Spectra by Means of Frequency Modulation. *Journal of the Audio Engineering Society*, 21:7, pp 526–534

SynthLab Documentation. 2020. www.willpirkle.com/synthlab-docs, Accessed on October 14, 2020

Index

For Product Safety Concerns and Information please contact our EU
representative GPSR@taylorandfrancis.com
Taylor & Francis Verlag GmbH, Kaufingerstraße 24, 80331 München, Germany

www.ingramcontent.com/pod-product-compliance
Ingram Content Group UK Ltd.
Pitfield, Milton Keynes, MK11 3LW, UK
UKHW030829080625
459435UK00014B/577